Instant Pot Cookbook

700 Easy & Delicious Recipes for Fast Cooking

Copyright © 2017 Luca Moretti
All rights reserved.

Table of Contents

Table of Contents 1

The Instant Pot Revolution 12
    How Fast Can I Cook my Meal? 13
    But, is it Worth The Money? 14
    Differences between the Instant Pot & Slow Cooker 15
    Versatility Unmatched 16
    Novel Ways To Use Your Instant Pot 17
    Saving you Time & Money 18
    How Safe Is The Instant Pot? 19
    How To Find Even More Instant Pot Recipes 20
    Instant Pot Cooking Times 21
    Instant Pot Cheat Sheet 28

Breakfast Recipes 29
    Cinnamon Cheesecake Oat Bowl 30
    Banana Breakfast Cake 31
    Island Breakfast Cobbler 32
    Pomegranate Jewel Porridge 33
    Tomato and Spinach Frittata 34
    Pumpkin Breakfast Pudding 35
    Wasabi Scotch Eggs 36
    Poached Egg Baskets 37
    Eggs a la Provence 38
    Porkers Breakfast Quiche 39
    Spicy Sunshine Oatmeal 40
    Mini Bacon Quiches 41
    Fruity Breakfast Risotto 42
    Brown Rice Muesli Bowl 43
    Cardamom and Coconut Rice 44
    Quirky Breakfast Quinoa 45
    Quinoa Rainbow Salad 46
    Savory Bread Pudding 47
    Millet and Date Pudding 48
    Indian Millet Pilaf 49
    Citrus Tapioca Pudding 50
    Chia and Almond Bowls 51
    Hash Brown Hodge-Podge 52

Fluffy Steel Cut Oatmeal 53
Almond Banana Oatmeal 54
Healthy Vegetable Crust-less Quiche 55
Quinoa with Fresh Berries 56
Healthy Breakfast Porridge 57
Quick Raspberry Breakfast Oatmeal 58
Honey Cinnamon Apples 59
Green Chili Quiche 60
Decadent Vanilla Oats 61
Mushroom and Oatmeal Breakfast Risotto 62
Speedy Pear and Walnut Oats 63
Coconut Blueberry Oatmeal 64
Simple Breakfast Muffins 65
French Toast with a Fruity Twist 66
Spicy Breakfast Burrito 67
Apple Raisins Oatmeal 68
Perfect Kale Quinoa 69
Breakfast Burritos 70
Cheesy Beef Breakfast Rolls 71
Italian Sausages and Pepper Pot 72
Speedy Breakfast Tacos 73
Double-Cheesy Grits 74
Cinnamon Rooibos Lentil Bowl 75
Pecan Pie Sweet Potatoes 76
Vanilla Strawberry Cobbler 77
Breakfast Bread Pudding 78
Creamy Almond Peach Quinoa 79

Poultry Recipes 80

Chicken with Homemade Teriyaki Sauce 81
Italian Chicken Slices 82
Chicken Slices with Beans and Pineapples 83
Seared Chicken Breasts with Honey Sauce 84
Turkey Balls Marinated In Pasta Sauce 85
Asian Lemongrass Chicken 86
Dijon Chicken and Potatoes 87
Tropical Chicken Sandwiches 88
Moroccan Chicken 89
Hawaiian Chicken Buns 90
Greek Cacciatore Chicken 91
Honey BBQ Chicken Wings 92
Thai Chicken 93
Turkey Chili Zinger 94

Chicken Romano	95
Chicken In Tomatillo Sauce	96
Sherry and Ginger Duck	97
Turkey Meatballs with Mushrooms	98
Filipino Chicken	99
Creamy Turkey and Mash	100
Cucumber and Ginger Duck	101
Asparagus and Bacon Chicken	102
Simple Chicken Salad	103
Asian Chicken and Rice	104
Quick Chicken Curry	105
Crispy Dipping Chicken	106
Braised Pancetta Quail	107
Cranberry and Walnut Wings	108
Coriander and Garlic Chicken	109
Hot Sweet Chicken Wings	110
French Chicken Delight	111
Chicken Gumbo	112
Coca Cola Chicken	113
Duck Chili	114
Coq Au Vin	115
Italian Summer Chicken	116
Teriyaki Chicken	117
Creamy Bacon Chicken	118
Buffalo Blue Cheese Chicken	119
Bacon and Lentil Chicken	120
Chicken Curry with Eggplant	121
Chicken Chickpea Masala	122
Sesame Chicken	123
Apricot and Honey Chicken	124
Chicken and Dumpling Delight	125
Tossed Chicken and Noodles	126
Pomegranate Chicken with Walnuts	127
Creamy Garlic Goose	128
Creole Chicken Gumbo	129
Sweet Chili Goose	130
Indian Butter Chicken	131
Cheese and Broccoli Chicken	132
Rustic Chicken and Corn	133
Thai Chicken and Cabbage	134
Turkey Lasagna with Ricotta	135
Fish & Seafood Recipes	**136**

Rosemary Wild Salmon With Asparagus	137
Smoked Salmon with Spinach Pesto	138
Frozen Shrimp Rice	139
Bacon and Shrimp Grits with Tomato Sauce	140
Tangy Citrus Fish	141
Steamed Fish a la Corfu	142
Kerala Fish Curry	143
Mediterranean Cod Medley	144
Fennel Basted Salmon	145
Instant Saffron Salmon	146
Steamed Salmon With Cinnamon	147
Spicy Salmon Fillets	148
Tomato and Thyme Salmon Parcel	149
Healthy Salmon Burger	150
Creamy Fish and Potatoes	151
Marinated Salmon and Raspberries	152
Crustless Fish Pie	153
Jambalaya	154
Hot Tuna and Noodle Salad	155
Cheesy Mushroom Tuna	156
Asian Roasted Mackerel	157
Crumbed Mackerel with Lemon	158
Steamed Garlic Mussels	159
Mussels Neapolitan	160
Mussels and Spicy Sauce	161
Mussels and Spicy Sausage	162
Cioppino Deluxe	163
Boozy Chorizo Clams	164
Stuffed Clams	165
Crab in a Jiffy	166
Shrimp Teriyaki	166
Saffron Shrimp Delight	167
Shrimp Paella	168
Red-Hot Shrimp Curry	169
Mild Shrimp Curry	170
Quick Shrimp Creole	171
Shrimp and Parmesan Pasta	172
Shrimp Risotto	173
Seafood Gumbo	174
Greek Herbed Octopus	175
Stuffed Squid	176
Squid Masala	177
Italian Braised Squid	178

Meat Recipes 179
    Pomegranate Molasses Roasted Chuck 180
    Spicy Minced Lamb with Peas and Tomato Sauce 181
    Roasted Lamb Shanks with Vegetables 182
    Classic Meatloaf stuffed with Mozzarella 183
    Baracoa-Style Shredded Beef 184
    Beef Shawarma with Tahini Sauce 185
    Red Pepper Flakes Beef Ribs with Rice 186
    Simple Corned Beef 187
    Beef Bourguignon 188
    Asian Beef Curry 189
    Beef Stroganoff 190
    Beef Chili 191
    Bordeaux Pot Roast 192
    Beef Hot Pot 193
    Veal and Mushroom Symphony 194
    Beef and Pasta Casserole 195
    Chinese Beef and Broccoli 196
    Brisket and Cabbage Hodgepodge 197
    Merlot Lamb Shanks 198
    Mediterranean Lamb 199
    Creamy Lamb Curry 200
    Lamb and Vegetable Hotpot 201
    Moroccan Lamb 202
    Lamb Ragout 203
    Mexican Style Lamb 204
    Goat and Tomato Pot 205
    Spicy Taco Meat 206
    Spicy Beef Barbacoa 207
    Pork Carnitas 208
    Sweet and Savory Pork Chops 209
    Easy Ranch Season Pork Chops 210
    Asian Pork 211
    BBQ Ribs 212
    Mustard Infused Meatloaf 213
    Tasty Beef Curry 214
    Delicious Lamb Curry 215
    Gluten Free Beef Rice 216
    Lentil Beef Stew 217
    Classic Garlic Herb Pot Roast 218
    Apple Pork Tenderloin 219
    Jalapeno Beef 220
    Spicy Beef with Tomato Sauce 221

Spicy Goat and Potatoes 222
Apple Cider Pork 223
Creamy Mushroom Pork Chops 224
Tangy Pulled Pork 225
Chinese BBQ Pork 226
Hot Pepper Pork Chops 227
Pork Chops and Creamy Garlic Potatoes 228
Hot Sweet Ribs 229
Simple Beef Tacos 230
Pulled Pork Tamales 231
Mexican Pork Tostadas 232
Meatball Delight 233
Italian Meatballs 234

Soups & Stew Recipes 235

Onion Soup with Gruyere Cheese 236
Lobster Whip Cream Bisque 237
Hot Broccoli Cheddar Soup 238
Chicken Broth Noodle Soup 239
Pea Ham Soup 240
Toscana Coconut Soup 241
Hearty Vegetable Stew 242
Simple Vegetable Beef Soup 243
Healthy Vegetable Steak Soup 244
Beef Mushroom Stew 245
Chicken and Corn Chowder 246
Butternut and Chicken Soup 247
Cheesy Potato Soup 248
Split Pea Soup 249
Hearty Beef and Beans Soup 250
Old-Fashioned Chicken Noodle Soup 251
Chicken and Wild Rice Soup 252
Creamy Tomato Soup 253
Vegetable Lamb Stew 254
Creamy Zuppa Toscana 255
Minestrone Soup 256
Carrot and Ginger Soup 257
Country Ham and Bean Soup 258
Lentil and Spinach Soup 259
Cream of Asparagus Soup 260
Creamed Artichoke Soup 261
Cream of Broccoli Soup 262
Curried Celery Soup 263

Cheeky Chestnut Soup 264
Cauliflower and Cream Cheese Soup 265
Turkey and Sweet Potato Soup 266
Chicken Chili Soup 267
Broccoli and Bacon Soup 268
Chorizo, Chicken and Kale Soup 269
Endive and Ginger Soup 270
Chicken Enchilada Soup 271
Hearty Beef and Barley Soup 272
Pork and Mixed Vegetable Stew 273
Colombian Chicken Stew 274
Chicken and Potato Hot Pot 275
Simple Fish Chowder 276
Italian Chickpea Stew 277
Moroccan Sweet Potato Stew 278
Spinach Stew with Turmeric 279
Turkey Stew with Cranberry Sauce 280
Mushroom and Beef Stew 281
Oxtail and Red Wine Stew 282
Tuscan Lamb Stew 283
Beer and Lamb Stew 284
German Kielbasa Stew 285
Italian Sausage Stew 286

Beans & Grain Recipes 287

Quick Black Beans 288
Mexican Charro Beans 289
Mashed Beans with Jalapeno 290
Pinto Beans with Garlic Bread 291
Quick Lemon Rice 292
Black Bean Avocado Bowl 293
Pinto Beans Risotto with Pepper Jack Cheese 294
Risotto with Salmon Crumble 295
Barley Mushroom Risotto 296
Barley and Parmesan Risotto 297
Cracked Wheat a la Mumbai 298
Bulgur Pilaf 299
Israeli Couscous 300
Creamy Millet and Peas 301
Spicy Oats 302
Olive and Feta Quinoa 303
Mexican Cranberry Beans 304
Cranberry and Kale Pasta 305

Shiitake and Cranberry Bean Ensemble 306
Cranberry Bean Chili 307
Indian Lentils 308
Chickpea Curry 309
Chickpeas and Dumplings 310
Chickpea Pesto 311
Kidney Bean Etouffee 312
Rajma Kidney Bean Curry 313
Cajun Kidney Beans 314
Black Beans and Chorizo 315
Spicy Mexican Black Beans 316
Chili Lime Black Beans 317
White Beans and Shrimp 318
Grandma's Baked Beans 319
Bengal Mung Beans 320
Indian Style Mung Feast 321
Navy Beans with Bacon and Cabbage 322
Full Mudammas 323
Butter Beans and Bacon 324
Split Pea and Squash Curry 325
Pea and Pineapple Curry 326

Vegetables & Sides **327**

Artichoke Hearts with Garlic 328
Blue Cheese Beet Crumble 329
Mexican Stuffed Bell Peppers 330
Stuffed Bell Peppers with Beef 331
Brussels Sprouts with Bacon 332
Brussels Sprouts with Parmesan 333
Turmeric Cabbage and Sausages 334
Sweet and Spicy Cabbage 335
Cauliflower and Spinach Pasta 336
Endives with Ham 337
Eggplant Ratatouille 338
Eggplant Supreme 339
Babaganoush 340
Fennel Risotto 341
Smoked Kale and Bacon 342
Crispy Potatoes 343
Zucchinis and Cherry Tomatoes 344
Spicy Turnips 345
Stuffed Tomatoes 346
Rosemary Baby Potatoes 347

Indian-style Potato Cubes 348
Wild Rice, Faro and Cherry Pilaf 349
Quinoa Pilaf 350
Quinoa with Almonds 351
Mushroom Risotto 352
Simple Pumpkin Risotto 353
Spicy Veggie Rice 354
Herby Mashed Potatoes 355
Saffron Risotto 356
Farro with Cherries 357
Herbed Polenta 358
Mexican Rice 359
Cauliflower and Barley Risotto 360
Lemon, Parmesan and Pea Risotto 361
Spinach and Goat Cheese Risotto 362
Creamy Rice and Artichoke Pilaf 363
Potatoes Au Gratin 364
Crunchy Sweet Potato Casserole 365
Classic French Fries 366
Pineapple and Cauliflower Rice 367
Red Beans and Herb Rice 368
Golden Cauliflower Mash 369
Garlic and Parmesan Asparagus 370
"Drunken" Peas with Pancetta 371
Eggplant and Anchovies 372
Ginger Bok Choy 373

Sauce Recipes 374
Eggplant Oregano Dip 375
Hot Double Cheese Corn Dip 376
Something Meaty Sauce 377
Infused Mushroom Sauce 378
Overnight Marinara Sauce 379
Cream Cheese Corn Dip with Cotija 380
Classic Salsa Recipe 381
Ancho Chili Sauce 382
BBQ Sauce 383
Giblet Gravy 384
Zucchini Pesto 385
Cheese and Tomato Sauce 385
Mushroom Sauce 386
Spicy Mango Chutney 387
Tomato Chutney 388

Date and Tomato Sauce	389
Green Tomato Sauce	390
Orange and Ginger Sauce	390
Plum Sauce	391
Simple Onion Sauce	391
Spiced Pineapple Sauce	392
Clementine and Cranberry Sauce	392
Chili Orange Sauce	393
Sriracha Hot Sauce	394
Pomegranate Sauce	394
Mustard Sauce	395
Apricot Sauce	396
Creamy Broccoli Sauce	396
Eggplant Sauce	397
Cherry Sauce	398
Elderberry Honey Sauce	398
Pear and Cinnamon Sauce	399
Melon and Wine Sauce	399
Gingered Guava Sauce	400
Peaches & Whiskey Sauce	400
Peach Sauce	401
Quince Sauce	401
Creamy Parsley Sauce	402
Cilantro Sauce	403
Chestnut Sauce	404
Spiced Rhubarb Sauce	404

Jams & Spreads **405**

Mixed Berry Breakfast Jam	406
Instant Lemon Marmalade	406
Orange Marmalade	407
Pear and Apple Jam	407
Mixed Berry Jam	408
Peach and Ginger Jam	409
Raspberry Curd	409
Blackberry Jam	410
Berry Compote	410
Cinnamon Apple Butter	411
Candied Lemon Peel	412
Chickpea Spread	413
Mushroom Pate	414
Ricotta Cheese Spread	415
Pumpkin Butter	415

    Chili Jam 416

Dessert Recipes 417
    Chocolate Cheesecake 418
    Apple Bread 419
    Pumpkin Chocolate Cake 420
    Banana Bread 421
    Chocolate Lava Cake 422
    Tasty Apple Crisp 423
    Grandma's Baked Apples 423
    Decadent Chocolate Fondue 424
    Classic Tapioca Pudding 424
    Steamed Cranberry and Apricot Pudding 425
    Mini Pumpkin Pies 426
    Upside-Down Apple Cake 427
    Brownie Cake with Almonds 428
    Crème Brûlée 429
    Old-Fashioned Bread Pudding 430
    Poached Pears with Wine Sauce 431
    Rich Ruby Pears 431
    Citrus Ricotta Cake 432
    Pumpkin Rice Pudding 433
    Key Lime Pie 434
    Spiced Carrot Cake 435
    Zucchini Nut Bread 436
    Samoa Cheesecake 437
    Autumn Cobbler 438
    Pina Colada Rice Pudding 439
    Caramel Custard Flan 440
    Decadent Chocolate Pudding 441
    Sticky Date Pudding 442
    Simple Chocolate Cake 443
    Carrot and Pecan Pudding 444
    Eggnog Cheesecake 445
    Lemon Crème Pots 446

Conclusion 447

The Instant Pot Revolution

I'm sure you've heard of the Instant pot by now. It's been the hot new cooking appliance for the past few months, and it does not look like it is going anywhere.
Chances are that you've seen it on the shelves of your local superstore, on Amazon, or perhaps you've come across one of the many blogs, social media posts, or celebrity followers singing the praises of this fresh take on the old-fashioned pressure cooker.

I've always been intrigued by the idea of a pressure cooker, but to be perfectly honest, it has always scared me. The Instant Pot is the perfect solution for people like me, who like the idea of cooking a tender roast in a fraction of the time that it takes in the oven or slow cooker.

While our mothers and grandmothers were comfortable using a stovetop pressure cooker, most men and women of this generation have been intimidated by the ominous hissing sound and the potential of having it explode at any moment. Because of this, pressure cooking has fallen out of favor in the last few decades. All that has now changed with the arrival of the Instant Pot - a self-contained, electrical pressure cooker with plenty of built in safety features.

With the promise of being able to cook a meal in 3 to 10 minutes of pressure cooking, it is no surprise that this new electric appliance is quickly gaining a large fan base. Instant Pots are flying off the shelves, and you can find plenty of fans online who share their favorite recipes, tips, and adaptations on blogs and popular Instant Pot Facebook groups.

The Instant Pot is a self-contained unit that sits neatly on your counter top and plugs into a power outlet. It takes up about as much space as a rice cooker or a small slow cooker. The difference is it's a smart pressure cooker that's controlled through an intuitive digital interface. You tell it how long you want to cook your meal under pressure, set the timer and you're good to go. It automatically brings up and holds the pressure and temperature at a safe level and will not allow you to open the pot while it's pressurized. This makes it as easy to operate as a microwave, if not easier.

It is not surprising then, that this new take on an old kitchen tool is quickly gaining popularity. The actual cooking is very hands-off and automated. You simply set it, and then walk away until you're food is ready. It has all the advantages of using the slow cooker, but takes a fraction of the time. Perfect when you want to get a home cooked meal on the table fast.

How Fast Can I Cook my Meal?

One of the big appeals of the Instant pot when you first start to look at it is how quickly it claims to cook food. I know it's what first attracted me to this new kitchen appliance. Being able to cook an entire Sunday dinner in 15 minutes or less sounded very appealing, but also a little too good to be true.

Let's take a closer look at how fast the Instant Pot actually cooks your food.

Let me start by pointing out that it does indeed cook pretty fast. It really shines on dishes like stews or roasts that would otherwise take a long time on the stove or in the oven, and even longer in the slow cooker.

Truth be told, the claims that it can cook chicken breast in 5 minutes, or a roast in 20 minutes, are a little misleading. While that is the time the food needs to cook under pressure, the actual time before you can eat is longer because it has to come up to pressure first. This process can take anywhere from ten minutes to half an hour. The fuller the pot, the colder (or even frozen) the ingredients, and the bigger the cut of meat, the longer it will take to come up to pressure. Once it does, the countdown timer will start.

After the food has cooked for the allotted time, it takes a little while before you can safely open the pot and serve your meal. There are two options and which one you choose is dependent on the meal you're preparing. The first option is to release the pressure through the vent in the lid which causes hot steam to escape and the pressure to decrease within a matter of minutes. Once this process is completed you'll be able to open the lid and serve the food once it has cooled to an edible temperature.

The second option is a process called Natural Pressure Release (NPR). Whenever a recipe calls for this, you shouldn't turn the valve to release the pressure. Instead, you let the pot sit until the pressure releases on its own. This process takes about 25 to 45 minutes and allows the food to continue cooking, until the pressure valve drops down and you are able to open the pot. It's important to allow for this additional time when preparing a meal in the Instant Pot.

All in all, you won't be able to cook your meals in a matter of minutes. You have to factor in the time it will take for the pot to come up to pressure, and for some recipes, additional time to allow the pressure to slowly drop back down.

Does this mean the Instant Pot isn't fast? Of course not.

It's still a much quicker method of cooking roasts, beans and the likes than any other cooking style. In short it's not super-fast for everything, but great for things that take a long time otherwise.

As an added bonus, once you add everything to the pot, it is hands-free cooking. You don't have to stir pots or babysit the food. Instead, you can work on something else, allocated your time to something more productive, spend some quality time with the family, or just relax a bit while dinner cooks itself.

But, is it Worth The Money?

Let's take a look at the instant pot and whether or not it's worth spending the money on one. Depending on the time of year, and what kind of deal you can find, the average Instant Pot will set you back anywhere from $70 to $150. While this doesn't make it the cheapest kitchen appliance on the market, it's also nowhere near the highest.

On the other hand you can pick up a stovetop pressure cooker or basic slow cooker for around $25. Does that mean the Instant Pot is overpriced, or something you shouldn't consider buying? I don't think so. While the Instant Pot may not be the right choice for everyone, it can quickly become one of your most valued and most often used appliances.

The inexpensive stove-top pressure cooker will do you no good if you're too intimidated to use it, or end up keeping it in the back of the cabinet because you don't have the time and patience to keep an eye on the pressure and adjust the stovetop as needed. If you have young children underfoot, you may not be comfortable using a traditional pressure cooker due to possible safety issues, so the Instant Pot provides a great alternative.

If you're good at planning ahead and starting dinner first thing in the morning to slow cook a roast, you may not need an Instant Pot. If on the other hand, you're like me and forget to get it started, the Instant Pot may just be the solution you need to get dinner on the table quickly.

Last but not least, let's talk hard cash. The expense of buying the Instant Pot will easily be worth it, if it keeps you from going out to eat, or picking up food on your way home. If you know you can get dinner cooked in 45 minutes without having to stir pots, it becomes a lot easier to go home and start that pot of chili, or the pot roast, and relax while it cooks. If it keeps you from ordering out even just once a week, it won't be long before the Instant Pot pays for itself!

At the end of the day, the decision is yours to make. If you aren't sure if you'll actually use it, the Instant Pot may be a waste of money. If on the other hand, you think you'll use it quite a bit then keep it on your counter and use it as your pressure cooker, slow cooker, and rice cooker, it will be an investment that's well worth it. Look through some recipes, borrow a friend's Instant Pot if possible, and see if this seems like the type of appliance that will work well for you and your lifestyle.

Differences between the Instant Pot & Slow Cooker

When you start to look into the benefits of using an Instant Pot, you may notice that there's quite a bit of overlap with the benefits of using a slow cooker. Both appliances are good at cooking large, inexpensive cuts of meat like pork and beef roasts for example. Both are great at cooking beans, soups, stews, chilies and the likes. Both are also great for busy home cooks, since they allow you put everything in, turn it on, and let the food cook itself. No stirring pots and watching the stove required.

In addition, both are electric appliances that sit on your counter top and plug into an available outlet. You can move them around as needed, they use up approximately the same amount of space, and you can take them with you to family get-togethers and vacations. They even both excel at keeping food piping hot until you're ready to eat.

The biggest difference between the Instant Pot and the Slow Cooker is cooking time. The slow cooker is designed to cook your meal low and slow. The average slow cooker dish takes six to ten hours to cook. The instant pot on the other hand will cook most meals in under an hour from start to finish.

Another big difference is that while a slow cooker is just that, a device that cooks your meals low and slow, the Instant Pot can replace your rice cooker as well as your slow cooker since it has a slow cooker setting. Depending on the model you choose, you can even replace your yogurt maker with it.

In this recipe book you will find many slow cooker recipes, showcasing that the instant pot can quite easily remove the need for multiple kitchen appliances that waste space and often go unused because they are sitting in y our basement, garage or at the back of your kitchen cupboard.

If you want more versatility in one appliance and the ability to cook a wholesome home cooked meal in a very short time, the Instant Pot is the way to go. I encourage you to give it a try and see if it becomes one of the most used kitchen appliances in your house like it has in mine.

If on the other hand you are comfortable with your slow cooker and good about planning ahead long enough to start your dinner in it, you may find that you have no need for an Instant Pot. Similarly, if you think the hissing and steaming, or simply the idea of having a pressure cooking device in your kitchen scares you then you're probably better off sticking to your slow cooker. That being said, with the safety features built in and the easy to use digital display, using an instant pot is just as simple and easy as your favorite slow cooker. If you're feeling a little intimidated, I encourage you to get one and give it a try. After preparing your first two or three meals in it, you'll be wondering what you were worried about in the first place.

Versatility Unmatched

One of my favorite things about the Instant Pot is how versatile it is. You can cook a wide variety of dishes in this popular new electric appliance. In chapter we're going to take a quick look at how you can cook breakfast, lunch, and dinner in this electric pressure cooker. This will come in handy when your stove is out, it's too hot to cook inside, you're on vacation, or when you're cooking with your Instant Pot in your dorm room for example.

Of course these aren't the only times the versatility of the Instant pot will come in handy. I like to use my Instant Pot multiple times per week and cook a wide variety of dishes in it for any time of the day. Let me quickly run you through some family favorites for breakfast, lunch and dinner.

Breakfast In The Instant Pot
Let's start with the first meal of the day – breakfast. There are all sorts of great dishes you can make in the Instant Pot. With the sauté function, you can even use it to scramble up some eggs or cook sausage in a pinch.

Where the Instant Pot really shines is with oatmeal. Some of the best tasting steel cut oats come from cooking them in this popular electric appliance. No constant stirring required for creamy and nutritious oats.

You can even hard boil a large quantity of eggs in your Instant Pot. Perfect for make ahead breakfast meals that last you all week long.

Lunch In The Instant Pot
Since the Instant Pot does such a great job at fixing soups and stews, it's perfect for lunchtime cooking as well. With a quick google search you'll be able to find plenty of yummy recipes to try as well as lots of directions for adapting your own favorite recipes.

It's also a great way to cook one pot meals including pasta and rice dishes that are perfect for lunch. And let's not forget about everyone's favorite – Mac and Cheese. If on the other hand you're in the mood for a nice salad, try boiling eggs for it in the instant pot, or even making an entire batch of potato salad in it from start to finish.

Dinner In The Instant Pot
Last but not least, let's talk about dinner. This is where the Instant pot really shines. It's great for easy weeknight dinners that can be cooked from start to finish in the instant pot like a nice big batch of beef stew, or your favorite chicken dish for example.

Pressure cookers have always been the best way to deal with large roasts and tougher cuts of meat. Cook your pot roast or a big batch of homemade pulled pork in the slow cooker for a nice Sunday dinner.

And let's not forget about side dishes. From various rice dishes to mashed, or scalloped potatoes, the instant pot can take care of your main side dish for you while you're busy cooking anything else.

Novel Ways To Use Your Instant Pot

Some fun and unusual stuff you can do. I.e. make vanilla extract, cheese cake, and can in the instant pot

So you have an Instant Pot and you've been using it regularly to cook all the typical pressure cooker dishes. You put it to good use for your Sunday roast, whip up a quick last minute dinner during the week, and even cook oatmeal in it a few times per week for breakfast. In short, the Instant Pot has become a staple appliance in your home.

Then you start to wonder what else this electric pressure cooker can do. I'm here with some fun ideas for unusual ways to make the most from your Instant Pot. While these may not be the things you will be making on a weekly or even monthly basis, they are fun to try and have their good uses.

Bake A Cheese Cake

The Instant Pot makes some of the yummiest and easiest cheese cakes. Yes, that's right. You can sort of bake in your instant pot. You'll need a spring form that fits inside your instant pot, a rack for the baking pan to sit in and of course a delicious cheese cake recipe.

A quick search will bring up an almost endless supply of yummy recipes to try. Pick one and start stirring your pot. Before long you'll be making one of your favorite indulged desserts in the Instant Pot. This is perfect for when you want to impress your guests or bring something unusual to the office pot luck.

Can Some Jam

Traditional pressure cookers are great for canning all sorts of fruits and vegetables. While the Instant Pot wasn't designed with canning and food preservation in mind, you can do a little small batch canning in it.

This is perfect if you want to turn some of those ripe fruits from the local farmers market into some artisan jam. Use the Instant Pot to preserve and pressure seal your jars. Since you're processing in small batches, you can try out various different and fun recipes and end up with some delicious jams and preserves to enjoy throughout the year.

Make Homemade Vanilla Extract

Do you use vanilla extract in your cooking and baking? I go through quite a bit, particularly during the holiday season. There's nothing quite like real vanilla extract, but let's be honest, it's outrageously pricey. Why not make your own homemade vanilla extract in your Instant Pot?

That's right... you can make your own homemade version using real vanilla beans and vodka or other high spirit. Not only is it some of the best tasting extract you'll ever use, it's also a wonderful gift to give to loved ones.

Saving you Time & Money

We're all busy and spending less and less time at home. As a result, it's hard to find the time to cook a nice home cooked meal. We simply can't spend hours and hours in the kitchen stirring pots. Heck most of us don't even have the time or energy at the end of the day for a quick 30 minute meal cooked from scratch.

The end result is that we rely on convenience food and takeout. While those options certainly save a good bit of time, we end up paying a lot more for our food. Let's not even mention the fact that it isn't always the healthiest food out there and we're not sure what ingredients and preservatives are in the food.

What if there was a way to save both time and money, and still get wholesome, home cooked meals on those nights when you don't have a lot of time or energy left. There is and the solution to your problem is the Instant Pot. Not only does it cook your food faster than just about any other method of cooking, it is also very hands-free. You can even cook frozen meat and veggies for those days when you forget to thaw ahead of time.

This means that you can come home, throw some ingredients in the Instant Pot, turn it on, and then focus your attention on something else. This means that you can help your kids with homework, start a load of laundry, catch up on work email, or just sit back and relax for half an hour before dinner is served.

In other words, the Instant Pot saves you time in two different ways. It will take less time overall to cook the food, and most of the cooking time doesn't require you to be there, stirring pots and playing an active role in the cooking process. That's a big deal and something you'll come to appreciate when you start to use your Instant Pot regularly.

An Instant Pot is a bit of an investment, even when you can find a great "Black Friday" style deal on it. On average, you can expect to spend about $100 for this electric pressure cooker. The good news is that it won't take you long to recoup this investment, as mentioned in the previous chapters.

An instant pot allows you to cook more at home instead of going out to eat, or ordering takeout. This alone will save you anywhere from $5 to $50 per family meal. But it doesn't stop there. The Instant Pot really shines with inexpensive cuts of meat like roasts, whole chickens and even more frugal fare like beans and rice. If you get in the habit of making just one frugal meal per week using your pressure cooker, those savings will quickly add up.

You can go even further by cooking double batches and taking leftovers for lunch instead of buying it. Saving time and money with an Instant Pot is quick, easy, and almost automatic. The only trick is that you have to actually get in the habit of using it regularly.

How Safe Is The Instant Pot?

Pressure cookers have been around for a long time, and just as long have the incidents of them exploding in the kitchen due to user error. While they are a great cooking tool and most of us can remember a grandmother, aunt, or other relative having one and cooking with it regularly, most of us in this day and age have been more than a little bit intimidated by the regular stove top models.

I can't say I blame you, if you feel the same. We're in the same boat. While I love the idea of being able to cook food quickly and in a healthy way by cooking it under pressure, I have never been comfortable being in the same room with one, not to mention actually using it. The hissing, steaming, and rattling alone is enough to send the bravest of home cooks to the hills.

Thankfully there's a new pressure cooker kid on the block – the Instant Pot and it's much safer and more convenient to use than the standard stove top models. It has a total of 10 built in safety features that will keep you and your loved ones safe and secure. Combined they ensure that it is almost impossible to go wrong due to user error or equipment failure.

Let's take the locking mechanism as an example. With a regular stove-top pressure cooker, it's easy to try to lift the lid while the container is still under pressure and burn yourself with the hot steam that will escape violently. The Instant Pot lid will not open until the pressure is back to normal.

Automatic pressure control and pressure regulators keep the pressure in the pot under control. This means you can't generate the kind of pressure inside your pot that could cause it to explode all over your kitchen. If you ask me, that's a very good thing.

It even has sensors built in that keep temperature in check and keep you from burning you food in cases where there isn't enough liquid in the pot to build up the appropriate cooking pressure. Instead of continuing to heat on high and burning the food inside the pressure cooker, it simply switches to the keep warm function, allowing you to add liquid and start over.

You can check the Instant Pot website for full details on all 10 safety features of the Instant Pot and how they make pressure cooking safer than ever. As long as you make sure the device isn't damaged and keep the sealing ring, lid, and vent clean, cooking in this smart new appliance is as safe as anything else you do in the kitchen.

Yes, there's still a bit of hissing steam before your cooker hits full pressure and the safety valve closes, but that just makes it fun and exciting. After the first few times of using your Instant Pot, you won't even think twice about it. Give it a try. I think you'll love this fast new way to cook healthy, homemade meals.

How To Find Even More Instant Pot Recipes

You bought an Instant Pot, brought it home, and got it set up. You did your water test, boiled some eggs in it, and maybe even made a handful of dishes from recipes on the Instant Pot website or in the included recipe guide. Now that you're comfortable using this new electric appliance, you're ready to branch out and start to look for some other fun recipes to try, other than the 700 provided in this book. Here are some of the best places both online and offline to find Instant Pot Recipes.

Go Old School With Cookbooks And Recipes Cards

Since the Instant Pot has been so popular for the past few months, there are plenty of traditional cookbooks (along with eBook versions) being published. Browse through your local bookstore, or head on over to Amazon.com to see what's available right now.

If you have friends or family members who are Instant Pot fans, ask them for their favorite recipes and jot them down on recipe cards. If there's a group of you, you can start to regularly exchange recipes. If someone brings an Instant Pot dish to a potluck or gathering, ask them for the recipe. It won't take you long to establish a nice little library of tried and true recipes.

Blogs And Google Searches

If you're looking for something specific, doing a quick Google search is always a great idea. You'll be able to find chicken thigh specific recipes, or instant pot ready recipes for spaghetti and meatballs.

Along the way, you'll likely come across all sorts of different blogs where fellow Instant Pot users share their experiences and recipes. Bookmark them, or simply browse around when you come across them for plenty of fresh recipe ideas. Try the recipes as is, or use them as inspiration to come up with your own take on a dish.

Go Social With Pinterest And Facebook Groups

Last but not least, let's not forget about social media. Pinterest is a great source of Instant Pot recipes. Do a quick search and follow a few Instant Pot or Pressure Cooker boards for plenty of new recipe ideas in your Pinterest Feed.

By far my favorite way to come across new recipes to try or get suggestions for recipe adaptations, is Facebook groups. There are several good Instant Pot specific groups you can join and participate in. You'll find a wealth of information in these groups along with all sorts of helpful tips and ideas.

Instant Pot Cooking Times
(Credit: www.instantpot.com)

As with conventional cooking, cooking with the Instant Pot® is full of personal choices, creativity, a lot of science, and little experimentation. No two people have exactly the same tastes, preferences of tenderness and texture of food. The purpose of the Cooking Time Tables is to provide you with a reference, however you are encouraged to experiment and find the time settings that best suit your personal preferences.

There are other factors that may affect the cooking time. Different cuts of meat and diverse types of rice, for example, may require different cooking times to yield the same tenderness or texture.

When cooking frozen food, there is no need to defrost the food in the microwave first. However, frozen food will prolong the pre-heating time and cooking time by a few minutes, depending on the amount of food.

The timing indicated within the Cooking Time Tables are based on the cooking pressure within the range of 10.15–11.6 psi.

SEAFOOD & FISH

The cooking time for seafood is typically short. The best result is achieved with the original juice being retained in the food. Steaming is the ideal cooking method, however stewing the food will also produce great results.

When steaming seafood, you will need at least one 1 cup (250 mL) of water, and an ovenproof or steel bowl on a trivet. When seafood or fish are over-cooked, their texture becomes tough. Unless that's the intended result, you should control the cooking time precisely. Normally, you'll need to use the steam release handle to release the pressure and stop cooking as soon as the programmed cooking period is over. An alternative is to take the natural cooling time (7 – 10 minutes) into consideration.

Seafood & Fish	FRESH Cooking Time (minutes)	FROZEN Cooking Time (minutes)
Crab, whole	2 – 3	4 – 5
Fish, whole	4 – 5	5 – 7
Fish, fillet	2 – 3	3 – 4
Fish, steak	3 – 4	4 – 6
Lobster	2 – 3	3 – 4
Mussels	1 – 2	2 – 3
Seafood soup or stock	7 – 8	8 – 9
Shrimp or Prawn	1 – 3	2 – 4

RICE & GRAINS

If you would like to cook some specialty rice or grains, please use the following grain : water ratio.

The provided Rice Measuring Cup (180 mL) can be used to measure the required grain to water ratios. One cup of grain yields about one adult serving.

Rice & Grains	Water Quantity Ratio (grain : water)	Cooking Time (minutes)
Barley, pearl	1 : 2 ½	20 – 22
Barley, pot	1 : 3 – 1 : 4	25 – 30
Congee, thick	1 : 4 – 1 : 5	15 – 20
Congee, thin	1 : 6 – 1 : 7	15 – 20
Couscous	1 : 2	2 – 3
Corn, dried / halved	1 : 3	25 – 30
Kamut, whole	1 : 2	10 – 12
Millet	1 : 1.75	10 – 12
Oats, quick cooking	1 : 2	2 – 3
Oats, steel-cut	1 : 3	3 – 5
Porridge, thin	1 : 6 – 1 : 7	5 – 7
Quinoa, quick cooking	1 : 1.25	1
Rice, Basmati	1 : 1	4
Rice, Brown	1 : 1	20 – 22
Rice, Jasmine	1 : 1	4
Rice, white	1 : 1	4
Rice, wild	1 : 2	20 – 25
Sorghum	1 : 3	20 – 25
Spelt berries	1 : 1 ½	25 – 30
Wheat berries	1 : 3	20 – 25

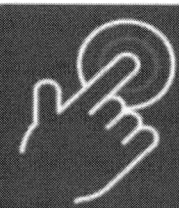

INSTANT TIP: Use the Smart Programs

Instant Pot®'s built-in [Rice] and [Multigrain] Smart Programs provide the optimal method of cooking rice and grains.

DRIED BEANS, LEGUMES, & LENTILS

There are a few things to be aware of when cooking dried beans and legumes:

- Dried beans double in volume and weight after soaking or cooking. To avoid overflow, please do not fill the inner pot more than half capacity to allow for expansion.
- When cooking dried beans, use enough liquid to cover the beans.

Beans and legumes are less likely to be over-cooked, but if they are undercooked the texture is typically unpleasant. Please consider the cooking time as the minimal time.

Dried Beans, Legumes, & Lentils	DRY Cooking Time (minutes)	SOAKED Cooking Time (minutes)
Adzuki / Azuki / Aduki	16 – 20	4 – 6
Anasazi	20 – 25	5 – 7
Black beans	20 – 25	4 – 6
Black-eyed peas	6 – 7	4 – 5
Chickpeas (chickpeas, garbanzo bean, or kabuli)	35 – 40	10 – 15
Cannellini beans	25 – 30	6 – 9
Gandules, pigeon peas	25 – 30	4 – 9
Great Northern beans	25 – 30	7 – 8
Kidney beans, red	15 – 20	7 – 8
Kidney beans, white / Cannellini	25 – 30	6 – 9
Lentils, green	4 – 6	N/A
Lentils, brown	4 – 6	N/A
Lentils, red, split	1 – 2	N/A
Lentils, yellow, split (moong dal)	1 – 2	N/A
Lima beans	12 – 14	3 – 6
Navy beans	20 – 25	3 – 4
Pinto beans	25 – 30	7 – 9
Peas	6 – 10	N/A
Scarlet runner	20 – 25	6 – 8
Soy beans	35 – 45	18 – 20

INSTANT TIP: Save Time, Soak the Beans

Although not strictly necessary, soaking the dried beans can speed up cooking significantly. Immerse the beans in 4 times their volume of water for 4-6 hours.

MEAT (POULTRY, BEEF, PORK, & LAMB)

There are a few things to be aware of when cooking meat:

- Raw meat is perishable and should not be left at room temperature for more than 2 hours (or 1 hour if room temperature is above 32°C / 90°F). When using the [Delay Start] program, do not set time for more than 1-2 hours. We recommend to pre-cook the meat and select the automatic [Keep Warm] or [Warm] program to maintain the food at serving temperature.
- Do not try to thicken the sauce before cooking. Corn starch, flour or arrow-root may deposit on the bottom of the inner pot and block heat dissipation. As a result, the pressure cooker may overheat.

You may want to brown the meat by selecting the [Sauté] program to seal the juices before pressure cooking.

Meat	Cooking Time (minutes)
Beef, stew meat	20 / 450 gm / 1 lb
Beef, meat ball	5 / 450 gm / 1 lb
Beef, dressed	20 – 25 / 450 gm / 1 lb
Beef (pot roast, steak, rump, round, chuck, blade or brisket (small chunks)	20 / 450 gm / 1 lb
Beef (pot roast, steak, rump, round, chuck, blade or brisket (large chunks)	15 / 450 gm / 1 lb
Beef, ribs	20 – 25
Beef, shanks	25 – 30
Beef, oxtail	40 – 50
Chicken, breasts (boneless)	6 – 8
Chicken, whole 2-2.5 Kg	8 / 450 gm / 1 lb
Chicken, cut with bones	10 – 15
Chicken, bones for stock	12 – 15
Duck, portions with bones	12 – 15
Duck, whole	10 / 450 gm / 1 lb

Meat	Cooking Time (minutes)
Ham, slices	9 – 12
Ham, picnic shoulder	8 / 450 gm / 1 lb
Lamb, cubes	10 – 15
Lamb, stew meat	12 – 15
Lamb, leg	15 / 450 gm / 1 lb
Pheasant	8 / 450 gm / 1 lb
Pork, loin roast	20 / 450 gm / 1 lb
Pork, butt roast	15 / 450 gm / 1 lb
Pork, ribs	15 – 20
Turkey, breast (boneless)	7 – 9
Turkey, breast (whole)	20 – 25
Turkey, drumsticks (leg)	15 – 20
Veal, chops	5 – 8
Veal, roast	12 / 450 gm / 1 lb
Quail, whole	8 / 450 gm / 1 lb

INSTANT TIP: Seasoning Beef— Try these on Your Next Meal

Beef: (approximately 500 g or 1 lb)
- 50 g (2 oz) butter, 2 cloves crushed garlic, 2 sprigs fresh thyme
- 50 g (2 oz) butter, 2 cloves crushed garlic, 2 sprigs fresh parsley
- 50 g (2 oz) butter, 2 tbsp (30 mL) fresh chives, 1 tbsp (15 mL) grainy mustard
- 1 tbsp (15 mL) olive oil, 2 sprigs fresh thyme, 50 g (2 oz) cooked bacon

VEGETABLES

When steaming vegetables, you will need 1 cup (250 mL) of water and an ovenproof or steel bowl on a trivet.

Due to short pressure keeping period, leaving the pressure cooker naturally cooling down without using the steam release will add some extra cooking time to the food. (Natural Release — see page 7).

Vegetables	FRESH Cooking Time (minutes)	FROZEN Cooking Time (minutes)
Artichoke, whole & trimmed	9 – 11	11 – 13
Artichoke, hearts	4 – 5	5 – 6
Asparagus, whole or cut	1 – 2	2 – 3
Beans, green, yellow or wax, whole, trim ends and strings	1 – 2	2 – 3
Beetroot, small / whole	11 – 13	13 – 15
Beetroot, large / whole	20 – 25	25 – 30
Broccoli, florets	1 – 2	2 – 3
Broccoli, stalks	3 – 4	4 – 5
Brussel sprouts, whole	2 – 3	3 – 4
Cabbage, red, purple or green, shredded	2 – 3	3 – 4
Cabbage, red, purple or green, wedges	3 – 4	4 – 5
Carrots, sliced or shredded	2 – 3	3 – 4
Carrots, whole or chunked	6 – 8	7 – 9
Cauliflower florets	2 – 3	4 – 5
Celery, chunks	2 – 3	3 – 4
Collard Greens	4 – 5	5 – 6

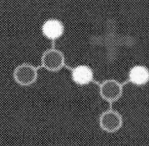 **INSTANT TIP:** Steaming Vegetables Preserves Vitamins

When cooking vegetables, fresh or frozen, it's recommended to use steaming to preserve vitamins and minerals to the maximum. Steaming also retains the nature look of the vegetable, adding aesthetic value to your dish.

Vegetables	FRESH Cooking Time (minutes)	FROZEN Cooking Time (minutes)
Corn (kernels)	1 – 2	2 – 3
Corn (on the cob)	3 – 4	4 – 6
Eggplant (slices or chunks)	2 – 3	3 – 4
Endive	2 – 3	4 – 5
Escarole (chopped)	3 – 4	4 – 6
Green beans (whole)	2 – 3	4 – 5
Greens (chopped)	2 – 3	4 – 5
Leeks	2 – 3	3 – 4
Mixed vegetables	3 – 4	4 – 6
Okra	2 – 3	3 – 4
Onions (sliced)	2 – 3	4 – 5
Parsnips (chunks)	3 – 4	4 – 6
Peas (in the pod)	2 – 3	4 – 5
Peas (green)	2 – 3	4 – 5
Potatoes (cubed)	2 – 3	3 – 4
Baby potatoes (whole)	3 – 4	4 – 6
Large potatoes (whole)	2 – 3	3 – 4
Pumpkin (small pieces)	2 – 3	4 – 5
Pumpkin (larges pieces)	3 – 4	4 – 6
Rutabaga (slices)	2 – 3	4 – 5
Rutabaga (chunks)	2 – 3	4 – 5
Spinach	2 – 3	3 – 4
Acorn squash (slices)	3 – 4	4 – 6
Butternut squash (slices)	2 – 3	3 – 4
Sweet Potato (cubes)	2 – 3	4 – 5
Sweet Potato Large (whole)	3 – 4	4 – 6
Sweet Potato Small (whole)	2 – 3	4 – 5
Sweet Pepper (slices or chunks)	2 – 3	4 – 5
Tomatoes (quarters)	N/A	4 – 5

Instant Pot Cheat Sheet
(Credit: www.onegoodthingbyjillee.com)

- Use natural release for red meat, and use quick release for everything else.
- If there is a range of cooking times, choose a time based on the size of the item you're cooking.
- Everything on this list is meant to be cooked on the manual setting on "high".

Use this cheat sheet to make your next meal an *instant* success!

BEEF ROAST  35-40 MINUTES	**DRY BLACK OR PINTO BEANS**  Cover beans with water 26 MINUTES	**BONELESS RIBS**  25 MINUTES	**CHICKEN BREASTS** 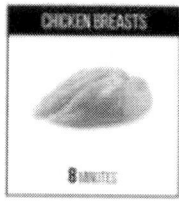 8 MINUTES	**CHICKEN THIGHS**  9 MINUTES
WHOLE CHICKEN  Use sauté function to brown first with a little oil 6 MINUTES PER POUND	**CORN ON THE COB**  3-4 MINUTES	**FISH FILLET (FRESH)**  2-3 MINUTES	**FISH FILLET (FROZEN)**  3-4 MINUTES	**HARD-BOILED EGGS**  Add 1 cup water and use metal rack 4 MINUTES
QUICK OATS  Oats : Water 1 : 1.8 5 MINUTES	**STEEL-CUT OATS**  Oats : Water 1 : 1.8 10 MINUTES	**PASTA**  Cover noodles with water 4 MINUTES	**PORK CHOPS**  Use sauté function to brown first with a little oil 5 MINUTES	**PORK ROAST**  Use sauté function to brown first with a little oil 45-55 MINUTES
WHOLE POTATOES  Add 1 cup water and use metal rack 12-15 MINUTES	**BROWN RICE**  Rice : Water 1 : 1.25 25 MINUTES	**WHITE RICE**  Rice : Water 1 : 1 12 MINUTES	**WILD RICE**  Rice : Water 1 : 1.8 27 MINUTES	**VEGGIES (CHUNKS)**  Add 1 cup water and use metal rack 1-3 MINUTES

ONEGOODTHINGBYJILLEE.COM

Breakfast Recipes

Cinnamon Cheesecake Oat Bowl

(**Prep Time:** 10 MIN| **Cook Time:** 13 MIN| **Serve:** 4)

Ingredients:

1 cup steel-cut oats
3 ½ cups water
a pinch of salt
1 tbsp butter
¾ cup raisins
1 tsp cinnamon
¼ cup brown sugar
2 tbsp white sugar
2 ounces cream cheese, soft
1 tsp milk

Directions:

1. Select Sauté mode on your instant pot, add butter and melt.
2. Add oats, toast for 3 minutes, stirring constantly.
3. Add a pinch of salt and the water, cover and cook on High for 10 minutes.
4. Release the pressure naturally for 5 minutes and uncover.
5. Add raisins, stir and set aside.
6. Meanwhile, mix cinnamon with brown sugar in a bowl.
7. In another bowl, mix white sugar, cream cheese and milk and stir well.
8. Transfer oats mixture to breakfast bowls and top each serving with cinnamon mixture
9. Top with cream cheese blend and enjoy!

(**Calories** 140|**Fat** 3 g| **Protein** 4 g| **Fiber** 3 g| **Carbohydrates** 26 g)

Banana Breakfast Cake

(**Prep Time:** 10 MIN| **Cook Time:** 55 MIN| **Serve:** 5)

Ingredients:

1 cup water
1 ½ cups sugar
2 cups flour
3 bananas, peeled and mashed
2 eggs
½ cup butter, softened
2 tsp baking powder
A pinch of salt
1 tsp cinnamon
1 tsp nutmeg

Directions:

1. In a bowl, mix eggs, butter and sugar and stir well.
2. Add salt, baking powder, cinnamon and nutmeg and stir again.
3. Add bananas and flour and stir again.
4. Grease a spring form pan with some butter, pour the batter in it and cover the pan with a paper towel and tin foil
5. Add 1 cup water to your instant pot, place the pan in the pot, cover and cook on High for 55 minutes.
6. Release the pressure quickly, remove the pan, leave to cool down, cut, serve and enjoy!

(**Calories** 326|**Fat** 11 g| **Protein** 4.3 g| **Fiber** 1.1 g| **Carbohydrates** 55 g)

Island Breakfast Cobbler

(**Prep Time:** 10 MIN| **Cook Time:** 15 MIN| **Serve:** 4)

Ingredients:

1 plum, chopped
1 pear, chopped
1 apple chopped
2 tbsp honey
½ tsp cinnamon, ground
3 tbsp coconut oil
¼ cup pecans, chopped
¼ cup coconut, shredded
2 tbsp sunflower seeds

Directions:

1. Put all fruit into a heat proof dish, add coconut oil, cinnamon and honey, toss to coat.
2. Place the dish in the steamer basket of your instant pot, cover and cook on High for 10 minutes.
3. Release the pressure naturally, take out the dish and transfer fruit to a bowl.
4. In the same baking dish, mix coconut with sunflower seeds and pecans and stir.
5. Transfer these to your instant pot, set it on Sauté mode and toast them for 5 minutes.
6. Add these to fruit in the bowl, toss to coat, serve and enjoy!

(**Calories** 150|**Fat** 7 g| **Protein** 6 g| **Fiber** 1.1 g| **Carbohydrates** 12 g)

Pomegranate Jewel Porridge

(**Prep Time:** 5 MIN| **Cook Time:** 2 MIN| **Serve:** 2)

Ingredients:

1 cup porridge oats
A pinch of salt
1 cup water
¾ cup pomegranate juice
Seeds from 1 pomegranate

Directions:
1. Put oats in your instant pot.
2. Add water, a pinch of salt and pomegranate juice, stir, cover and cook on High for 2 minutes.
3. Release the pressure quickly, add those ruby red pomegranate seeds, stir well, divide into bowls and enjoy!

(**Calories** 200|**Fat** 2.8 g| **Protein** 7.3 g| **Fiber** 4.4 g| **Carbohydrates** 40 g)

Tomato and Spinach Frittata

(Prep Time: 10 MIN| Cook Time: 20 MIN| Serve: 6)

Ingredients:

½ cup milk
Salt and black pepper to taste
12 eggs
3 cups baby spinach, chopped
3 green onions, sliced
1 cup tomato, diced
4 tomatoes, sliced
¼ cup parmesan, grated
1 ½ cups water

Directions:

1. Put the water in your instant pot.
2. In a bowl, mix the eggs with salt, pepper and milk and stir well.
3. Put diced tomato, spinach and green onions in a baking dish and mix them together.
4. Pour the egg mixture over the spinach mixture, spread tomato slices on top and sprinkle parmesan over.
5. Arrange this in the steamer basket of your instant pot, cover and cook on High for 20 minutes.
6. Release the pressure and brown the top of the frittata in a preheated broiler.
7. Cut into wedges and serve.

(Calories 200|Fat 10.1 g| Protein 10 g| Fiber 1.8 g| Carbohydrates 16 g)

Pumpkin Breakfast Pudding

(**Prep Time:** 20 MIN| **Cook Time:** 15 MIN| **Serve:** 6)

Ingredients:

3 cups water
1 tbsp soft butter
1 cup pumpkin puree
1 cup steel-cut oats
¼ cup maple syrup
2 tsp cinnamon
1 tsp pumpkin pie spice
A pinch of salt

Directions:

1. Select Sauté mode on your instant pot, melt butter and add oats and cook for 3 minutes.
2. Add pumpkin puree, water, cinnamon, salt, maple syrup and pumpkin spice, stir, cover and cook on High for 10 minutes.
3. Release the pressure naturally for 10 minutes, stir oats granola, leave to cool for 10 minutes, serve and enjoy!

(**Calories** 200|**Fat** 7 g| **Protein** 5 g| **Fiber** 3 g| **Carbohydrates** 33 g)

Wasabi Scotch Eggs

(**Prep Time:** 10 MIN| **Cook Time:** 15 MIN| **Serve:** 4)

Ingredients:
1 pound sausage, ground
1 tbsp vegetable oil
4 eggs
2 cups water
Mayonnaise and wasabi to serve

Directions:

1. Put the eggs in the instant pot, add 1 cup water, cover and cook on High for 6 minutes.
2. Release the pressure for 6 minutes, uncover, remove the eggs and put them in a bowl filled with ice water.
3. Peel the eggs and place them on a working surface.
4. Divide sausage mixture into 4 balls, flatten them, place 1 egg in the center of each sausage piece, wrap meat around each egg and put them all on a plate.
5. Set your instant pot on Sauté mode, add the oil and heat
6. Add scotch eggs, brown them all over and transfer them to a plate.
7. Add the rest of the water to your instant pot, arrange the eggs in the steamer basket of the pot, cover and cook on High for 6 minutes more.
8. Release the pressure quickly and divide the eggs among plates, slice in half and serve with a blend of mayonnaise and wasabi to taste.

(**Calories** 300|**Fat** 21 g| **Protein** 12 g| **Fiber** 0 g| **Carbohydrates** 16 g)

Poached Egg Baskets

(**Prep** Time: 10 MIN| **Cook** Time: 10 MIN| **Serve**: 2)

Ingredients:

1 bunch rucola leaves
2 eggs
2 bell peppers, ends cut off
2 slices mozzarella cheese
2 slices whole wheat bread, toasted
1 cup water

For the sauce:
1 ½ tsp mustard
2/3 cup homemade mayonnaise
Salt to taste
1 tsp turmeric powder
1 tsp lemon juice
3 tbsp orange juice
1 tbsp white wine vinegar

Directions:
1. In a bowl, mix mayo with salt, turmeric, mustard, lemon juice, orange juice and vinegar, stir well, cover the bowl and keep in the fridge until needed.
2. Break an egg in each bell pepper, place them in the steamer basket of your instant pot, cover the basket with tin foil, add the water in the pot and cook on Low for 5 minutes.
3. Release the pressure naturally and uncover.
4. Place a slice of toast on each plate, top with sliced cheese, some rucola leaves and finish up with poached egg pepper baskets.
5. Drizzle the sauce all over and serve immediately.

(**Calories** 129|**Fat** 8 g| **Protein** 12 g| **Fiber** 1 g| **Carbohydrates** 9 g)

Eggs a la Provence

(**Prep Time**: 10 MIN| **Cook Time**: 20 MIN| **Serve**: 6)

Ingredients:

1 yellow onion, finely chopped
6 eggs
1 cup ham, cooked and crumbled
1 cup kale leaves, chopped
½ cup heavy cream
Salt and black pepper to taste
1 tsp herbs de Provence
1 cup cheddar cheese, grated
1 cup water

Directions:
1. In a bowl, mix eggs with salt, pepper, heavy cream, onion, kale, cheese and herbs, whisk very well and pour into a heat proof dish.
2. Put 1 cup water in your instant pot, place dish in the steamer basket, cover and cook on High for 20 minutes.
3. Release the pressure, uncover, remove the dish, and serve.

(**Calories** 189|**Fat** 12.3 g| **Protein** 20.3 g| **Fiber** 1 g| **Carbohydrates** 1 g)

Porkers Breakfast Quiche

(**Prep Time:** 10 MIN| **Cook Time:** 30 MIN| **Serve:** 4)

Ingredients:

½ cup milk
6 eggs, whisked
Salt and black pepper to taste
4 bacon slices, cooked and crumbled
1 cup sausage, already cooked and ground
½ cup ham, diced
1 cup cheese, shredded
2 green onions, chopped
1 ½ cups water

Directions:

1. Put the water in your instant pot and set aside.
2. In a bowl, mix eggs with salt, pepper, milk, sausage, ham, bacon, onions and cheese and stir well.
3. Pour mixture into a baking dish, cover with some tin foil, place in the steamer basket of your instant pot, cover and cook on High for 30 minutes.
4. Release the pressure for 10 minutes, uncover, take the quiche out and leave to cool for a few minutes.
5. Cut the quiche and serve.

(**Calories** 220|**Fat** 3.4 g| **Protein** 15.3 g| Fiber 1.1 g| **Carbohydrates** 22 g)

Spicy Sunshine Oatmeal

(Prep Time: 20 MIN| Cook Time: 13 MIN| Serve: 6)

Ingredients:

1 cup steel-cut oats
4 cups water
1 tbsp butter
3 tbsp maple syrup
A pinch of salt
2 tsp cinnamon
1 tsp pie spice
1 cup grated carrots
¼ cup chia seeds
¾ cup raisins

Directions:
1. Select the Sauté mode on your instant pot, add butter and melt.
2. Add oats, and toast, stirring, for 3 minutes.
3. Add carrots, water, maple syrup, cinnamon, spice and a pinch of salt, stir, cover and cook on High for 10 minutes.
4. Release the pressure naturally for 10 minutes, add raisins and chia seeds, stir and set oatmeal aside for 10 minutes to cool, divide it in bowls and serve immediately.

(Calories 145|Fat 3 g| Protein 3.5 g| Fiber 1.3 g| Carbohydrates 25 g)

Mini Bacon Quiches

(**Prep Time**: 10 MIN| **Cook Time**: 10 MIN| **Serve**: 4)

Ingredients:

1 ½ cups water
1 green onion, chopped
4 bacon slices, cooked and crumbled
4 tbsp cheddar cheese, shredded
¼ tsp lemon pepper
4 eggs
A pinch of salt

Directions:

1. In a bowl, mix eggs with a pinch of salt and lemon pepper and whisk well.
2. Divide green onion, bacon and cheese on muffin cups.
3. Add eggs and stir a bit.
4. Put the water in your instant pot, add muffin cups in the steamer basket, cover and cook on High for 10 minutes.
5. Release the pressure quickly, divide the egg muffins onto plates and enjoy them right away.

(**Calories** 70|**Fat** 2.4 g| **Protein** 4.6 g| Fiber 1 g| Carbohydrates 1.5 g)

Fruity Breakfast Risotto

(**Prep Time:** 10 MIN| **Cook Time:** 12 MIN| **Serve:** 4)

Ingredients:

1 ½ cups Arborio rice
1 ½ tsp cinnamon powder
1/3 cup brown sugar
A pinch of salt
2 tbsp butter
2 apples, cored and sliced
1 cup apple juice
3 cups milk
½ cup cherries, dried

Directions:

1. Set your instant pot on Sauté mode, add butter and melt.
2. Add rice, stir constantly for 5 minutes.
3. Add sugar, apples, apple juice, milk, a pinch of salt and the cinnamon, mix well, cover and cook on High for 6 minutes.
4. Release the pressure naturally for 6 minutes, uncover, add cherries, stir, cover and leave for flavors to blend for 5 more minutes.
5. Divide into breakfast bowls and serve right away. Delicious!

(**Calories** 160|**Fat** 16 g| **Protein** 11 g| **Fiber** 3 g| **Carbohydrates** 30 g)

Brown Rice Muesli Bowl

(**Prep Time:** 5 MIN| **Cook Time:** 7 MIN| **Serve:** 4)

Ingredients:

1 cup cooked brown rice
1 cup boiling water
½ cup coconut chips
1 cup coconut milk
½ cup maple syrup
¼ cup raisins
¼ cup almonds
A pinch of cinnamon powder
A pinch of salt

Directions:

1. Put the rice in a pot, add the boiling water, simmer on Medium heat for 1 minute to warm rice, drain and transfer it to your instant pot.
2. Add milk, coconut chips, almonds, raisins, salt, cinnamon and maple syrup, stir well, cover and cook on High for 5 minutes.
3. Release pressure quickly, transfer rice to breakfast bowls and enjoy.

(**Calories** 240|**Fat** 7 g| **Protein** 13 g| **Fiber** 9.5 g| **Carbohydrates** 45 g)

Cardamom and Coconut Rice

(**P**rep Time: 10 MIN| **C**ook Time: 35 MIN| **S**erve: 4)

Ingredients:

6 ½ cups water
¾ cup sugar
2 cups black rice, washed and rinsed
2 cinnamon sticks
A pinch of salt
5 cardamom pods, crushed
3 cloves
½ cup coconut, grated
Chopped mango for serving

Directions:

1. Put the rice in your instant pot, add a pinch of salt and the water and stir.
2. In a cheesecloth bag, mix cardamom with cinnamon and cloves and tie it closed.
3. Place this in the pot with the rice, cover and cook on Low for 35 minutes.
4. Release the pressure naturally, uncover, stir, add coconut and set your pot to Sauté mode.
5. Cook for 10 minutes, discard bag of spices, transfer to breakfast bowls and serve with chopped mango to garnish.

(**C**alories 118|**F**at 1 g| **P**rotein 8 g| **F**iber 1 g| **C**arbohydrates 21 g)

Quirky Breakfast Quinoa

(**Prep Time:** 10 MIN| **Cook Time:** 10 MIN| **Serve:** 6)

Ingredients:

2 ¼ cups water
1 ½ cups quinoa, rinsed
2 tbsp maple syrup
A pinch of salt
¼ tsp cinnamon powder
½ tsp vanilla extract
Fresh berries for serving
Milk for serving
Almonds, sliced for serving

Directions:

1. In your instant pot, add water, quinoa, vanilla, cinnamon, salt and maple syrup.
2. Stir, cover and cook on High for 10 minutes.
3. Release the pressure naturally, fluff quinoa with a fork, divide it into breakfast bowls, add milk and stir.
4. Top with almonds and berries and serve.

(**C**alories 100|**F**at 3 g| **P**rotein 2 g| Fiber 1 g| **C**arbohydrates 4 g)

Quinoa Rainbow Salad

(**Prep Time:** 10 MIN| **Cook Time:** 15 MIN| **Serve:** 8)

Ingredients:

For the salad:
2 garlic cloves, minced
2 ¼ cups water
1 ½ cups quinoa, rinsed
A pinch of salt
2 tomatoes, chopped
1 cucumber, chopped
1 jalapeno pepper, chopped
1 cup corn, already cooked
½ cup scallions, finely chopped
1 ½ cups chickpeas, already cooked
2/3 cup parsley leaves, finely chopped
1/3 cup mint leaves, chopped
1 avocado, pitted, peeled and diced

For the dressing:
3 tbsp veggie stock
¼ cup lime juice
Black pepper to taste
½ tsp chipotle chili pepper

Directions:

1. In your pressure cooker, mix quinoa with 1 garlic clove, a pinch of salt and the water, stir, cover and cook on High for 1 minute.
2. Release the pressure, uncover instant pot, fluff quinoa with a fork and leave it to cool.
3. Transfer quinoa to a bowl, add tomatoes, cucumber, jalapeno pepper, corn, scallions, chickpeas, parsley, mint and avocado.
4. To make the dressing, mix veggie stock with black pepper to taste, 1 garlic clove, lime juice and chipotle chili pepper and stir very well.
5. Pour dressing over salad, toss and serve.

(**Calories** 239|**Fat** 6.4 g| **Protein** 9 g| **Fiber** 7.7 g| **Carbohydrates** 39 g)

Savory Bread Pudding

(**Prep Time**: 10 MIN| **Cook Time**: 25 MIN| **Serve**: 6)

Ingredients:

1 cup water
Cooking spray
4 tbsp butter
1 cup onions, thinly sliced
1 cup mushrooms, sliced
1 cup ham, diced
¼ cup sugar
3 eggs, whisked
2 cups half and half
½ tsp mustard, dry
Salt and black pepper to taste
1 cup Swiss cheese, grated
½ tsp thyme, dried
14 ounces loaf, cubed

For the sauce:
1 ½ cups rice wine vinegar
½ cup mustard
2 tbsp maple syrup
Salt and black pepper to taste

Directions:

1. Heat up a pan over medium heat, add butter and melt.
2. Add onions, stir and cook for 2 minutes.
3. Add ham, stir again, cook for 2 minutes more, take off heat and set aside.
4. Spray a pan with some cooking oil.
5. In a bowl, mix eggs with sugar, half and half, thyme, half of the Swiss cheese, salt, pepper, bread cubes, mushroom, ham and onions. Mix and stir well.
6. Pour this into greased pan, place it in the steamer basket of your instant pot, also add the water in the instant pot, cover with tin foil, cover and cook on High for 25 minutes.
7. Meanwhile, to make the sauce, heat up a small pot over medium heat, add dry mustard, salt, pepper, vinegar and maple syrup, stir well and cook for 2-3 minutes.

8. Release pressure from the pot, uncover, take pan out and sprinkle the rest of the cheese on top, put in preheated broiler and brown for a few minutes.
9. Divide bread pudding onto plates, drizzle the sauce on top and serve.

(**Calories** 270| **Fat** 12 g| **Protein** 10 g| Fiber 2 g| **Carbohydrates** 14 g)

Millet and Date Pudding

(**Prep Time:** 10 MIN| **Cook Time:** 10 MIN| **Serve:** 4)

Ingredients:

14 ounces coconut milk
7 ounces water
2/3 cup millet
A pinch of salt
4 dates, pitted
Honey for serving

Directions:

1. Put the millet in your instant pot, add milk, dates and a pinch of salt and stir.
2. Add the water, stir again, cover and cook on High for 10 minutes.
3. Release the pressure naturally, uncover, divide the pudding in bowls, top with honey and serve.

(**Calories** 240| **Fat** 2 g| **Protein** 8 g| Fiber 2.6 g| **Carbohydrates** 25 g)

Indian Millet Pilaf

(**Prep Time:** 10 MIN| **Cook Time:** 10 MIN| **Serve:** 4)

Ingredients:

1 tbsp ghee
1 tsp cardamom, crushed
3 cumin seeds
1 large bay leaf
1 inch cinnamon stick
2 cups organic millet
1 white onion, chopped
Salt to taste
3 cups water

Directions:
1. Set your instant pot on Sauté mode, add ghee and heat
2. Add cumin, cinnamon, cardamom and bay leaf, stir and cook for 1 minute.
3. Add onion, stir and cook for 4 minutes.
4. Add millet, salt and water, stir, cover and cook on High for 1 minute.
5. Release the pressure naturally and fluff the mixture with a fork, transfer to bowls and serve.

(**Calories** 100|**Fat** 3.1 g| **Protein** 2.5 g| **Fiber** 1.3 g| **Carbohydrates** 16 g)

Citrus Tapioca Pudding

(Prep Time: 5 MIN| Cook Time: 10 MIN| Serve: 4)

Ingredients:

1 ½ cups water
1/3 cup tapioca pearls
1 ¼ cup whole milk
Zest from ½ lemon
½ cup sugar

Directions:
1. Put 1 cup water in your instant pot.
2. Put tapioca pearls in a heat proof bowl add milk, ½ cup water, lemon zest and sugar.
3. Stir mixture, place the bowl in the steamer basket of the pot, cover and cook on High for 10 minutes.
4. Release the pressure, transfer pudding to serving cups and enjoy!

(Calories 122|Fat 2 g| Protein 5 g| Fiber 0 g| Carbohydrates 21 g)

Chia and Almond Bowls

(**Prep Time:** 2 Hours| **Cook Time:** 3 MIN| **Serve:** 4)

Ingredients:

½ cup chia seeds
2 cups almond milk
¼ cup almonds
¼ cup coconut, shredded
4 sugar

Directions:
1. Put chia seeds in your instant pot, add milk, almonds and coconut flakes.
2. Stir, cover and cook on High for 3 minutes.
3. Release the pressure quickly, divide the pudding in bowls, sprinkle each with a tsp of sugar and serve.

(**Calories** 130|**Fat** 12 g| **Protein** 14 g| **Fiber** 22 g| **Carbohydrates** 2 g)

Hash Brown Hodge-Podge

(**Prep Time:** 10 MIN| **Cook Time:** 7 MIN| **Serve:** 4)

Ingredients:

8 ounces sausage, ground
1 package hash browns, frozen
1/3 cup water
1 yellow onion, chopped
1 green bell pepper, chopped
1 cup cheddar cheese, grated
Salt and black pepper to taste
4 eggs, whisked
Salsa for serving

Directions:

1. Set your instant pot on Sauté mode, add sausage, stir and cook for 2 minutes.
2. Drain excess fat, add bell pepper and onion, stir and FRY for 2 more minutes.
3. Add hash browns, water, eggs, salt and cheese, stir, cover and cook on Low for 4 minutes.
4. Release the pressure quickly, dish up and serve with salsa.

(**Calories** 300|**Fat** 16 g| **Protein** 17 g| **Fiber** 4 g| **Carbohydrates** 30 g)

Fluffy Steel Cut Oatmeal

(**Prep Time:** 3 MIN| **Cook Time:** 3 MIN| **Serve:** 3)

Ingredients:

1 cup steel cut oats
1/2 Tsp ground cinnamon
1 tbsp maple syrup
3 cups almond milk
1/8 Tsp salt
1/4 cup fresh strawberries, sliced
1 tbsp almonds, sliced

Directions:

1. Add almond milk and oats into the instant pot and stir well.
2. Seal instant pot with lid and select MANUAL button and set the timer for 3 minutes.
3. Allow releasing steam naturally.
4. Open lid carefully and give a nice stir.
5. Add maple syrup, cinnamon and stir well.
6. Pour oatmeal into serving bowls and top with sliced strawberries and almonds.
7. Serve and enjoy.

(**Calories** 689| **Fat** 60 g| **Protein** 9.6 g| **Carbohydrates** 37.9 g)

Almond Banana Oatmeal

(**Prep Time:** 5 MIN| **Cook Time:** 3 MIN| **Serve:** 3)

Ingredients:

1 cup steel cut oats
1 tsp ground cinnamon
2 bananas, sliced
3 cups almond milk
1/2 cup almonds, sliced
1 tbsp honey

Directions:

1. Add oats, almond milk, cinnamon, and banana into the instant pot and stir well.
2. Seal instant pot with lid and select MANUAL button and set the timer for 3 minutes.
3. Allow releasing steam naturally then open the lid.
4. Stir oatmeal and pour into serving bowls.
5. Top with sliced almonds and drizzle with honey.
6. Serve and enjoy.

(Calories 840| Fat 67.2 g| Protein 13.4 g| Carbohydrates 59.5 g)

Healthy Vegetable Crust-less Quiche

(**P**rep Time: 10 MIN| **C**ook Time: 30 MIN| **S**erve: 8)

Ingredients:

8 eggs
1 1/2 cups mozzarella cheese, shredded
1/4 cup green onions, chopped
1 bell pepper, chopped
1/2 cup flour
1/2 cup almond milk
1 cup cherry tomatoes, halved
1/4 Tsp black pepper
1/4 Tsp salt

Directions:

1. Pour 1 cup water into the instant pot then place trivet into the pot.
2. In a mixing bowl, whisk together eggs, flour, milk, pepper, and salt.
3. Add 1 cup cheese, tomatoes, bell pepper, and green onion and mix well.
4. Take one heat proof dish which fits into your instant pot and sprays with cooking spray.
5. Pour egg mixture into the prepared dish and cover dish with foil.
6. Place dish into the instant pot.
7. Seal pot with lid and cook on HIGH pressure for 30 minutes.
8. Release steam quickly than open the lid.
9. Remove dish carefully from the pot.
10. Remove foil and add remaining cheese on top of quiche and again cover dish with foil until cheese is melted.
11. Serve and enjoy.

(**C**alories 151| **F**at 9.1 g| **P**rotein 8.6 g| **C**arbohydrates 9.6 g)

Quinoa with Fresh Berries

(Prep Time: 5 MIN| Cook Time: 1 MIN| Serve: 6)

Ingredients:

1 1/2 cups quinoa, rinsed and drained
1/4 Tsp ground cinnamon
1/2 Tsp vanilla extract
2 tbsp honey
2 1/4 cups water
2 tbsp sliced almonds
1/4 cup blueberries
1/4 cup raspberries
1/8 Tsp salt

Directions:

1. Add quinoa, vanilla, honey, water, and salt in instant pot.
2. Seal pot with lid and cook on high pressure for 1 minute.
3. Quick release steam then opens the lid carefully.
4. Fluff quinoa using a fork and add in the serving bowl.
5. Top with sliced almonds, fresh raspberries, and strawberries.
6. Serve and enjoy.

(**Calories** 197| **Fat** 3.6 g| **Protein** 6.6 g| **Carbohydrates** 35.1 g)

Healthy Breakfast Porridge

(**Prep Time:** 5 MIN| **Cook Time:** 5 MIN| **Serve:** 2)

Ingredients:

1/4 cup pumpkin seeds
1 tbsp honey
2 tsp butter, melted
1 cup water
1/2 cup shredded coconut, unsweetened
1/2 cup pecan, halves
1/2 cup cashews
1/4 cup blueberries
2 strawberries, halves

Directions:

1. Add pumpkin seeds, shredded coconut, pecan, and cashews in food processor and process until it looks like meal.
2. Transfer mixture into the steel bowl and stir in honey, butter, and water.
3. Place bowl in instant pot and seal pot with lid.
4. Select porridge button and set the timer for 3 minutes.
5. Quick release steam then opens the lid carefully.
6. Stir well and pour into the serving bowls.
7. Top with strawberries and blueberries.
8. Serve and enjoy.

(**Calories** 465| **Fat** 36.9 g| **Protein** 10.8 g| **Carbohydrates** 30 g)

Quick Raspberry Breakfast Oatmeal

(**Prep Time:** 5 MIN| **Cook Time:** 5 MIN| **Serve:** 1)

Ingredients:

1/3 cup oats
1/3 cup fresh raspberries
1 tbsp chia seeds
1/3 cup Greek yogurt
1/3 cup almond milk
1/2 Tsp vanilla
1/8 Tsp salt

Directions:

1. Pour 1 1/2 cups water into the instant pot.
2. Add all ingredients into the pint size jar and cover jar top with foil.
3. Place the jar in a pot and select MANUAL button and set the timer for 6 minutes.
4. Allow to releasing steam its own then open the lid.
5. Carefully remove the jar from the pot and set aside to cool slightly.
6. Stir well and serve.

(Calories 402| **Fat** 24.6 g| **Protein** 12.1 g| **Carbohydrates** 36.8 g)

Honey Cinnamon Apples

(**Prep Time:** 3 MIN| **Cook Time:** 2 MIN| **Serve:** 4)

Ingredients:

3 medium apples, peel, core and sliced
1 tsp honey
1 tsp ground cinnamon
2 tbsp water

Directions:

1. Add all ingredients into the instant pot and stir well.
2. Seal pot with lid and cook on HIGH pressure for 2 minutes.
3. Release steam quickly than open the lid.
4. Stir well and serve warm.

(Calories 94|Fat 0.3 g| Protein 0.5 g| Carbohydrates 25 g)

Green Chili Quiche

(Prep Time: 10 MIN| Cook Time: 30 MIN| Serve: 8)

Ingredients:

8 eggs
2 cup Monterey Jack cheese
20 oz can green chilies, drained and chopped
2 cups half and half
1 tsp ground cumin
1/2 Tsp black pepper
1 tsp salt

Directions:

1. Pour 2 cups water into the instant pot and place trivet into the pot.
2. In a bowl, beat together eggs, 1 cup cheese, cumin, half and half, green chilies, black pepper, and salt.
3. Take one heat proof dish which fits into your instant pot and sprays with cooking spray.
4. Pour egg mixture into the prepared dish and cover dish with foil.
5. Place dish into the instant pot.
6. Seal pot with lid and cook on HIGH pressure for 20 minutes.
7. Allow to releasing steam by its own then open.
8. Remove dish carefully and set aside for few minutes to cool.
9. Remove foil and add remaining cheese over top of quiche and broil quiche under a hot broiler for 5 minutes.
10. Serve and enjoy.

(Calories 263|Fat 20.1 g| Protein 14.8 g| Carbohydrates 6.6 g)

Decadent Vanilla Oats

(**Prep Time:** 10 MIN| **Cook Time:** 10 MIN| **Serve:** 4)

Ingredients:

1 cup milk
1 cup steel-cut oats
2 ½ cups water
2 tbsp sugar
A pinch of salt
1 tsp espresso powder
2 tsp vanilla extract
Whipped cream for serving
Grated chocolate for serving

Directions:

1. In your instant pot, mix oats with water, sugar, milk, salt and espresso powder and stir well.
2. Cover and cook on High for 10 minutes.
3. Release the pressure for 10 minutes, take the lid off, add vanilla extract, stir and allow to cool for 5 minutes.
4. Divide into bowls and serve with whipped cream and grated chocolate.

(**Calories** 250|**Fat** 3.1 g| **Protein** 5 g| **Carbohydrates** 43 g| **Fiber** 5.4 g)

Mushroom and Oatmeal Breakfast Risotto

(**Prep Time:** 10 MIN| **Cook Time:** 15 MIN| **Serve:** 4)

Ingredients:

- 1 small yellow onion, chopped
- 1 cup steel-cut oats
- 2 garlic cloves, minced
- 2 tbsp butter
- ½ cup water
- 14 ounces canned chicken stock
- 3 thyme springs, chopped
- 2 tbsp extra virgin olive oil
- ½ cup gouda, grated
- 8 ounces mushroom, sliced
- Salt and black pepper to taste

Directions:

1. Select Sauté mode on your instant pot, add butter and melt it.
2. Add onions, stir and sauté for 3 minutes.
3. Add garlic and sauté for another 1 minute.
4. Add oats, stir and cook for a further minute.
5. Lastly, add water, salt, pepper, stock and thyme, cover and cook on High for 10 minutes.
6. Release the pressure and set the pot aside.
7. Meanwhile, heat up a pan with the olive oil over medium heat, add mushrooms and fry for 3 minutes.
8. Add them to the instant pot and add more salt and pepper to taste.
9. Lastly, add gouda, stir and serve.

(**Calories** 300|**Fat** 14 g| **Protein** 20.5 g| **Fiber** 6.7 g| **Carbohydrates** 30.2 g)

Speedy Pear and Walnut Oats

(**Prep Time:** 5 MIN| **Cook Time:** 6 MIN| **Serve:** 4)

Ingredients:

1 cup water
2 cups milk
1 tbsp soft butter
A pinch of salt
¼ cup brown sugar
½ tsp cinnamon powder
1 cup rolled oats
½ cup walnuts, chopped
2 cups pear, peeled and chopped
½ cup raisins

Directions:

1. In a heat proof dish, mix milk, sugar, butter, salt, oats, cinnamon, raisins, pears and walnuts and stir well.
2. Place the dish in the steamer basket of the pot, add 1 cup water to the pot, cover and cook on High for 6 minutes.
3. Release the pressure quickly, divide oatmeal into bowls, serve and enjoy!

(**Calories** 250|**Fat** 10 g| **Protein** 7 g| **Fiber** 11.3 g| **Carbohydrates** 14 g)

Coconut Blueberry Oatmeal

(Prep Time: 5 MIN| Cook Time: 3 MIN| Serve: 4)

Ingredients:

1 cup fresh blueberries
1 cup steel cut oats
1/8 Tsp cinnamon
1 tbsp maple syrup
3 cups coconut milk
1/8 Tsp salt

Directions:

1. Add all ingredients into the instant pot and mix well.
2. Seal pot with lid and cook on HIGH pressure for 3 minutes.
3. Allow to releasing steam by its own then open.
4. Stir well and serve.

(Calories 525| Fat 44.4 g| Protein 7.1 g| Carbohydrates 32.5 g)

Simple Breakfast Muffins

(Prep Time: 5 MIN| Cook Time: 8 MIN| Serve: 4)

Ingredients:

4 eggs
4 bacon slices, cooked and crumbled
2 tbsp green onion, diced
4 tbsp cheddar cheese, shredded
1/4 Tsp ground black pepper
1/4 Tsp salt

Directions:

1. Pour 1 1/2 cups water into the instant pot and place steamer basket in pot.
2. Beat eggs with black pepper and salt in large bowl.
3. Add shredded cheese and green onion in egg mixture and stir well.
4. Pour egg mixture into the muffin cup and place on the steamer basket.
5. Seal pot with lid and select MANUAL HIGH pressure for 8 minutes.
6. Quick release steam then opens the lid carefully.
7. Carefully remove muffin cups from the pot and serve immediately.

(Calories 195|Fat 14.7 g| Protein 14.4 g| Carbohydrates 1 g)

French Toast with a Fruity Twist

(**Prep Time:** 10 MIN| **Cook Time:** 30 MIN| **Serve:** 6)

Ingredients:

For the orange sauce:
¼ cup orange juice
½ cup sugar
2 cups cranberries
A pinch of salt
¼ tsp cinnamon, ground

For the toast:
2 cups milk
3 eggs, whisked
4 tbsp melted butter
½ cup sugar
Zest from 1 orange, grated
A pinch of salt
1 tsp vanilla extract
1 loaf bread, cubed
1 cup water

Directions:

1. Heat up a small pot over medium heat, add cranberries, orange juice, ¼ tsp cinnamon, a pinch of salt and ½ cup sugar, stir well and simmer for 5 minutes.
2. Pour this mixture into a greased pan and set aside.
3. In a bowl, add milk, melted butter, ½ cup sugar, eggs, vanilla extract, a pinch of salt and orange zest and mix well.
4. Add bread cubes and stir again.
5. Pour this mixture over the cranberries and sauce in greased pan and place in the steamer basket of your instant pot. Add the water at the bottom, cover and cook on High for 25 minutes.
6. Release the pressure, take the pan out and serve.

(**Calories** 300|**Fat** 14 g| **Protein** 14 g| **Carbohydrates** 80 g| **Fiber** 2 g)

Spicy Breakfast Burrito

(**Prep Time:** 10 MIN| **Cook Time:** 13 MIN| **Serve:** 6)

Ingredients:

4 eggs
3/4 Tsp taco seasoning
2 lbs potatoes, cubed
1/2 Tsp chili powder
3/4 cup ham steak cubed
1 jalapeno pepper, diced
1 medium onion, chopped
1/2 Tsp salt

Directions:

1. In a medium bowl, beat together eggs, taco seasoning, 1 tbsp water, and salt.
2. Add jalapeno, ham, potatoes, and onion in a bowl and mix well.
3. Pour egg mixture into the pot which fits into your instant pot and cover pot with foil.
4. Pour 1 cup water into the instant pot then place a trivet in the pot.
5. Place egg mixture pot on a trivet.
6. Seal instant pot with lid and select MANUAL button and set the timer for 13 minutes.
7. Allow releasing steam by its own then open the lid.
8. Carefully remove the pot from the instant pot and remove foil.
9. Fill burritos and serve.

(Calories 193|Fat 5.1 g| Protein 10.2 g| Carbohydrates 27.1 g)

Apple Raisins Oatmeal

(Prep Time: 5 MIN| Cook Time: 4 MIN| Serve: 4)

Ingredients:

1 cup steel cut oats
1/4 cup raisins
1/8 Tsp ground cinnamon
3 tbsp butter
2 tbsp maple syrup
1 cup apple, diced
2 1/2 cups almond milk

Directions:

1. Add all ingredients into the instant pot and stir well.
2. Seal pot with lid and select MANUAL button and set timer for 5 minutes/
3. Quick release steam then opens the lid carefully.
4. Stir well and serve.

(Calories 581|Fat 45.9 g| Protein 6.7 g| Carbohydrates 43.8 g)

Perfect Kale Quinoa

(**P**rep Time: 5 MIN| **C**ook Time: 1 MIN| **S**erve: 4)

Ingredients:

2 cups quinoa, rinsed and drained
3 kale leaves, chopped
1 tbsp lemon juice
3 cups vegetable stock
1/4 cup fresh cilantro, chopped
1/4 Tsp salt

Directions:

1. Add quinoa, kale, vegetable stock, and salt into the instant pot and stir well.
2. Seal pot with lid and select MANUAL button and set the timer for 1 minute.
3. Allow to releasing steam by its own then open.
4. Fluff quinoa well and add lemon juice and cilantro.
5. Serve and enjoy.

(Calories 348|Fat 5.7 g| Protein 14 g| Carbohydrates 61.8 g)

Breakfast Burritos

(**Prep Time:** 15 MIN| **Cook Time:** 15 MIN| **Serve:** 6)

Ingredients

8 ounces pork meat, ground
Salt and black pepper to taste
1 tsp thyme, dry
1 tsp sage, dry
1 tsp fennel seed, crushed
1 tsp brown sugar
A pinch of nutmeg
½ tsp red pepper flakes, crushed
1 tbsp water
1 ½ cups water
6 tortilla shells
8 eggs
A drizzle of olive oil
¼ cup milk
Cheddar cheese, shredded for serving
Salsa for serving

Directions:

1. In a bowl, mix pork with salt, pepper, thyme, sage, fennel, pepper flakes, nutmeg, sugar and 1 tbsp water, stir very well, cover the bowl and keep it in the fridge for now.
2. Brush tortilla shells with some olive oil, arrange them on a baking sheet, cover them with tin foil and seal edges.
3. In a heat proof dish, mix eggs with salt, pepper and milk and whisk well.
4. Add pork mixture, stir and cover the dish with some tin foil.
5. Place dish in the steamer basket of your instant pot, add wrapped tortilla shells on top, add 1 ½ cups water to the pot, cover and cook on High for 15 minutes.
6. Release the pressure and take tortilla shells and eggs and meat mixture out of the pot.
7. Unwrap tortilla shells, fill them with the savory mixture and top with salsa and cheddar cheese. Arrange on plates and enjoy!

(**Calories** 380|**Fat** 25 g| **Protein** 21 g| **Fiber** 11 g| **Carbohydrates** 19 g)

Cheesy Beef Breakfast Rolls

(**Prep Time:** 10 MIN| **Cook Time:** 40 MIN| **Serve:** 8)

Ingredients:

2 tbsp brown sugar
4 pound beef roast, cut into small chunks
Salt and black pepper to taste
2 tsp paprika
2 ½ tsp garlic powder
2 tsp mustard powder
2 tsp onion flakes
3 cups beef stock
1 tbsp balsamic vinegar
2 tbsp Worcestershire sauce
4 tbsp butter, soft
8 hoagie rolls
8 slices provolone cheese

Directions:

1. Put the meat in your instant pot.
2. Add salt, pepper, paprika, garlic powder, mustard powder, onion flakes, stock, vinegar and Worcestershire sauce, stir well, cover and cook on High for 40 minutes.
3. Release the pressure quickly, transfer meat to a cutting board. Strain the liquid and keep it in a bowl.
4. Shred meat and divide among rolls after you've buttered them.
5. Add provolone cheese on top, place rolls in preheated broiler and broil until cheese melts.
6. Dip sandwiches in the sauce from the pot and devour them.

(**Calories** 340|**Fat** 21 g| **Protein** 34 g| **Fiber** 2 g| **Carbohydrates** 12 g)

Italian Sausages and Pepper Pot

(**Prep Time:** 10 MIN| **Cook Time:** 25 MIN| **Serve:** 5)

Ingredients:

15 ounces tomato sauce
28 ounces canned tomatoes, diced
10 Italian sausages
4 green bell peppers, cut into thin strips
1 cup water
4 garlic cloves, minced
1 tbsp basil, dried
1 tbsp Italian seasoning

Directions:
1. Put tomatoes, tomato sauce, basil, water, garlic, sausages, bell peppers and Italian seasoning in your instant pot and stir gently.
2. Cover and cook on High for 25 minutes.
3. Release the pressure quickly, serve and enjoy!

(**Calories** 400|**Fat** 31 g| **Protein** 23 g| **Fiber** 1 g| **Carbohydrates** 8 g)

Speedy Breakfast Tacos

(**Prep** Time: 10 MIN| **Cook** Time: 5 MIN| **S**erve: 4)

Ingredients:

1 pound turkey meat, ground
1 tbsp Worcestershire sauce
1 tbsp extra virgin olive oil
1 ¼ cups beef stock
2 tsp corn flour
1 ½ tsp cumin, ground
1 tbsp chili powder
¼ tsp onion powder
¼ tsp garlic powder
¼ tsp dried onions
½ tsp paprika
¼ tsp oregano, dried
A pinch of cayenne pepper
Salt and black pepper to taste
Tacos shells for serving

Directions:

1. Set your instant pot on Sauté mode, add oil and heat
2. Add meat and ½ cup stock, stir and brown for a few minutes.
3. Discard excess fat, add the rest of the stock, Worcestershire sauce, corn flour, cumin, chili powder, garlic and onion powder, dried onions, paprika, oregano, salt, pepper and cayenne pepper, cover and cook on High for 5 minutes.
4. Release the pressure naturally, uncover, stir again and divide it into taco shells. Serve immediately.

(Calories 240|Fat 11. g| **P**rotein 31.1 g| Fiber 1 g| Carbohydrates 3.4 g)

Double-Cheesy Grits

(**Prep Time:** 10 MIN| **Cook Time:** 10 MIN| **Serve:** 4)

Ingredients:

2 tbsp coconut oil
1 ¾ cup half and half
1 cup stone ground grits
3 cups water
2 tsp salt
3 tbsp butter
4 ounces cheddar cheese, grated
Butter for serving

Directions:

1. Set your instant pot on Sauté mode, add grits and toast them for 3 minutes, stirring constantly.
2. Add oil, half and half, water, salt, butter and cheese. Stir, cover and cook on High for 10 minutes.
3. Release the pressure naturally and leave cheesy grits to cool for 15 minutes, transfer to breakfast bowls, add butter on top and serve.

(**Calories** 280|**Fat** 13 g| **Protein** 13.2 g| **Fiber** 1 g| **Carbohydrates** 26 g)

Cinnamon Rooibos Lentil Bowl

(**Prep Time:** 10 MIN| **Cook Time:** 25 MIN| **Serve:** 4)

Ingredients:

3 cups rooibos tea
1 tbsp cinnamon, ground
1 cup red lentils, soaked for 4 hours and drained
2 apples, diced
1 tsp cloves, ground
1 tsp turmeric, ground
Maple syrup to taste
Coconut milk for serving

Directions:

1. Put lentils in your instant pot, add rooibos tea, stir, cover and cook on High for 15 minutes.
2. Release pressure, uncover, add cinnamon, apples, turmeric and cloves, stir well, cover and cook on High for a further 15 minutes.
3. Release pressure quickly, divide the lentil mixture in bowls and add coconut milk and maple syrup to taste.

(**Calories** 140|**Fat** 1.2 g| **Protein** 5 g| **Fiber** 8.4 g| **Carbohydrates** 35 g)

Pecan Pie Sweet Potatoes

(**Prep Time:** 10 MIN| **Cook Time:** 10 MIN| **Serve:** 8)

Ingredients:

1 cup water
1 tbsp lemon peel
½ cup brown sugar
¼ tsp salt
3 sweet potatoes peeled and sliced
¼ cup butter
¼ cup maple syrup
1 cup pecans chopped
1 tbsp cornstarch
Whole pecans for garnish

Directions:

1. Put the water in your instant pot, add lemon peel, brown sugar and salt and stir.
2. Add potatoes, cover and cook on High for 15 minutes.
3. Release the pressure and transfer the potatoes on a serving plate.
4. Select Sauté mode on your instant pot, add the butter and melt it.
5. Add pecans, maple syrup, cornstarch and stir very well.
6. Pour this sauce over the potatoes, garnish with whole pecans and serve!

(**Calories** 230|**Fat** 13 g| **Protein** 6 g| **Fiber** 4 g| **Carbohydrates** 15 g)

Vanilla Strawberry Cobbler

(**Prep Time:** 5 MIN| **Cook Time:** 12 MIN| **Serve:** 2)

Ingredients:

3/4 cup strawberries, sliced
1/3 cup butter
3/4 cup almond milk
1 1/2 Tsp baking powder
1 tsp vanilla
1/2 cup sugar, granulated
1 1/4 cups flour
Pinch of salt

Directions:

1. Add all ingredients except strawberries into the large bowl and whisk well.
2. Add sliced strawberries and fold well.
3. Spray ramekins with cooking spray.
4. Pour batter into the ramekins.
5. Pour 1 1/2 cups water into the instant pot and place trivet into the pot.
6. Place ramekins on a trivet.
7. Seal pot with lid and select MANUAL HIGH pressure for 12 minutes.
8. Allow releasing steam naturally for 5 minutes then open the lid.
9. Serve and enjoy.

(Calories 977|Fat 53.1 g| Protein 10.8 g| Carbohydrates 120.8 g)

Breakfast Bread Pudding

(Prep Time: 5 MIN| Cook Time: 10 MIN| Serve: 2)

Ingredients:

1 egg
2 cups bread, cubed
1/4 cup condensed milk
1/4 cup milk
1 tsp vanilla extract

Directions:

1. In a medium bowl, beat together egg, vanilla, milk, and condensed milk until well blended.
2. Add bread cubes to egg mixture and mix well and set aside until all liquid absorbed.
3. Pour bread mixture into the heat proof dish.
4. Pour 1 cup water into the instant pot and place trivet in the pot.
5. Place pudding mixture dish on a trivet.
6. Seal pot with lid and select MANUAL HIGH pressure for 10 minutes.
7. Quick release steam then opens the lid carefully.
8. Serve warm and enjoy.

(Calories 269|Fat 7.3 g| Protein 9.5 g| Carbohydrates 40.5 g)

Creamy Almond Peach Quinoa

(**Prep Time:** 5 MIN| **Cook Time:** 6 MIN| **Serve:** 4)

Ingredients:

2 cups quinoa, rinsed and drained
1 1/2 half and half
1 tsp vanilla
2 cups fresh peaches, chopped
2 cups almond milk
1 cup water
2 tbsp butter

Directions:

1. Add butter into the instant pot and select sauté.
2. Once butter is melted then add quinoa and stir for 2 minutes.
3. Add milk, water and vanilla and stir well.
4. Seal pot with lid and select MANUAL button and set the timer for 4 minutes.
5. Release steam quickly than open the lid.
6. Stir in half and half and peaches.
7. Serve and enjoy.

(Calories 682|Fat 40.5 g| Protein 15.8 g| Carbohydrates 68.6 g)

Poultry Recipes

Chicken with Homemade Teriyaki Sauce

(Prep Time: 10 MIN| Cook Time: 15 MIN| Serve: 6)

Ingredients:

2/3 cup gluten free tamari
½ cup pure apple cider vinegar
5 tbsp honey
3 tbsp dry sherry
1 tbsp corn starch
3 tbsp water
2 chicken breast
2 tbsp extra-virgin olive oil
Salt, to taste
Freshly ground black pepper, to taste
3 cloves garlic, crushed
½ ground ginger
2 bell pepper
2 carrots
1 cup long grain rice, rinsed
Water, for cooking
1 cup broccoli florets
2/3 cup edamame
Sesame seeds (optional)

Directions:

1. Start off by preparing the Teriyaki sauce, heat the Instant Pot over medium heat. In a bowl, whisk together the tamari, apple cider, honey, sherry and corn starch. Pour into the pot and stir in some water, about 3 tablespoons.
2. Set the Instant Pot to "Sauté" mode and bring the sauce to a boil. When the sauce thickens to the desired consistency, remove the pot from the heat and pour the sauce in a heatproof bowl.
3. Cut the chicken breasts into cubes and chop the bell peppers into long strips. Dice the carrots and place aside.
4. Clean the Instant Pot and return to the heat on "Sauté" mode, add the olive oil and chicken. Season with salt and pepper and cook the chicken for 4 minutes. Stir in the garlic and ground ginger.
5. Next, add the bell pepper strips with the carrots and edamame.
6. Pour about 2/3 of the Teriyaki sauce in the pot along with 1 cup of water.

7. Set the timer for 6 minutes. When the time is finished, allow the pressure to be released automatically.
8. Uncover the pot and transfer the contents to serving platter, and garnish with sesame seeds and serve hot.

(Calories 376|Fat 8.7| Protein 17.9 g| Carbohydrates 51.6g)

Italian Chicken Slices

(Prep Time: 10 MIN| Cook Time: 15 MIN| Serve: 6)

Ingredients:
2 lbs chicken breasts
1 large onion, diced
2 bell peppers, sliced
3 tbsp extra-virgin olive oil
Pinch of salt, to taste
1 cup marinara
¼ cup pesto
1 cup sliced mushrooms

Directions:
1. Cut the chicken breasts into slices, dice the onions and cut the bell peppers in strips.
2. Place the Instant Pot over medium heat and add the olive oil. Stir in onion and pepper. Season with salt and stir for 4 minutes.
3. Pour in the marinara and pesto into the pot. Add the chicken slices and mushrooms and stir to evenly coat.
4. Cover the pot and the timer for 10 minutes. When the time is finished, manually release the pressure and uncover the lid.
5. Transfer the chicken into a plate and drizzle with half the sauce. Serve warm with flat bread and some cheese. And you can also cook some rice using the leftover sauce.

(Calories 323|Fat 17.5| Protein 34.6g| Carbohydrates 5.9g)

Chicken Slices with Beans and Pineapples

(**Prep Time:** 10 MIN| **Cook Time:** 30MIN| **Serve:** 8)

Ingredients:
2 lbs chicken breasts
2/3 cup salsa
1/3 cup buffalo wild wings hot sauce
1 cup packed brown sugar
1 ½ cup sliced pineapples
1 ½ cup sweet corn
1 ½ cup black beans
1 ½ cup green chilies, chopped
2 tsp garlic powder
1 tsp onion powder
1 ½ tsp smoked paprika
1 tsp red pepper flakes
¾ tsp salt, to taste
2 tbsp extra-virgin olive oil

Directions:
1. Chop the chicken breasts into slices and place in a bowl. Add the rest of the ingredients except the olive oil and using your hands, make sure that the slices are fully covered with marinade.
2. Place the Instant Pot over medium heat and add the olive oil. Place the chicken in the pot and cover with the lid.
3. Set the Instant Pot on "Meat/Stew" and timer for 30 minutes.
4. When the time is finished, carefully release the pressure from the pot and uncover the lid.
5. Serve the chicken slices warm and top with avocado slices. Serve hot with some rice and sour cream.

(Calories 515|Fat 13.5g| Protein 43.1 g| Carbohydrates 57.4g)

Seared Chicken Breasts with Honey Sauce

(Prep Time: 10 MIN| Cook Time: 26MIN| Serve: 8)

Ingredients:
4 chicken breasts
Salt, to taste
Freshly ground black pepper, to taste
1 cup organic honey
1/3 cup soy sauce
1 onion, diced
4 tbsp ketchup
2 tbsp extra-virgin olive oil
3 cloves garlic, crushed
½ tsp red pepper flakes
2 tbsp corn starch
5 tbsp water

Directions:
1. Sear the chicken breast diagonally and place aside. Dice the onion and crush the garlic cloves,
2. Make the honey sauce: In a bowl whisk together the honey and soy sauce. Add in the diced onion and crushed garlic.
3. Stir in the ketchup, olive oil and red pepper flakes.
4. Place the Instant Pot over medium heat, add in the seared chicken breasts and pour the honey sauce over it.
5. Set the pot on "Meat" and the timer for 20 minute. Once the time is finished, carefully release the pressure and uncover the pot.
6. Transfer the chicken to a plate and leave the sauce in the pot. In a cup melt the cornstarch in the water.
7. Return the Instant Pot over medium heat and set on "Sauté" and pour in the cornstarch water.
8. Stir the sauce until it thickens for about 6 minutes. Return the chicken breasts into the pot and flip in the sauce.
9. Transfer the chicken to serving plate and drizzle with the sauce. Serve hot with some rice or noodles.

(Calories 245|Fat 4.87| Protein 11.8 g| Carbohydrates 41.6g)

Turkey Balls Marinated In Pasta Sauce

(Prep Time: 10 MIN| Cook Time: 15 MIN| Serve: 4)

Ingredients:
3 tbsp extra-virgin olive oil
1 large onion, finely chopped
3 zucchini, diced
8oz mushroom slices
1 ½ cup pasta sauce
2/3 cup water
1 lbs lean minced turkey
2/3 cup long grain rice
1 ½ tsp Italian seasoning
1 ½ tsp salt
Fresh basil, to garnish
Freshly grated Parmesan cheese, to serve

Directions:
1. Place the Instant Pot over medium heat and set on "Sauté". Add the olive oil and stir in the onion for 4 minute until translucent. Next, add the zucchini and mushrooms, stir for 4 more minutes.
2. Pour in t hasta sauce and allow it to simmer for 5 minutes.
3. Meanwhile, in a bowl, mix together the minced meat with the rice and seasonings. Shape into small balls and place in a plate.
4. Start dropping the turkey balls into the pot, carefully one by one.
5. Set the Instant Pot on "Keep Warm" and choose "Poultry", cover and allow it to cook for 15 minutes.
6. Carefully release the pressure when the time is finished and transfer the meatballs into a platter. Garnish with fresh basil and serve hot with some rice and Parmesan cheese.

(Calories 610|Fat 29.6g| Protein 40.6g| Carbohydrates 49.3g)

Asian Lemongrass Chicken

(**Prep Time:** 10 MIN| **Cook Time:** 20 MIN| **Serve:** 5)

Ingredients:

1 bunch lemongrass, rough bottom removed and trimmed
1 inch piece ginger root, chopped
4 garlic cloves, crushed
2 tbsp fish sauce
3 tbsp coconut aminos
1 tsp Chinese five spice
10 chicken drumsticks
1 cup coconut milk
Salt and black pepper to taste
1 tsp ghee
¼ cup cilantro, finely chopped
1 yellow onion, chopped
1 tbsp lime juice

Directions:

1. In your food processor, mix lemongrass with ginger, garlic, coconut aminos, fish sauce and five spice and pulse well.
2. Add coconut milk and pulse again.
3. Set your instant pot on Sauté mode, add ghee and melt it.
4. Add onion, stir and fry for 5 minutes.
5. Add chicken pieces, salt and pepper, and cook for 1 minute, stirring constantly.
6. Add coconut milk and lemongrass mix, stir, cover, set on "Poultry" mode and cook for 15 minutes on High.
7. Release the pressure quickly, uncover, add more salt and pepper and lime juice. Serve with cilantro sprinkled on top.

(**Calories** 400|**Fat** 18 g| **Protein** 20 g| **Fiber** 2 g| **Carbohydrates** 6 g)

Dijon Chicken and Potatoes

(**Prep Time**: 15 MIN| **Cook Time**: 15 MIN| **Serve**: 4)

Ingredients:

2 tbsp extra virgin olive oil
2 pounds chicken thighs, skinless and boneless
¾ cup chicken stock
¼ cup lemon juice
2 pounds red potatoes, peeled and cut into quarters
3 tbsp Dijon mustard
2 tbsp Italian seasoning
Salt and black pepper to taste

Directions:
1. Set your instant pot on Sauté mode, add the oil and heat
2. Add chicken thighs, salt and pepper, stir and brown for 2 minutes.
3. In a bowl, mix stock with mustard, Italian seasoning and lemon juice and stir well.
4. Pour this over chicken, add potatoes, cover and cook on High for 15 minutes.
5. Release the pressure quickly, uncover and serve.

(**Calories** 190|**Fat** 6 g| **Protein** 18 g| **Fiber** 3.3 g| **Carbohydrates** 23 g)

Tropical Chicken Sandwiches

(**Prep Time:** 10 MIN| **Cook Time:** 15 MIN| **Serve:** 8)

Ingredients:

6 chicken breasts, skinless and boneless
12 ounces canned orange juice
2 tbsp lemon juice
15 ounces canned peaches and their juice
1 tsp soy sauce
20 ounces canned pineapple and its juice, chopped
1 tbsp cornstarch
¼ cup brown sugar
8 hamburger buns
8 grilled pineapple slices, for serving

Directions:

1. In a bowl, mix orange juice with soy sauce, lemon juice, canned pineapples pieces, peaches and sugar and stir well.
2. Pour half of this mix into your instant pot, add chicken and pour the rest of the sauce over meat.
3. Cover and cook on High for 12 minutes.
4. Release the pressure quickly and put chicken on a cutting board, shred meat and set aside.
5. In a bowl, mix cornstarch with 1 tbsp cooking juice and stir well.
6. Transfer the sauce to a pot, add cornstarch mixture and chicken, stir and cook for a few more minutes.
7. Divide this chicken mixture onto hamburger buns, top with grilled pineapple pieces and serve.

(**Calories** 240|**Fat** 4.6 g| **Protein** 14 g| **Fiber** 4 g| **Carbohydrates** 21 g)

Moroccan Chicken

(**Prep Time:** 10 MIN| **Cook Time:** 25 MIN| **Serve:** 4)

Ingredients:

6 chicken thighs
2 tbsp extra virgin olive oil
10 cardamom pods
2 bay leaves
½ tsp coriander
1 tsp cloves
½ tsp cumin
½ tsp ginger
½ tsp turmeric
½ tsp cinnamon, ground
1 tsp paprika
2 yellow onions, chopped
2 tbsp tomato paste
5 garlic cloves, chopped
¼ cup white wine
1 cup green olives
1 cup chicken stock
¼ cup cranberries, dried
Juice of 1 lemon
½ cup parsley, finely chopped

Directions:

1. In a bowl, mix bay leaf with cardamom, cloves, coriander, ginger, cumin, cinnamon, turmeric and paprika and stir.
2. Set your instant pot on Sauté mode, add the oil and heat up.
3. Add chicken thighs, brown for a few minutes and transfer to a plate.
4. Add onion to the pot, stir and cook for 4 minutes.
5. Add garlic, stir and cook for 1 minute.
6. Add wine, tomato paste, spices from the bowl, stock and chicken.

7. Stir, cover and cook on High for 15 minutes.
8. Release the pressure quickly, discard bay leaf, cardamom and cloves, add olives, cranberries, lemon juice and parsley, stir and divide chicken mixture onto plates and serve.

(**Calories** 381|**Fat** 10.2 g| **Protein** 4.3 g| **Fiber** 7.8 g| **Carbohydrates** 4 g)

Hawaiian Chicken Buns

(Prep Time: 5 MIN| Cook Time: 13 MIN| Serve: 6)

Ingredients:

3 lbs chicken boneless chicken breasts
2 cups pineapples, cubed
½ tsp salt, to taste
1 cup BBQ sauce, plus extra to serve
6 Hawaiian Buns

Directions:

1. Cut the chicken into thick slices and place in a bowl. Add the pineapples, salt and BBQ sauce. Toss the chicken slices until evenly coated.
2. Place the Instant Pot over medium heat and add the chicken with the sauce. Cover the pot and set on "Meat" and cook for 13 minutes.
3. Carefully release the pressure hen the time is finished and uncover the lid.
4. Fill the buns with chicken slices and add more BBQ sauce if desired and serve.

(**Calories** 260|**Fat** 1.9g| **Protein** 17.3g| **Carbohydrates** 43.3g)

Greek Cacciatore Chicken

(**Prep Time:** 10 MIN| **Cook Time:** 15 MIN| **Serve:** 4)

Ingredients:

1 cup chicken stock
Salt to taste
8 chicken drumsticks, bone-in
1 bay leaf
1 tsp garlic powder
1 yellow onion, chopped
28 ounces canned tomatoes and juice, crushed
1 tsp oregano, dried
½ cup black olives, pitted and sliced

Directions:

1. Set your instant pot on Sauté mode, add stock, bay leaf and salt and stir.
2. Add chicken, garlic powder, onion, oregano and tomatoes, stir, cover and cook on High for 15 minutes.
3. Release the pressure naturally, uncover, discard bay leaf, divide chicken onto plates, drizzle cooking liquid all over, sprinkle olives and serve.

(**Calories** 210|**Fat** 2.9 g| **Protein** 25.9 g| **Fiber** 2.4 g| **Carbohydrates** 9.5 g)

Honey BBQ Chicken Wings

(**Prep Time:** 10 MIN| **Cook Time:** 25 MIN| **Serve:** 4)

Ingredients:

2 pounds chicken wings
Salt and black pepper to taste
¾ cup honey BBQ sauce
A pinch of cayenne pepper
½ cup apple juice
1 tsp red pepper, crushed
2 tsp paprika
½ cup water
½ tsp basil, dried
½ cup brown sugar

Directions:

1. Put chicken wings in your instant pot.
2. Add BBQ sauce, apple juice, salt, pepper, red pepper, paprika, basil, sugar and water.
3. Stir, cover and cook on High for 10 minutes.
4. Release the pressure quickly, uncover and transfer chicken to a baking sheet, add sauce all over and place in preheated broiler for 7 minutes, flip chicken wings and broil for 7 more minutes before dishing onto plates and serving.

(**Calories** 147.5|**Fat** 2.2 g| **Protein** 21.8 g| Fiber 1 g| Carbohydrates 8 g)

Thai Chicken

(**Prep Time:** 10 MIN| **Cook Time:** 10 MIN| **Serve:** 4)

Ingredients:

2 pounds chicken thighs, boneless and skinless
½ cup fish sauce
1 cup lime juice
2 tbsp coconut nectar
¼ cup extra virgin olive oil
1 tsp ginger, grated
2 tsp cilantro, finely chopped
1 tsp mint, chopped

Directions:
1. Put chicken thighs in your instant pot.
2. In a bowl, mix lime juice with fish sauce, olive oil, coconut nectar, ginger, mint and cilantro and whisk well.
3. Pour this over chicken, cover and cook on High for 10 minutes.
4. Release the pressure quickly, divide Thai chicken on plates and serve.

(**Calories** 300|**Fat** 5 g| **Protein** 32 g| **Fiber** 4 g| **Carbohydrates** 23 g)

Turkey Chili Zinger

(Prep Time: 10 MIN| Cook Time: 10 MIN| Serve: 4)

Ingredients:

1 pound turkey meat, ground
Salt and black pepper to taste
5 ounces water
15 ounces chickpeas, already cooked
1 yellow onion, chopped
1 yellow bell pepper, chopped
3 garlic cloves, chopped
2 ½ tsp chili powder
1 ½tsp cumin
A pinch of cayenne pepper
12 ounces veggies stock

Directions:
1. Put turkey meat in your instant pot.
2. Add water, stir, cover and cook on High for 5 minutes.
3. Release the pressure quickly, uncover and add chickpeas, bell pepper, onion, garlic, chili powder, cumin, salt, pepper, cayenne pepper and veggie stock.
4. Stir, cover and cook on High for 5 minutes.
5. Release the pressure for 10 minutes, uncover and serve.

(Calories 224|Fat 7.7 g| **Protein** 19.7 g| **Fiber** 6.1 g| **Carbohydrates** 18 g)

Chicken Romano

(**Prep Time:** 10 MIN| **Cook Time:** 15 MIN| **Serve:** 4)

Ingredients:

6 chicken thighs, boneless and skinless and cut into medium chunks
Salt and black pepper to taste
½ cup white flour
2 tbsp vegetable oil
10 ounces tomato sauce
1 tsp white wine vinegar
4 ounces mushrooms, sliced
1 tbsp sugar
1 tbsp oregano, dried
1 tsp garlic, minced
1 tsp basil, dried
1 tsp chicken bouillon granules
1 yellow onion, chopped
1 cup Romano cheese, grated

Directions:

1. Set your instant pot on Sauté mode, add oil and heat
2. Add chicken pieces, stir and brown them for 2 minutes.
3. Add onion and garlic, stir and fry for 3 minutes more.
4. Add salt, pepper, flour and stir very well to avoid lumps.
5. Add tomato sauce, vinegar, mushrooms, sugar, oregano, basil and bouillon granules, stir cover and cook on High for 10 minutes.
6. Release the pressure for 10 minutes, uncover, add cheese, stir to melt and serve.

(**Calories** 450|**Fat** 11 g| **Protein** 61.2 g| **Fiber** 1 g| **Carbohydrates** 24.2 g)

Chicken In Tomatillo Sauce

(**Prep Time:** 10 MIN| **Cook Time:** 30 MIN| **Serve:** 8)

Ingredients:

1 pound chicken thighs, skinless and boneless
2 tbsp extra virgin olive oil
1 yellow onion, thinly sliced
1 garlic clove, crushed
4 ounces canned green chilies, chopped
1 handful cilantro, finely chopped
Salt and black pepper to taste
15 ounces canned tomatillos, chopped
5 ounces canned garbanzo beans, drained
15 ounces rice, already cooked
5 ounces tomatoes, chopped
15 ounces cheddar cheese, grated
4 ounces black olives, pitted and chopped

Directions:

1. Set your instant pot on Sauté mode, add oil and heat
2. Add onions, stir and fry for 5 minutes.
3. Add garlic, stir and cook 15 more seconds.
4. Add chicken, chilies, salt, pepper, cilantro and tomatillos, stir, cover and cook on 'Poultry' mode for 8 minutes.
5. Release the pressure quickly, uncover, take chicken out and shred it.
6. Return chicken to pot, add rice, beans, set instant pot on Sauté mode again and cook for 1 minute.
7. Add cheese, tomatoes and olives, stir, cook for 2 minutes more, ladle onto plates and serve.

(**Calories** 245|**Fat** 11.4 g| **Protein** 20 g| **Fiber** 1.3 g| **Carbohydrates** 14.2 g)

Sherry and Ginger Duck

(**Prep Time:** 10 MIN| **Cook Time:** 20 MIN| **Serve:** 4)

Ingredients:

1 duck, cut into small chunks
Black pepper to taste
1 potato, cut into cubes
1 inch ginger root, sliced
4 garlic cloves, minced
4 tbsp sugar
4 tbsp soy sauce
2 green onions, roughly chopped
4 tbsp sherry wine
A pinch of salt
¼ cup water

Directions:

1. Set your instant pot on Sauté mode, add duck pieces, stir and brown them for a few minutes.
2. Add garlic, ginger, green onions, soy sauce, sugar, wine, a pinch of salt, black pepper and water, stir, cover, set pot to 'Poultry' mode and cook for 18 minutes.
3. Release the pressure quickly, uncover, add potatoes, cover and cook on High for 5 minutes.
4. Release the pressure quickly, spoon braised duck onto plates and serve.

(**Calories** 238|**Fat** 18 g| **Protein** 19 g| **Fiber** 0 g| **Carbohydrates** 1 g)

Turkey Meatballs with Mushrooms

(Prep Time: 10 MIN| Cook Time: 40 MIN| Serve: 8)

Ingredients:

1 pound turkey meat, ground
1 yellow onion, minced
¼ cup parmesan cheese, grated
½ cup Panko bread crumbs
4 garlic cloves, minced
¼ cup parsley, chopped
Salt and black pepper to taste
1 tsp oregano, dried
1 egg, whisked
¼ cup milk
2 soy sauce
1 tsp fish sauce
12 cremini mushrooms, chopped
3 dried shiitake mushrooms, soaked in water, drained and chopped
1 cup chicken stock
2 tbsp extra virgin olive oil
2 tbsp butter
A splash of sherry wine
2 tbsp cornstarch mixed with 2 tbsp water

Directions:

1. In a bowl, mix turkey meat with parmesan cheese, salt, pepper to taste, yellow onion, garlic, bread crumbs, parsley, oregano, egg, milk, 1 tsp soy sauce and 1 tsp fish sauce, stir very well and shape 16 meatballs.
2. Heat up a pan with 1 tbsp oil over medium high heat, add meatballs, brown them for 1 minute on each side and transfer them to a plate.
3. Pour chicken stock in the pan, stir and take off heat.
4. Set your instant pot on Sauté mode, add 1 tbsp oil and 2 tbsp butter and heat them up.
5. Add cremini mushrooms, salt and pepper, stir and cook for 10 minutes.
6. Add dried mushrooms, sherry wine and the rest of the soy sauce and stir well.

7. Add meatballs, cover and cook on High for 6 minutes.
8. Release the pressure quickly, uncover, add cornstarch mix, stir well until sauce thickens, dish up onto plates and serve with rice if desired.

(**Calories** 330|**Fat** 16 g| **Protein** 28 g| **Fiber** 3 g| **Carbohydrates** 21 g)

Filipino Chicken

(**Prep Time:** 10 MIN| **Cook Time:** 15 MIN| **Serve:** 4)

Ingredients:

5 pounds chicken thighs
Salt and black pepper to taste
½ cup white vinegar
1 tsp black peppercorns
4 garlic cloves, minced
3 bay leaves
½ cup soy sauce

Directions:

1. Set your instant pot on 'Poultry' mode, add chicken, vinegar, soy sauce, salt, pepper, garlic, peppercorns and bay leaves, stir, cover and cook for 15 minutes.
2. Release the pressure for 10 minutes, uncover, discard bay leaves, stir, divide chicken on plates and enjoy!

(**Calories** 430|**Fat** 11 g| **Protein** 76 g| **Fiber** 1 g| **Carbohydrates** 2.4 g)

Creamy Turkey and Mash

(Prep Time: 10 MIN| Cook Time: 50 MIN| Serve: 3)

Ingredients:

2 turkey quarters
1 yellow onion, chopped
1 carrot, chopped
3 garlic cloves, minced
1 celery stalk, chopped
1 cup chicken stock
Salt and black pepper to taste
A splash of white wine
2 tbsp extra virgin olive oil
A pinch of rosemary, dried
2 bay leaves
A pinch of sage, dried
A pinch of thyme, dried
3 tbsp cornstarch mixed with 2 tbsp water
5 gold potatoes, cut into halves
2 tbsp parmesan cheese, grated
3.5 ounces cream
2 tbsp butter

Directions:

1. Season turkey with salt and pepper.
2. Put 1 tbsp oil in your instant pot, set pot on Sauté mode and heat
3. Add turkey, brown pieces for 4 minutes, transfer them to a plate and set aside.
4. Add ½ cup stock to pot and stir well.
5. Add 1 tbsp oil and heat
6. Add onion, stir and fry for 1 minute.
7. Add garlic, stir and cook for a further 20 seconds.
8. Add salt and pepper, carrot and celery, stir and fry for 7 minutes.
9. Add 2 bay leaves, thyme, sage and rosemary, stir and cook 1 minute longer.

10. Add wine, turkey and the rest of the stock.
11. Put potatoes in the steamer basket and also introduce it in the pot, cover and cook for 20 minutes on High.
12. Release the pressure for 10 minutes, uncover, transfer potatoes to a bowl and mash them.
13. Add salt, pepper, butter, parmesan and cream and mix well.
14. Divide turkey quarters onto plates and set your instant pot on Sauté mode again.
15. Add cornstarch mixture to pot and stir continuously while cooking for 2-3 minutes.
16. Drizzle sauce over turkey, add mashed potatoes on the side and serve.

(**Calories** 200| **Fat** 5 g| **Protein** 18 g| Fiber 4 g| **Carbohydrates** 19 g)

Cucumber and Ginger Duck

(**Prep Time:** 10 MIN| **Cook Time:** 40 MIN| **Serve:** 8)

Ingredients:

1 duck, chopped in medium pieces
1 cucumber, chopped
1 tbsp wine
2 carrots, chopped
2 cups water
Salt and black pepper to taste
1 inch ginger pieces, chopped

Directions:

1. Put duck pieces in your instant pot.
2. Add cucumber, carrots, wine, water, ginger, salt and pepper, stir, cover and cook on 'Poultry' mode for 40 minutes.
3. Release the pressure, serve and enjoy!

(**Calories** 189| **Fat** 2 g| **Protein** 22 g| Fiber 1 g| **Carbohydrates** 4 g)

Asparagus and Bacon Chicken

(**Prep Time:** 10 MIN| **Cook Time:** 30 MIN| **Serve:** 2)

Ingredients:

2 chicken breasts, skinless and boneless and butterflied
1 piece ham, halved and cooked
6 asparagus spears
16 bacon strips
4 mozzarella cheese slices
Salt and black pepper to taste
2 cup water

Directions:

1. In a bowl, mix chicken breasts with salt and 1 cup water, stir, cover and keep in the fridge for 30 minutes.
2. Pat dry chicken breasts and place them on a working surface.
3. Pile 2 slices of mozzarella, 1 piece ham and 3 asparagus pieces on each.
4. Add salt and pepper and roll up each chicken breast.
5. Place 8 bacon strips on a working surface, add chicken and wrap it in bacon.
6. Repeat this with the other chicken breast.
7. Put chicken rolls in the steamer basket of the pot, add 1 cup water in the pot before covering and cooking on High for 10 minutes.
8. Release the pressure quickly, pat dry rolls with paper towels and leave them on a plate.
9. Set your instant pot on Sauté mode, add chicken rolls and brown them on all sides for a few minutes.
10. Serve and enjoy!

(**Calories** 270|**Fat** 11 g| **Protein** 37 g| **Fiber** 1 g| **Carbohydrates** 6 g)

Simple Chicken Salad

(**Prep Time:** 55 MIN| **Cook Time:** 10 MIN| **Serve:** 2)

Ingredients:

1 chicken breast, skinless and boneless
3 cups water
Salt and black pepper to taste
1 tbsp mustard
3 garlic cloves, minced
1 tbsp balsamic vinegar
1 tbsp honey
3 tbsp extra virgin olive oil
Mixed salad greens
A handful of cherry tomatoes, cut into halves

Directions:

1. In a bowl, mix 2 cups water with salt to taste.
2. Add chicken to this mix, stir and keep in the fridge for 45 minutes.
3. Add 1 cup water to your instant pot, place chicken breast in the steamer basket of the pot, cover and cook on High for 5 minutes.
4. Release the pressure naturally, leave chicken breast on a plate for 8 minutes and cut into thin strips.
5. For the vinaigrette, mix garlic with salt and pepper to taste, mustard, honey, vinegar and olive oil and whisk very well.
6. In a salad bowl, mix chicken strips with salad greens and tomatoes.
7. Drizzle the vinaigrette on top and serve.

(**Calories** 140|**Fat** 2.5 g| **Protein** 19 g| **Fiber** 4 g| **Carbohydrates** 11 g)

Asian Chicken and Rice

(Prep Time: 15 MIN| Cook Time: 35 MIN| Serve: 2)

Ingredients:

3 chicken quarters cut into small pieces
2 carrots, cut into chunks
2 potatoes, cut into quarters
1 shallot, sliced
1 yellow onion, sliced
3 garlic cloves, minced
Salt and black pepper to taste
1 green bell pepper, chopped
7 ounces coconut milk
2 bay leaves
1 tbsp soy sauce
1 tbsp peanut oil
1 ½ tsp turmeric powder
1 tsp cumin, ground
1 ½ tbsp cornstarch mixed with 2 tbsp water

For the marinade:
1 tbsp soy sauce
½ tsp sugar
1 tbsp white wine
A pinch of white pepper
1 ½ cups water
1 ½ cups rice

Directions:
1. In a bowl, mix chicken with sugar, white pepper, 1 tbsp soy sauce and 1 tbsp white wine, stir and keep in the fridge for 20 minutes.
2. Set your instant pot on Sauté mode, add peanut oil and heat
3. Add onion and shallot, stir and fry for 3 minutes.
4. Add garlic, salt and pepper and cook for 2 minutes more.
5. Add chicken, stir and brown for 2 minutes.
6. Add turmeric and cumin, and continue cooking for a further minute.

7. Add bay leaves, carrots, potatoes, bell pepper, coconut milk and 1 tbsp soy sauce.
8. Stir everything, place steamer basket in the pot, place the rice in a bowl inside the basket,
9. Add 1 and ½ cups water in the bowl, cover and cook on High for 4 minutes.
10. Release the pressure naturally, take the rice out of the pot and divide among plates, add cornstarch to pot and thicken the sauce.
11. Serve chicken and sauce next to rice in bowls.

(**C**alories 200|**F**at 9 g| **P**rotein 26 g| **F**iber 1 g| **C**arbohydrates 22 g)

Quick Chicken Curry

(**P**rep **T**ime: 10 MIN| **C**ook **T**ime: 20 MIN| **S**erve: 4)

Ingredients:

15 ounces chicken breast, chopped
1 tbsp extra virgin olive oil
1 yellow onion, thinly sliced
6 potatoes, cut into halves
5 ounces canned coconut cream
1 bag chicken curry base
½ bunch coriander, chopped

Directions:

1. Set your instant pot on Sauté mode, add the oil and heat
2. Add chicken, stir and brown for 2 minutes.
3. Add onion, stir and fry for 1 minute.
4. In a bowl, mix curry base with coconut cream and stir.
5. Pour this over chicken, also add potatoes, cover and cook on High for 15 minutes.
6. Release pressure fast, uncover and serve with chopped coriander on top.

(**C**alories 120|**F**at 8.6 g| **P**rotein 14.8 g| **F**iber 1.2 g| **C**arbohydrates 6.11 g)

Crispy Dipping Chicken

(**Prep Time:** 10 MIN| **Cook Time:** 40 MIN| **Serve:** 4)

Ingredients:

4 garlic cloves, chopped
6 chicken thighs
1 yellow onion, thinly sliced
A pinch of rosemary, dried
1 cup cold water
1 tbsp soy sauce
Salt and black pepper to taste
2 tbsp cornstarch mixed with 2 ½ tbsp water
1 ½ cups Panko breadcrumbs
2 tbsp extra virgin olive oil
2 tbsp butter
1 cup white flour
2 eggs, whisked

Directions:

1. In your instant pot, mix garlic with onion, rosemary and 1 cup water.
2. Place chicken things in the steamer basket and place in the pot.
3. Cover and cook on High for 9 minutes.
4. Release the pressure naturally for 10 minutes and uncover.
5. Heat up a pan with the butter and oil over medium high heat.
6. Add 1 ½ cups breadcrumbs, stir, toast them and take them off heat.
7. Remove chicken thighs from pot, pat them dry, season with salt and pepper to taste, coat them with the flour, dip them in beaten egg and then coat them in toasted breadcrumbs.
8. Place chicken thighs on a lined baking sheet, place in the oven at 300 degrees F and bake for 10 minutes.
9. Meanwhile, set your instant pot on Sauté mode and heat up the cooking liquid.
10. Add 1 tbsp soy sauce, salt, pepper and cornstarch, stir until thick and bubbling and transfer to a bowl.
11. Take chicken thighs out of the oven, divide them on plates and serve with the sauce from the pot on the side.

(**C**alories 360|**F**at 7 g| **P**rotein 15 g| **F**iber 4 g| **C**arbohydrates 18 g)

Braised Pancetta Quail

(**Prep Time:** 10 MIN| **Cook Time:** 15 MIN| **Serve:** 2)

Ingredients:
2 quails, cleaned and emptied
3.5 ounces smoked pancetta, chopped
½ cup champagne
2 scallions, chopped
½ bunch thyme, chopped
½ bunch thyme
1 bay leaf
Salt and black pepper to taste
½ bunch rosemary, chopped
½ bunch rosemary
½ fennel bulb, cut into matchsticks
4 carrots, cut into thin matchsticks
A handful arugula
Lemon juice of 1 lemon
A drizzle of olive oil

Directions:
1. Put fennel and carrot in the steamer basket of your instant pot, add 2 cups water to the pot, cover, cook on High for 1 minute, release the pressure, rinse veggies with cold water, transfer them to a bowl and also keep the cooking liquid in a separate bowl.
2. Set your instant pot on Sauté mode, add shallots, pancetta, chopped rosemary, chopped thyme and bay leaf, salt and pepper, stir and fry for 4 minutes.
3. Stuff quail with whole rosemary and thyme and add to pot.
4. Brown on all sides, add champagne and cook for 2 minutes, stirring all the time.
5. Add cooking liquid from veggies, cover and cook on High for 9 minutes.
6. Release the pressure, take quail out of the pot and set aside.
7. Strain liquid from the pot into a pan, heat up over medium heat and simmer until it reduces by half.
8. Arrange arugula on a platter, add steamed fennel and carrots, a drizzle of oil, lemon juice and top with quail. Drizzle the sauce from the pan over the quail and serve.

(**Calories** 300|**Fat** 17 g| **Protein** 40 g| **Fiber** 0.2 g| **Carbohydrates** 0.2 g)

Cranberry and Walnut Wings

(**Prep Time:** 10 MIN| **Cook Time:** 20 MIN| **Serve:** 4)

Ingredients:

4 turkey wings
2 tbsp butter
2 tbsp vegetable oil
1 ½ cups cranberries
Salt and black pepper to taste
1 yellow onions, sliced
1 cup walnuts
1 cup orange juice
1 bunch thyme, roughly chopped

Directions:

1. Set your instant pot on Sauté mode, add butter and oil and heat up.
2. Add turkey wings, salt and pepper and brown them on all sides.
3. Take wings out of the pot, add onion, walnuts, cranberries and thyme, stir and cook for 2 minutes.
4. Add orange juice and return turkey wings to pot, stir, cover and cook on High for 20 minutes.
5. Release the pressure naturally, uncover and divide turkey wings on your plates.
6. Transfer cranberry mixture to a pan, heat up over medium heat and simmer for 5 minutes.
7. Drizzle sauce over turkey wings and serve.

(**Calories** 320|**Fat** 15.3 g| **Protein** 29 g| **Fiber** 2.1 g| **Carbohydrates** 16.4 g)

Coriander and Garlic Chicken

(**Prep Time:** 10 MIN| **Cook Time:** 35 MIN| **Serve:** 8)

Ingredients:

1 whole chicken

1 tbsp extra virgin olive oil
1 ½ tbsp lemon zest
1 cup chicken stock
1 tbsp thyme leaves
½ tsp cinnamon powder
Salt and black pepper to taste
1 tbsp cumin powder
2 tsp garlic powder
1 tbsp coriander powder

Directions:

1. In a bowl, mix cinnamon with cumin, garlic, coriander, salt, pepper and lemon zest and stir well.
2. Rub chicken with half of the oil, then rub it inside and out with spices mix.
3. Set your instant pot on Sauté mode, add the rest of the oil and heat
4. Add chicken and brown it on all sides for 5 minutes.
5. Add stock and thyme, stir, cover and cook on High for 25 minutes.
6. Release the pressure naturally and transfer chicken to a platter.
7. Add cooking liquid over it and serve.

(**Calories** 260|**Fat** 3.1 g| **Protein** 26.7 g| **Fiber** 1 g| **Carbohydrates** 4 g)

Hot Sweet Chicken Wings

(**Prep Time:** 10 MIN| **Cook Time:** 25 MIN| **Serve:** 6)

Ingredients:

12 chicken wings, cut in half (24 pieces)
1 pound celery, cut into thin matchsticks
¼ cup honey
4 tbsp hot sauce
Salt to taste
1 cup water
¼ cup tomato puree
1 cup yogurt
1 tbsp parsley, finely chopped

Directions:
1. Put 1 cup water into your instant pot.
2. Place chicken wings in the steamer basket of your pot, cover and cook on High for 19 minutes.
3. Meanwhile, in a bowl, mix tomato puree with hot sauce, salt and honey and stir very well.
4. Release the pressure from the pot, add chicken wings to honey mix and toss them to coat.
5. Arrange chicken wings on a lined baking sheet and place in preheated broiler for 5 minutes.
6. Arrange celery sticks on a platter and arrange chicken wings amongst them.
7. In a bowl, mix yogurt with parsley, stir well and place next to the platter.
8. Enjoy dipping!

(**Calories** 300|**Fat** 3.1 g| **Protein** 33 g| **Fiber** 2 g| **Carbohydrates** 14 g)

French Chicken Delight

(**Prep Time:** 10 MIN| **Cook Time:** 37 MIN| **Serve:** 4)

Ingredients:

6 chicken thighs
1 tsp vegetable oil
Salt and black pepper to taste
1 yellow onion, chopped
1 celery stalk, chopped
¼ pound baby carrots, cut into halves
½ tsp thyme, dried
2 tbsp tomato paste
½ cup white wine
15 ounces canned tomatoes, chopped
2 cups chicken stock
1 ½ pounds potatoes, chopped

Directions:

1. Set your instant pot on Sauté mode, add oil and heat
2. Add chicken pieces, salt and pepper to taste and brown them for 4 minutes on each side.
3. Take chicken out of the pot and set aside.
4. Add onion, carrots, celery, thyme and tomato paste to the pot, stir and cook for 5 minutes.
5. Add white wine and salt, stir and cook a further 3 minutes.
6. Add chicken stock, chicken pieces and chopped tomatoes.
7. Place the steamer basket in the pot, add potatoes to it, cover and cook on High for 30 minutes.
8. Release the pressure, take potatoes out of the pot and also take chicken pieces out.
9. Shred chicken meat and return to pot.
10. Also return potatoes, more salt and pepper, stir well and serve.

(**Calories** 237|**Fat** 12 g| **Protein** 30 g| **Fiber** 0 g| **Carbohydrates** 1 g)

Chicken Gumbo

(**Prep Time:** 10 MIN| **Cook Time:** 45 MIN| **Serve:** 4)

Ingredients:

1 pound smoky sausage, sliced
1 tbsp vegetable oil
1 pound chicken thighs, cut into halves
Salt and black pepper to taste

For the roux:
½ cup flour
¼ cup vegetable oil
1 tsp Cajun spice

Aromatics:
1 bell pepper, chopped
1 yellow onion, chopped
1 celery stalk, chopped
Salt to taste
4 garlic cloves, minced
2 quarts chicken stock
15 ounces canned tomatoes, chopped
½ pound okra
A dash of Tabasco sauce

For serving:
White rice, already cooked
½ cup parsley, chopped

Directions:
1. Set your instant pot on Sauté mode, add 1 tbsp oil and heat
2. Add sausage, brown for 4 minutes and transfer to a plate.
3. Add chicken pieces to pot, brown for 6 minutes and place next to the sausage.
4. Add ¼ cup vegetable oil to your pot and heat
5. Add Cajun spice, stir and cook for 5 minutes.

6. Add bell pepper, onion, garlic, celery, salt and pepper and fry for 5 minutes more.
7. Return chicken and sausage to the pot and stir.
8. Add stock, tomatoes and combine well.
9. Cover and cook on High for 10 minutes.
10. Release the pressure naturally for 15 minutes, uncover, add okra, set pot to Simmer mode and cook for 10 minutes.
11. Add more salt and pepper and the Tabasco sauce, stir well and dish up gumbo onto plates. Serve with rice on the side and parsley sprinkled on top.

(**C**alories 208|**F**at 15 g| **P**rotein 10 g| Fiber 1 g| Carbohydrates 8 g)

Coca Cola Chicken

(**P**rep Time: 10 MIN| **C**ook Time: 10 MIN| **S**erve: 4)

Ingredients:

1 yellow onion, minced
4 chicken drumsticks
1 tbsp balsamic vinegar
1 chili pepper, chopped
15 ounces Coca Cola
Salt and black pepper to taste
2 tbsp extra virgin olive oil

Directions:

1. Set your instant pot on Sauté mode, add the oil and heat
2. Add chicken pieces, stir and brown them on all sides and then transfer them to a plate.
3. Add vinegar, Coca Cola and chili to the pot, stir and simmer for 2 minutes.
4. Return chicken, add salt and pepper to taste, stir, cover and cook on High for 10 minutes.
5. Release the pressure quickly, uncover and dish up chicken portions onto plates. Enjoy!

(**C**alories 410|**F**at 23 g| **P**rotein 27 g| Fiber 1 g| Carbohydrates 24 g)

Duck Chili

(**Prep Time:** 10 MIN| **Cook Time:** 1 HOUR| **Serve:** 4)

Ingredients:

1 pound northern beans, soaked and rinsed
1 yellow onion, cut into half
1 garlic head, top trimmed off
Salt to taste
2 cloves
1 bay leaf
6 cups water

For the duck:
1 pound duck, ground
1 tbsp vegetable oil
1 yellow onion, minced
2 carrots, chopped
Salt and black pepper to taste
4 ounces canned green chilies and their juice
1 tsp brown sugar
15 ounces canned tomatoes and their juices, chopped
A handful cilantro, chopped

Directions:

1. Put the beans in your instant pot.
2. Add whole onion, garlic head, cloves, bay leaf, the water and salt to taste, stir, cover and cook on High for 25 minutes.
3. Release the pressure, uncover, discard solids and transfer beans to a bowl.
4. Heat up a pan with the oil over medium high heat, add carrots and chopped onion, season with salt and pepper to taste and cook for 5 more minutes.
5. Add duck, stir and cook for a further 5 minutes.
6. Add chilies and tomatoes, bring to a simmer and take off heat.
7. Pour this into your instant pot, cover and cook on High for 5 minutes.
8. Release pressure naturally for 15 minutes, add more salt and pepper, beans and brown sugar and serve with cilantro scattered on top.

(**Calories** 270|**Fat** 13 g| **Protein** 25 g| **Fiber** 26 g| **Carbohydrates** 15 g)

Coq Au Vin

(Prep Time: 10 MIN| Cook Time: 50 MIN| Serve: 4)

Ingredients:

2 pounds chicken pieces
4 ounces bacon, chopped
¼ cup peanut oil
2 brown onions, sliced
2 garlic cloves, crushed
14 ounces red wine
1 bay leaf
2 tbsp flour
7 ounces white mushrooms, sliced
1 cup parsley, finely chopped
Salt and black pepper to taste
12 small potatoes, cut into halves
2 tbsp cognac

Directions:

1. Set your instant pot on Sauté mode, add the oil and heat
2. Add chicken pieces, brown them on all sides and transfer them to a bowl.
3. Add bacon and onions to pot, stir and fry for 5 minutes.
4. Add garlic, stir for a further minute
5. Return chicken to pot, add flour and cognac, stir briskly to avoid lumps forming and cook for 1 minute.
6. Add salt, pepper, bay leaf and red wine, stir well, bring to a boil, cover pot and cook on High for 30 minutes.
7. Release the pressure quickly, add mushrooms to the pot and potatoes in the steamer basket, cover again and cook everything for 15 minutes.
8. Release the pressure again, take potatoes out and divide them onto plates.
9. Spoon the pieces of chicken on top, sprinkle parsley and serve.

(Calories 281|Fat 12.4 g| Protein 23 g| Fiber 2.2 g| Carbohydrates 15 g)

Italian Summer Chicken

(**Prep Time:** 10 MIN| **Cook Time:** 20 MIN| **Serve:** 6)

Ingredients:

1 tbsp extra virgin olive oil
2 pounds chicken breasts, skinless and boneless
Salt and black pepper to taste
¾ cup yellow onion, diced
½ cup green bell pepper, chopped
½ cup red bell pepper, chopped
¾ cup marinara sauce
2 tbsp pesto
¾ cup mushrooms, sliced
Cheddar cheese, shredded for serving

Directions:

1. Set your instant pot on Sauté mode, add the oil and heat.
2. Add onion, red and green bell pepper, salt and pepper to taste, fry for 4 minutes.
3. Add pesto, marinara sauce and chicken, stir, cover and cook on High for 12 minutes.
4. Release the pressure, uncover, remove chicken, place on a cutting board and shred,.
5. Discard 2/3 cup cooking liquid, add mushrooms to the pot, set it on Sauté mode again and fry them for 3 minutes.
6. Return chicken to the pot and mix well. Serve with shredded cheese on top.

(**Calories** 340|**Fat** 15 g| **Protein** 34 g| **Fiber** 3.5 g| **Carbohydrates** 10.1 g)

Teriyaki Chicken

(**P**rep Time: 10 MIN| **C**ook Time: 12 MIN| **S**erve: 6)

Ingredients:

2 pounds chicken breasts, skinless and boneless
2/3 cup teriyaki sauce
1 tbsp honey
½ cup chicken stock
Salt and black pepper to taste
A handful green onions, chopped
Cooked rice to serve

Directions:

1. Set your instant pot on Sauté mode, add teriyaki sauce and honey, stir and simmer for 1 minute.
2. Add stock, chicken, salt and pepper, cover and cook on High for 12 minutes.
3. Release the pressure quickly, take chicken breasts and place them on a cutting board and shred with 2 forks.
4. Remove ½ cup of cooking liquid, return shredded chicken to pot, add green onions, stir, divide among plates and serve with cooked rice.

(**C**alories 240|Fat 13 g| **P**rotein 34 g| Fiber 1 g| Carbohydrates 8 g)

Creamy Bacon Chicken

(**Prep Time:** 10 MIN| **Cook Time:** 20 MIN| **Serve:** 6)

Ingredients:

2 slices bacon, chopped
1 cup chicken stock
4 ounces cream cheese
1 ounce ranch seasoning
2 pounds chicken breasts, skinless and boneless
Green onions, chopped for serving

Directions:

1. Set your instant pot on Sauté mode, add bacon and fry for 4 minutes.
2. Add chicken, stock and seasoning, stir, cover and cook on High for 12 minutes.
3. Release the pressure, uncover, transfer chicken to a cutting board and shred it.
4. Remove 2/3 cup liquid from the pot, add cream cheese, set pot to Sauté mode again and cook for 3 minutes, stirring.
5. Return chicken to pot, stir, add green onions and serve.

(**Calories** 300|**Fat** 7 g| **Protein** 22 g| **Fiber** 3 g| **Carbohydrates** 23 g)

Buffalo Blue Cheese Chicken

(**Prep Time:** 10 MIN| **Cook Time:** 15 MIN| **Serve:** 6)

Ingredients:

2 pounds chicken breasts, skinless, boneless and cut into thin strips
½ cup celery, chopped
1 small yellow onion, chopped
½ cup buffalo sauce
½ cup chicken stock
¼ cup blue cheese, crumbled

Directions:

1. In your instant pot, mix onion with celery, buffalo sauce, stock and chicken, stir, cover and cook on High for 12 minutes.
2. Release the pressure, uncover, discard 2/3 cup of cooking liquid, add crumbled cheese, stir until cheese melts and then dish up and enjoy!

(**Calories** 190|**Fat** 9 g| **Protein** 14 g| Fiber 1 g| **Carbohydrates** 20 g)

Bacon and Lentil Chicken

(Prep Time: 10 MIN| Cook Time: 25 MIN| Serve: 4)

Ingredients:

8 ounces bacon, chopped
2 tbsp extra virgin olive oil
A drizzle of olive oil for serving
1 cup yellow onion, chopped
8 ounces lentils, dried
2 carrots, chopped
12 parsley springs, chopped
Salt and black pepper to taste
2 bay leaves
2 ½ pounds chicken pieces
1 quart chicken stock
2 tsp sherry vinegar

Directions:

1. Set your instant pot on Sauté mode, add the oil and heat.
2. Add bacon, stir and fry for 1 minute.
3. Add onions and fry for a further 2 minutes.
4. Add the rest of the ingredients except sherry vinegar, stir, cover and cook on High for 20 minutes.
5. Release pressure, take chicken pieces and place them on a cutting board.
6. Discard skin and bones, shred chicken and return to pot.
7. Set pot on Sauté mode again and cook for 7 more minutes.
8. Adjust seasoning, and add the sherry vinegar.
9. Drizzle some olive oil over the whole dish and serve.

(**Calories** 340|**Fat** 3.3 g| **Protein** 29 g| **Fiber** 23 g| **Carbohydrates** 30 g)

Chicken Curry with Eggplant

(**Prep Time:** 10 MIN| **Cook Time:** 25 MIN| **Serve:** 4)

Ingredients:

3 garlic cloves, crushed
2 tbsp vegetable oil
3 bird's eye chilies, cut into halves
1 inch piece finger, sliced
2 tbsp green curry paste
1/8 tsp cumin, ground
¼ tsp coriander, ground
14 ounces canned coconut milk
6 cups squash, cubed
8 chicken pieces
1 eggplant, cubed
Salt and black pepper to taste
1 tbsp fish sauce
4 cups spinach, chopped
½ cup cilantro, chopped
½ cup basil, chopped
Cooked barley for serving
Lime wedges, for serving

Directions:

1. Set your instant pot on Sauté mode, add oil and heat.
2. Add garlic, ginger, chilies, cumin and coriander, stir and cook for 1 minute.
3. Add curry paste and cook for 3 more minutes.
4. Add coconut milk, stir and simmer for 1 minute.
5. Add chicken, squash, eggplant, salt and pepper, stir, cover and cook on High for 20 minutes.
6. Release the pressure, uncover, add spinach, fish sauce, more salt and pepper, basil and cilantro, stir and divide among plates.
7. Serve with cooked barley on the side and lime wedges.

(**Calories** 160|**Fat** 8.2 g| **Protein** 6 g| **Fiber** 4.1 g| **Carbohydrates** 13.2 g)

Chicken Chickpea Masala

(**Prep Time:** 10 MIN| **Cook Time:** 25 MIN| **Serve:** 4)

Ingredients:

1 yellow onion, finely chopped
2 tbsp butter
4 garlic cloves, minced
1 tbsp ginger, grated
1 ½ tsp paprika
1 tbsp cumin, ground
1 ½ tsp coriander, ground
1 tsp turmeric, ground
Salt and black pepper to taste
A pinch of cayenne pepper
15 ounces canned tomatoes, crushed
¼ cup lemon juice
1 pound spinach, chopped
3 pounds chicken drumsticks and thighs
½ cup cilantro, chopped
½ cup chicken stock
15 ounces canned chickpeas, drained
½ cup heavy cream

Directions:
1. Set your instant pot on Sauté mode, add butter and melt it.
2. Add ginger, onion and garlic, stir and cook for 5 minutes.
3. Add paprika, cumin, coriander, cayenne, turmeric, salt, pepper, and stir cook for 30 seconds.
4. Add tomatoes and spinach, stir and cook for a further 2 minutes.
5. Add half of the cilantro, chicken pieces and stock, stir, cover and cook on High for 15 mins.
6. Release the pressure, uncover, add heavy cream, chickpeas, lemon juice, more salt and pepper, stir, set pot on Sauté mode again and simmer for 3 minutes.
7. Sprinkle the rest of the cilantro on top, stir, divide among plates and enjoy

(**Calories** 270|**Fat** 8 g| **Protein** 31 g| **Fiber** 7.6 g| **Carbohydrates** 30 g)

Sesame Chicken

(**Prep Time:** 10 MIN| **Cook Time:** 8 MIN| **Serve:** 4)

Ingredients:

2 pounds chicken breasts, skinless, boneless and chopped
½ cup yellow onion, chopped
Salt and black pepper to taste
1 tbsp vegetable oil
2 garlic cloves, minced
½ cup soy sauce
¼ cup ketchup
2 tsp sesame oil
½ cup honey
2 tbsp cornstarch
¼ tsp red pepper flakes
3 tbsp water
2 green onions, chopped
1 tbsp sesame seeds, toasted

Directions:

1. Set your instant pot on Sauté mode, add the oil and heat
2. Add garlic, onion, chicken, salt and pepper, stir and fry for 3 minutes.
3. Add pepper flakes, soy sauce and ketchup, stir, cover and cook on High for 3 minutes.
4. Release pressure quickly, add sesame oil and honey and stir.
5. In a bowl, mix cornstarch with water and stir well.
6. Add this to the pot, also add green onions and sesame seeds, stir well to prevent sauce clumping, divide among plates and hey presto, a delicious quick and easy meal!

(**Calories** 170|**Fat** 3.5 g| **Protein** 7 g| **Fiber** 2.9 g| **Carbohydrates** 16 g)

Apricot and Honey Chicken

(**Prep Time:** 10 MIN| **Cook Time:** 20 MIN| **Serve:** 4)

Ingredients:

1 chicken, cut into medium pieces
Salt and black pepper to taste
1 tbsp extra virgin olive oil
½ tsp paprika
¼ cup white wine
½ tsp marjoram, dried
¼ cup chicken stock

For the duck sauce:
2 tbsp white vinegar
¼ cup apricot preserves
1 ½ tsp ginger root, grated
2 tbsp honey

Directions:

1. Set your instant pot on Sauté mode, add oil and heat
2. Add chicken pieces, brown them on all sides and transfer to a bowl.
3. Season them with salt, pepper, marjoram and paprika and toss to coat.
4. Drain fat from pot, add stock and wine, stir and simmer for 2 minutes.
5. Return chicken to pot, cover and cook on High for 9 minutes.
6. Release the pressure, transfer chicken to serving dish and set aside.
7. Add apricot preserves to pot, ginger, vinegar and honey, set pot to Sauté mode again, stir and simmer sauce for 10 minutes.
8. Drizzle over chicken and enjoy!

(**Calories** 170|**Fat** 4 g| **Protein** 23 g| **Fiber** 3 g| **Carbohydrates** 9 g)

Chicken and Dumpling Delight

(**Prep Time:** 10 MIN| **Cook Time:** 20 MIN| **Serve:** 6)

Ingredients:

2 pounds chicken breasts, skinless and bone-in
4 carrots, chopped
1 yellow onion, chopped
3 celery stalks, chopped
¾ cup chicken stock
Salt and black pepper to taste
½ tsp thyme, dried

For the dumplings:
2 eggs
2/3 cup milk
1 tbsp baking powder
2 cups flour
1 tbsp chives

Directions:

1. In your instant pot, add chicken, onion, carrots, celery, stock, thyme, salt and pepper, stir, cover and cook on Low for 15 minutes.
2. Release the pressure quickly, transfer chicken to a bowl and keep warm.
3. To make the dumplings, in a bowl, mix eggs with salt, milk and baking powder and stir.
4. Add flour gradually and stir very well.
5. Set instant pot to Simmer mode and bring the liquid inside to a boil.
6. Shape dumplings in to small balls, drop them into stock, cover and cook on High for 7 minutes.
7. Shred chicken and add to the pot after you've released the pressure, stir. Serve chicken and dumplings with chives sprinkled on top.

(**Calories** 380|**Fat** 4.2 g| **Protein** 43 g| **Fiber** 2.9 g| **Carbohydrates** 40 g)

Tossed Chicken and Noodles

(**Prep Time:** 10 MIN| **Cook Time:** 20 MIN| **Serve:** 6)

Ingredients:

8 chicken thighs, skinless and boneless
3 carrots, chopped
2 garlic cloves, minced
1 yellow onion, chopped
3 celery stalks, chopped
6 cups chicken stock
1 bay leaf
2 sage springs
1 rosemary spring
5 thyme springs
Salt and black pepper to taste
1 tsp chicken seasoning
1 pound egg noodles
2 tbsp cornstarch
3 tbsp water
1 cup peas, frozen
Juice of 1 lemon
¼ cup parsley, chopped

Directions:

1. Set your instant pot on Sauté mode, add onion, garlic and celery, stir and brown for 4 minutes.
2. Add carrot, chicken, stock, bay leaf, thyme, rosemary, sage, chicken seasoning, salt and pepper to taste, stir and cook covered on Low for 10 minutes.
3. Release the pressure naturally, uncover, add egg noodles, cornstarch mixed with water, peas, lemon juice, parsley and more salt and pepper if needed.
4. Discard herbs springs, stir to check there are no lumps, divide among plates and serve.

(**Calories** 560|**Fat** 11.2 g| **Protein** 39 g| **Fiber** 5.2 g| **Carbohydrates** 77 g)

Pomegranate Chicken with Walnuts

(**P**rep Time: 10 MIN| **C**ook Time: 15 MIN| **S**erve: 6)

Ingredients:

10 chicken pieces
2 cups walnuts
Salt and black pepper to taste
3 tbsp extra virgin olive oil
1 yellow onion, chopped
¼ tsp cardamom, ground
½ tsp cinnamon, ground
2/3 cup pomegranate molasses
¾ cup water
2 tbsp sugar
Juice from ½ lemon
Pomegranate seeds for serving

Directions:

1. Heat up a pan over medium high heat, add walnuts and toast for 5 minutes.
2. Transfer them to your food processor, blend well, transfer to a bowl and set aside.
3. Set your instant pot on Sauté mode, add 2 tbsp oil and heat
4. Add chicken pieces, salt and pepper, brown them on all sides and transfer them to a plate.
5. Add the rest of the oil to the pot, add onion and fry for 3 minutes.
6. Add cardamom and cinnamon, stir and cook for 1 minute.
7. Add ground walnuts, pomegranate molasses, lemon juice, chicken and sugar, mix well, cover and cook on High for 7 minutes.
8. Release the pressure, uncover, add more salt and pepper and serve with the sauce from the pot. Sprinkle pomegranate seeds on top.

(**C**alories 200|**F**at 1 g| **P**rotein 17 g| **F**iber 4 g| **C**arbohydrates 27 g)

Creamy Garlic Goose

(**Prep Time:** 10 MIN| **Cook Time:** HOUR| **S**erve: 5)

Ingredients:

1 goose breast, fat trimmed off and cut into pieces
1 goose leg, skinless
1 goose thigh, skinless
Salt and black pepper to taste
3 ½ cups water
2 tsp garlic, minced
1 yellow onion, chopped
12 ounces canned mushroom cream
Toasted bread for serving

Directions:

1. Put all goose meat in your instant pot.
2. Add onion, salt, pepper, water and garlic, stir, cover and cook on Low for 1 hour.
3. Release the pressure, uncover, add mushroom cream, set pot on Simmer mode and cook everything for 5 minutes.
4. Divide into bowls and serve with toasted bread on the side.

(**Calories** 345|**Fat** 7.8 g| **Protein** 428.4 g| **Fiber** 1 g| **Carbohydrates** 1 g)

Creole Chicken Gumbo

(Prep Time: 10 MIN| Cook Time: 15 MIN| Serve: 4)

Ingredients:

8 ounces shrimp, peeled and deveined
8 ounces sausages, sliced
8 ounces chicken breasts, skinless, boneless and chopped
2 tbsp extra virgin olive oil
1 tsp Creole seasoning
2 tsp thyme, dried
A pinch of cayenne pepper
2 tsp Worcestershire sauce
1 dash Tabasco sauce
3 garlic cloves, minced
1 yellow onion, chopped
1 green bell pepper, chopped
3 celery stalks, chopped
1 cup white rice
1 cup chicken stock
2 cups canned tomatoes, chopped
3 tbsp parsley, chopped
Salt amd pepper to tast

Directions:

1. In a bowl, mix Creole seasoning with thyme and cayenne and stir.
2. Set your instant pot on Sauté mode, add the oil and heat
3. Add chicken and brown for a few minutes.
4. Add sausage slices, stir and cook for 3 minutes.
5. Add shrimp and half of the seasoning mix, stir and cook for 2 minutes.
6. Transfer everything to a bowl and set aside.
7. Add garlic, onions, celery and bell peppers to your instant pot.
8. Add the rest of the seasoning mix, sir and cook for 10 minutes.
9. Add rice, stock, tomatoes, Tabasco sauce and Worcestershire sauce, stir, cover and cook on High for 8 minutes.

10. Release the pressure, return chicken, sausage and shrimp to the rice mixture, stir, cover and set instant pot aside for 5 minutes for flavors to develop.
11. Serve in bowls for a delicious spicy feast!

(**Calories** 269| **Fat** 5.9 g| **Protein** 28.4 g| **Fiber** 2.4 g| **Carbohydrates** 23.5 g)

Sweet Chili Goose

(**Prep Time:** 10 MIN| **Cook Time:** 15 MIN| **Serve:** 4)

Ingredients:

1 goose breast half, skinless, boneless and cut into thin slices
¼ cup extra virgin olive oil
1 sweet onion, chopped
2 tsp garlic, chopped
Salt and black pepper to taste
¼ cup sweet chili sauce

Directions:

1. Set your instant pot on Sauté mode, add the oil and heat
2. Add onion and garlic and fry for 2 minutes.
3. Add goose breast slices, salt and pepper to taste, stir and cook for 2 minutes on each side.
4. Add sweet chili sauce, stir, cover and cook on High for 5 minutes.
5. Release pressure quickly and serve for a yummy feast!

(**Calories** 190| **Fat** 8 g| **Protein** 29 g| **Fiber** 1 g| **Carbohydrates** 1 g)

Indian Butter Chicken

(**P**rep Time: 10 MIN| **C**ook Time: 15 MIN| **S**erve: 6)

Ingredients:

10 chicken thighs, skinless and boneless
2 jalapeno peppers, chopped
28 ounces canned tomatoes and their juice, chopped
2 tbsp cumin, ground
2 tbsp ginger, chopped
½ cup butter
Salt and black pepper to taste
¾ cup heavy cream
2 tbsp garam masala
¾ cup Greek yogurt
2 tbsp cumin seeds, toasted and ground
2 tbsp cornstarch
2 tbsp water
¼ cup cilantro, chopped

Directions:

1. In your food processor, mix tomatoes with ginger and jalapenos and blend well.
2. Set your instant pot on Sauté mode, add butter and melt it.
3. Add chicken, stir and brown for 3 minutes on each side.
4. Transfer chicken pieces to a bowl and set aside.
5. Add paprika and ground cumin to your pot, stir and cook for 10 seconds.
6. Add tomatoes, salt, pepper, yogurt, heavy cream and chicken pieces, stir, cover and cook on High for 5 minutes.
7. Release the pressure naturally for 15 minutes, uncover, add cornstarch mixed with the water, garam masala and cumin seeds and stir well.
8. Add cilantro, stir and serve with naan bread.

(**C**alories 380|**F**at 29 g| **P**rotein 24 g| **F**iber 2 g| **C**arbohydrates 8 g)

Cheese and Broccoli Chicken

(**Prep Time:** 10 MIN| **Cook Time:** 15 MIN| **Serve:** 6)

Ingredients:

2 chicken breasts, skinless and boneless
1 tbsp butter
1 tbsp extra virgin olive oil
½ cup yellow onion, chopped
14 ounces canned chicken stock
Salt and black pepper to taste
A pinch of red pepper flakes
1 tbsp parsley, dried
2 tbsp water
2 tbsp cornstarch
3 cups broccoli, steamed and chopped
1 cup cheddar cheese, shredded
4 ounces cream cheese, cubed

Directions:

1. Set your instant pot on Sauté mode, add butter and oil and heat up.
2. Add chicken breasts, salt and pepper, brown on all sides and transfer to a bowl.
3. Add onion to the pot, stir and fry for 5 minutes.
4. Add more salt, pepper, stock, parsley, pepper flakes and return chicken breasts to the pot.
5. Stir, cover and cook on High for 5 minutes.
6. Release the pressure quickly, transfer chicken to a cutting board, chop it into bite size pieces and return to pot.
7. Add cornstarch mixed with water, shredded cheese and cream cheese and stir until all the cheese dissolves.
8. Add broccoli, stir, set the pot on Simmer mode and cook for 5 minutes.
9. Divide among plates and serve.

(**Calories** 280|**Fat** 13 g| **Protein** 30 g| **Fiber** 4 g| **Carbohydrates** 23 g)

Rustic Chicken and Corn

(**Prep Time:** 10 MIN| **Cook Time:** 25 MIN| **Serve:** 4)

Ingredients:

8 chicken drumsticks
Salt and black pepper to taste
1 tsp extra virgin olive oil
½ tsp garlic powder
3 scallions, chopped
½ yellow onion, chopped
1 tomato, chopped
¼ cup cilantro, chopped
1 garlic clove, minced
2 cups water
8 ounces tomato sauce
1 tbsp chicken bouillon
2 corn on the cob, husked and cut into halves
½ tsp cumin, ground

Directions:

1. Set your instant pot on Sauté mode, add oil and heat up.
2. Add onions, tomato, scallions and garlic, stir and fry for 3 minutes.
3. Add cilantro, stir and cook for 1 minute.
4. Add tomato sauce, water, bouillon, cumin, garlic powder, chicken, salt, pepper and top with the corn.
5. Cover and cook on High for 20 minutes.
6. Release the pressure quickly, uncover, add more salt and pepper if needed, divide chicken and corn on plates and serve.

(**Calories** 320|**Fat** 10 g| **Protein** 42 g| **Fiber** 3 g| **Carbohydrates** 18 g)

Thai Chicken and Cabbage

(Prep Time: 10 MIN| Cook Time: 30 MIN| Serve: 3)

Ingredients:

1 ½ pounds chicken thighs, boneless
1 green cabbage, roughly chopped
1 tbsp vegetable oil
Salt and black pepper to taste
2 chili peppers, chopped
1 yellow onion, chopped
4 garlic cloves, chopped
3 tbsp curry paste
A pinch of cayenne pepper
½ cup white wine
10 ounces coconut milk
1 tbsp fish sauce
Cooked fragrant rice for serving

Directions:

1. Set your instant pot on Sauté mode, add oil and heat
2. Add chicken, season with salt and pepper, stir, brown for a few minutes and transfer to a bowl.
3. Add garlic, chili peppers and onions to the pot, stir and cook for 4 minutes.
4. Add curry paste, stir and fry for 2 minutes more to release flavors.
5. Add wine, cabbage, coconut milk, cayenne, fish sauce, chicken pieces, salt and pepper, stir, cover and cook on High for 20 minutes.
6. Release the pressure naturally, uncover, stir your mixture and serve on top of rice in bowls.

(**Calories** 260|**Fat** 5.5 g| **Protein** 30.2 g| **Fiber** 4.9 g| **Carbohydrates** 15.2 g)

Turkey Lasagna with Ricotta

(Prep Time: 15 MIN| Cook Time: 30 MIN| Serve: 8)

Ingredients:
2 lbs ground turkey
5 cups baby spinach leaves
1 cup ricotta
1 cup mozzarella cheese, grated
1 can crushed tomatoes
3 tsp dried oregano
2 tsp thyme
3 tbsp fresh parsley, finely chopped
1 tsp salt
1 tsp freshly ground black pepper
1 tsp onion powder
1 tsp garlic powder
8 lasagna sheets
3 cups water

Directions:
1. In a bowl mix together the ricotta and mozzarella and place aside.
2. In another bowl, mix the crushed tomatoes with the oregano, thyme, parsley, salt, pepper, onion and garlic powder.
3. Start layering the lasagna in a heatproof dish that fits inside the Instant Pot.
4. Spread one tablespoon of the tomatoes sauce and layer some of the lasagna sheets. Spread more of the tomatoes sauce on the sheets and top with a layer of each of the following: cheese, minced meat and spinach. Top with more sauce and place the rest of the lasagna. Repeat the layering process until you run out of lasagna sheets. Sprinkle with leftover cheese and cover tightly with aluminum foil.
5. Place the Instant Pot over medium heat, pour in water and carefully place the lasagna dish inside the pot on the trivet.
6. Cover the pot and manually set the timer for 30 minutes. When the time is done, carefully release the pressure.
7. Uncover the pot and remove the foil. To allow the lasagna to brown.
8. Carefully take out the lasagna dish out of the pot and serve hot.

(Calories 787|Fat 22.3| Protein 63.6 g| Carbohydrates 90.6g)

Fish & Seafood Recipes

Rosemary Wild Salmon With Asparagus

(Prep Time: 10 MIN| Cook Time: 5 MIN| Serve: 4)

Ingredients:

2 lbs frozen salmon, thawed
Salt, to taste
Freshly ground black pepper, to taste
2 tbsp rosemary
¼ cup extra-virgin olive oil
1 package asparagus
1 cup cherry tomatoes
1 cup water

Directions:

1. In a bowl place the salmon and season it with salt and pepper on each side. Pour in 1 tablespoon of olive oil and half the lemon juice.
2. Place the Instant Pot over medium heat, pour the water and remaining lemon juice and insert the rack.
3. Place the salmon on the rack and top with the rosemary, asparagus and half the tomatoes.
4. Chop the remaining tomatoes in halves and place aside.
5. Cover and set the timer on 4 minutes. Carefully release the pressure when the time is finished.
6. Carefully transfer the salmon onto a serving plate, discard the rosemary. And arrange the asparagus on top of salmon.
7. Add the halved tomatoes next to the salmon. Drizzle some olive oil and sprinkle with a pinch of salt and pepper, to taste.
8. Serve warm!

(Calories 435|Fat 27| Protein 46 g| Carbohydrates 5.4g)

Smoked Salmon with Spinach Pesto

(Prep Time: 10 MIN| Cook Time: 5 MIN| Serve: 4)

Ingredients:

1 lbs Spinach leaves
1/4 cup pine nuts
3 cloves of garlic, crushed
1/3 cup extra-virgin olive oil
1 ¼ cup Parmesan cheese, freshly grated
Pinch of salt, to taste
¼ tsp freshly ground black pepper, to taste
1 package pasta shells
Water for cooking
1 package smoked salmon
Zest of 1 lemon
1 cup heavy cream
Kosher salt, to taste
Freshly ground black pepper, to taste
Lemon juice, to serve

Directions:
1. Start off by making the spinach pesto. In a food processor combine half the spinach, pine nuts, garlic, olive oil, ¾ cup of Parmesan cheese, salt and pepper. Pulse until smooth.
2. Cook the pasta in the Instant Pot over medium heat. Fill about half the Instant Pot with water and add the pasta. Set the timer for 4 minutes.
3. Chop the smoked salmon into bite sized pieces.
4. When the time is finished, release the pressure and uncover. Set the Instant Pot on "Sauté" mode and toss in the salmon with the lemon zest and cream.
5. Stir and season with salt and pepper. Add the remaining Parmesan cheese and spinach.
6. Keep stirring until the spinach wilts and then transfer to a serving plate.
7. Serve warm with lemon juice.

(Calories 482|Fat 39.9| Protein 17.6 g| Carbohydrates 18.4g)

Frozen Shrimp Rice

(Prep Time: 10 MIN| Cook Time: 6 MIN| Serve: 4)

Ingredients:

3 tbsp unsalted butter
1 cup long grain rice
3 garlic cloves, minced
1 1/3 cup broth
Kosher salt, to taste
Freshly ground black pepper, to taste
1 can black beans, rinsed
2 lbs frozen shrimps
Juice of 1 lemon
½ cup fresh cilantro, finely chopped

Directions:
1. Place the Instant Pot over medium heat and set on "Sauté" mode.
2. Melt the butter and add in the rice. toss the rice until golden in the butter and stir in the garlic.
3. Season with salt and pepper and pour in broth. Add the beans, shrimps and lemon juice.
4. Cover the pot and set the timer on 6 minutes.
5. When the time is finished, manually release the pressure.
6. Uncover the lid and give the rice a toss.
7. Transfer to serving plate and garnish with fresh cilantro.

(Calories 672|Fat 14.2| Protein 62.1 g| Carbohydrates 71.8)

Bacon and Shrimp Grits with Tomato Sauce

(Prep Time: 10 MIN| Cook Time: 5 MIN| Serve: 4)

Ingredients:

2 lbs frozen shrimps, thawed
1 tbsp Cajun Seasonings
5 strips smoked bacon
1 onion
2 bell peppers
2 cloves garlic, crushed
3 tbsp white vinegar
1 can tomatoes
Juice of ½ lemon
1/3 cup chicken stock
Dash of hot sauce
Kosher salt, to taste
Freshly ground black pepper
3 tbsp heavy cream
1 scallion, finely chopped
2/3 cup grits
1 cup water
1 cup full fat milk
2 tbsp unsalted butter

Directions:

1. Place t In a bowl, toss the thawed shrimps with the spices.
2. Place the Instant Pot over medium heat and set on "Sauté" mode. Chop the bacon strips into small pieces and toss in the pot and stir for 3 minutes until crispy. Transfer to a plate and stir in the onions and peppers into the pot.
3. Stir and add the garlic.
4. Remove the pot from the heat and pour in the vinegar. Keep stirring until nothing sticks to the bottom.
5. Add the tomatoes with lemon juice, chicken stock and hot sauce. Season with salt and pepper.
6. In a heatproof bowl that fits into the pot, combine the grits with the water, milk. Season with extra salt and pepper and mix to combine.
7. Insert the wire rack into the pot so that you can place the heatproof bowl on top of it.
8. Cover the pot and set the timer for 10 minutes. Once the time is over, allow the pressure to be release automatically.

9. Uncover the pot and carefully take out the bowl and place it aside.
10. Return the Instant Pot on medium heat and remove the wire rack.
11. Toss in the shrimps and cover the pot. Set on " Keep Warm" and allow it to cook for 10 minutes on low heat.
12. Using a fork, fluff out the grits mixture and add the butter.
13. When the time is finished, uncover the pot and add in the shrimps and cream. Set on "Sauté" mode and stir for a minutes.
14. Place the grits into serving plates and top with shrimps and drizzle some of the sauce. Top with bacon slices and chopped scallions. Serve hot.

(Calories 496|Fat 20.8| Protein 54.6 g| Carbohydrates 21.5g)

Tangy Citrus Fish

(**Prep Time:** 10 MIN| **Cook Time:** 7 MIN| **Serve:** 4)

Ingredients:

4 white fish fillets
4 spring onions, chopped
A drizzle of extra virgin olive oil
A small piece of ginger, chopped
Salt and black pepper to taste
Juice and zest from 1 orange
1 cup fish stock

Directions:

1. Pat dry fish fillets, season with salt, pepper and rub them with the olive oil.
2. Put stock, ginger, orange juice, orange zest and onions in your instant pot.
3. Put fish fillets in the steamer basket, cover and cook on High for 7 minutes.
4. Release the pressure, divide fish onto plates and drizzle the orange sauce on top.

(**Calories** 326|**Fat** 2 g| **Protein** 23 g| **Fiber** 0.4 g| **Carbohydrates** 10 g)

Steamed Fish a la Corfu

(**Prep Time:** 10 MIN| **Cook Time:** 10 MIN| **Serve:** 4)

Ingredients:

4 white fish fillets
1 cup olives, pitted and chopped
1 pound cherry tomatoes, cut into halves
A pinch of thyme, dried
1 garlic clove, minced
A drizzle of olive oil
Salt and black pepper to taste
1 cup water

Directions:

1. Put the water in your instant pot.
2. Put fish fillets in the steamer basket of the pot.
3. Add tomatoes and olives on top.
4. Also add garlic, thyme, oil, salt and pepper.
5. Cover and cook on Low for 10 minutes.
6. Release the pressure, uncover and serve.

(**C**alories 157|**F**at 3.2 g| **P**rotein 29 g| **F**iber 0 g| **C**arbohydrates 0 g)

Kerala Fish Curry

(**Prep Time:** 10 MIN| **Cook Time:** 15 MIN| **Serve:** 6)

Ingredients:

6 fish fillets, cut into medium pieces
1 tomato, chopped
14 ounces coconut milk
2 onions, sliced
2 capsicums, cut into strips
2 garlic cloves, minced
6 curry leaves
1 tbsp coriander, ground
1 tbsp ginger, finely grated
½ tsp turmeric, ground
2 tsp cumin, ground
Salt and black pepper to taste
½ tsp fenugreek, ground
1 tsp hot pepper flakes
2 tbsp lemon juice

Directions:
1. Set your instant pot on Sauté mode, add oil and curry leaves and fry for 1 minute.
2. Add ginger, onion and garlic, stir and cook a further 2 minutes.
3. Add coriander, turmeric, cumin, fenugreek and hot pepper and cook 2 minutes.
4. Add coconut milk, tomatoes, fish and capsicum, stir, cover and cook on Low for 5 minutes.
5. Release the pressure naturally, add salt and pepper to taste, serve in bowls with a squeeze of lemon juice.

(**Calories** 230|**Fat** 10 g| **Protein** 23 g| **Fiber** 1.1 g| **Carbohydrates** 12 g)

Mediterranean Cod Medley

(**Prep Time:** 10 MIN| **Cook Time:** 10 MIN| **Serve:** 4)

Ingredients:

4 cod fillets
17 ounces tomatoes, cut into halves
1 garlic clove, crushed
1 cup olives, pitted and chopped
2 tbsp capers, drained and chopped
Salt and black pepper to taste
1 tbsp parsley, chopped
1 tbsp extra virgin olive oil

Directions:

1. Put tomatoes on the bottom of a heat proof bowl.
2. Add parsley, salt and pepper and toss to coat.
3. Place fish fillets on top, add olive oil, salt, pepper, garlic, olives and capers.
4. Place the bowl in the steamer basket of the pot, cover and cook on High for 5 minutes.
5. Release the pressure naturally and serve your Mediterranean feast!

(**Calories** 170|**Fat** 9 g| **Protein** 23 g| Fiber 1 g| **Carbohydrates** 4 g)

Fennel Basted Salmon

(**Prep Time:** 10 MIN| **Cook Time:** 5 MIN| **Serve:** 4)

Ingredients:

16 ounces salmon fillet, skin on
Zest from 1 lemon
4 scallions, chopped
3 black peppercorns
½ tsp fennel seeds
1 bay leaf
1 tsp white wine vinegar
2 cups chicken stock
½ cup dry white wine
¼ cup dill, chopped
Salt and black pepper to taste

Directions:

1. Put salmon in the steamer basket of your instant pot and season with salt and pepper.
2. Add stock, scallions, lemon zest, peppercorns, fennel, vinegar, bay leaf, wine, stock and dill to your pot.
3. Cover and cook on High for 5 minutes.
4. Release the pressure, uncover pot and divide salmon on your plates and keep warm.
5. Set the pot on Simmer mode and cook the liquid for a few minutes more to reduce liquid.
6. Drizzle over salmon and serve.

(**Calories** 140|**Fat** 4 g| **Protein** 23 g| **Fiber** 0 g| **Carbohydrates** 2 g)

Instant Saffron Salmon

(**Prep** Time: 5 MIN| **Cook** Time: 5 MIN| **Serve**: 2)

Ingredients:

2 wild salmon fillets, frozen
Salt and black pepper to taste
½ cup jasmine rice
1 cup chicken stock
¼ cup vegetable soup mix, dried
1 tbsp butter
A pinch of saffron

Directions:

1. In your instant pot, mix stock with rice, soup mix, butter and saffron and stir.
2. Season salmon with salt and pepper, place in the steamer basket of your pot, cover and cook on High for 5 minutes.
3. Release the pressure and serve salmon on plates, with saffron rice on the side.

(**Calories** 300|**Fat** 8 g| **Protein** 25 g| Fiber 0.5 g| Carbohydrates 30 g)

Steamed Salmon With Cinnamon

(**Prep Time:** 10 MIN| **Cook Time:** 10 MIN| **Serve:** 2)

Ingredients:

2 salmon fillets, skin on
1 bay leaf
1 cup water
1 cinnamon stick
3 cloves
1 tbsp canola oil
1 cup baby carrots
2 cups broccoli florets
Salt and black pepper to taste
Lime wedges for serving

Directions:

1. Put the water in your instant pot.
2. Add bay leaf, cinnamon stick and cloves.
3. Place salmon fillets in the steamer basket of your pot after you've brushed them with canola oil.
4. Season with salt and pepper, add broccoli and carrots, cover and cook on High for 6 minutes.
5. Release the pressure for 4 minutes, uncover, portion out the salmon and veggies onto plates.
6. Drizzle the sauce from the pot over salmon after you've discarded cinnamon, cloves and bay leaf and serve with lime wedges on the side.

(**Calories** 170|**Fat** 4.5 g| **Protein** 17 g| **Fiber** 3.7 g| **Carbohydrates** 13 g)

Spicy Salmon Fillets

(**Prep Time:** 10 MIN| **Cook Time:** 5 MIN| **Serve:** 4)

Ingredients:

4 salmon fillets
2 tbsp assorted chili pepper
Juice of 1 lemon
1 lemon, sliced
1 cup water
Salt and black pepper to taste

Directions:

1. Place salmon fillets in the steamer basket of your pot, add salt, pepper, lemon juice, lemon slices and chili pepper.
2. Add 1 cup water to the pot, cover and cook on High for 5 minutes.
3. Release the pressure, divide salmon and lemon slices amongst plates and serve.

(**Calories** 120|**Fat** 2 g| **Protein** 5 g| Fiber 0.5 g| **Carbohydrates** 13 g)

Tomato and Thyme Salmon Parcel

(**Prep Time:** 10 MIN| **Cook Time:** 15 MIN| **Serve:** 4)

Ingredients:

4 salmon fillets
1 lemon, sliced
1 white onion, chopped
3 tomatoes, sliced
4 thyme springs
4 parsley springs
3 tbsp extra virgin olive oil
Salt and black pepper to taste
2 cups water

Directions:

1. Drizzle the oil onto a piece of parchment paper.
2. Add a layer of tomatoes, salt and pepper.
3. Drizzle some oil again, add fish and season them with salt and pepper.
4. Drizzle some more oil, add thyme and parsley springs, onions, lemon slices, salt and pepper.
5. Fold and tuck ends of packet underneath, place in the steamer basket of your instant pot.
6. Add 2 cups water to the pot, cover and cook on Low for 15 minutes.
7. Release the pressure, uncover, open packet carefully (be careful of the steam). Divide contents onto plates and serve.

(**Calories** 180|**Fat** 5 g| **Protein** 31 g| **Fiber** 1 g| **Carbohydrates** 0 g)

Healthy Salmon Burger

(**Prep Time:** 10 MIN| **Cook Time:** 10 MIN| **Serve:** 4)

Ingredients:

1 tsp extra virgin olive oil
½ cup Panko crumbs
1 pound salmon meat, minced
2 tbsp lemon zest
Salt and black pepper to taste
Mustard for serving
Tomatoes slices for serving
Arugula leaves for serving

Directions:

1. Put salmon in your food processor and blend it.
2. Transfer to a bowl, add Panko, salt, pepper and lemon zest and stir well.
3. Shape 4 patties and place them on a working surface.
4. Set your instant pot on Sauté mode, add oil and heat
5. Add patties, fry for 3 minutes on each side and put them onto hamburger buns.
6. Serve with tomatoes, arugula and mustard. Yummy!

(**Calories** 170|**Fat** 9 g| **Protein** 22 g| **Fiber** 0 g| **Carbohydrates** 1 g)

Creamy Fish and Potatoes

(**Prep Time:** 10 MIN| **Cook Time:** 25 MIN| **Serve:** 6)

Ingredients:

17 ounces white fish, cut into medium chunks
1 yellow onion, chopped
13 ounces potatoes, peeled and cut into chunks
13 ounces milk
Salt and black pepper to taste
14 ounces chicken stock
14 ounces water
14 ounces half and half
2 tsp cornflour mixed with water

Directions:
1. In your instant pot mix fish with onion, potatoes, water, milk and stock.
2. Cover and cook on High for 10 minutes.
3. Release the pressure, uncover and set the pot on Simmer mode.
4. Add salt, pepper, half and half, cornflour mixture and stir while it thickens. Then cook for 10 minutes.
5. Divide in bowls and serve.

(**Calories** 194|**Fat** 4.4 g| **Protein** 17 g| Fiber 2 g| **Carbohydrates** 21 g)

Marinated Salmon and Raspberries

(**Prep Time:** 2 HOURS| **Cook Time:** 5 MIN| **Serve:** 6)

Ingredients:

6 salmon steaks
2 tbsp extra virgin olive oil
4 leeks, sliced
2 garlic cloves, minced
2 tbsp parsley, chopped
1 cup clam juice
2 tbsp lemon juice
Salt and white pepper to taste
1 tsp sherry
1/3 cup dill, finely chopped
Raspberries for serving

<u>For the raspberry vinegar:</u>
2 pints red raspberries
1 pint cider vinegar

Directions:
1. Mix red raspberries with vinegar and stir well.
2. Add salmon steaks and leave aside in the fridge for 2 hours.
3. Set your instant pot on Sauté mode, add oil and heat
4. Add parsley, leeks and garlic, stir and fry for 2 minutes.
5. Add clam and lemon juice, sherry, salt, pepper and dill and stir.
6. Add salmon steaks, cover and cook on High for 3 minutes.
7. Release pressure, uncover and serve salmon with leeks and fresh raspberries.

(**Calories** 670|**Fat** 46 g| **Protein** 81 g| **Fiber** 1 g| **Carbohydrates** 18 g)

Crustless Fish Pie

(**Prep Time:** 10 MIN| **Cook Time:** 20 MIN| **Serve:** 4)

Ingredients:

1 pound cod fillets, cut into medium pieces
2 tbsp parsley, chopped
4 ounces bread crumbs
2 tsp lemon juice
2 eggs, whisked
2 ounces butter
½ pint milk
½ pint shrimp sauce
Salt and black pepper to taste
½ pint water

Directions:

1. In a bowl, mix fish with crumbs, lemon juice, parsley, salt and pepper and stir.
2. Heat up a pan with the butter over medium high heat.
3. Put milk in a pot and bring to a boil over medium high heat.
4. Pour butter and milk over egg and stir very well.
5. Add this to fish and set aside for 3 minutes.
6. Pour everything into a greased pudding dish and place in the steamer basket of your pot.
7. Add ½ pint water to the pot, cover and cook on High for 15 minutes.
8. Release the pressure, uncover and serve your fish pie with shrimp sauce.

(**Calories** 200|**Fat** 3 g| **Protein** 9 g| **Fiber** 1 g| **Carbohydrates** 8 g)

Jambalaya

(Prep Time: 10 MIN| Cook Time: 4 MIN| Serve: 8)

Ingredients:

1 pound chicken breast, chopped
1 pound shrimp, peeled and deveined
2 tbsp extra virgin olive oil
1 pound sausage, already cooked and chopped
2 cups onions, chopped
1 ½ cups rice
2 tbsp garlic, chopped
2 cups green, yellow and red bell peppers, chopped
3 ½ cups chicken stock
1 tbsp Creole seasoning
1 tbsp Worcestershire sauce
1 cup tomatoes, crushed

Directions:

1. Set your instant pot on Sauté mode, add chicken and Creole seasoning, brown on all sides and transfer to a bowl.
2. Add oil and heat.
3. Add peppers, onions and garlic, stir and fry for 2 minutes.
4. Add rice, stir and cook for 2 more minutes.
5. Add tomato puree, stock, Worcestershire sauce and return chicken, stir, cover and cook for 10 minutes.
6. Release the pressure, add sausage and shrimp, stir, cover and cook on High for 2 minutes.
7. Release the pressure, uncover, and serve in bowls.

(Calories 250|Fat 13 g| Protein 27 g| Fiber 1 g| Carbohydrates 22 g)

Hot Tuna and Noodle Salad

(**Prep Time:** 10 MIN| **Cook Time:** 15 MIN| **Serve:** 4)

Ingredients:

8 ounces egg noodles
½ cup red onion, chopped
1 tbsp extra virgin olive oil
1 ¼ cups water
14 ounces canned tomatoes, chopped and mixed with oregano, basil and garlic
Salt and black pepper to taste
14 ounces canned tuna, drained
8 ounces artichoke hearts, drained and chopped
1 tbsp parsley, chopped
Crumbled feta cheese

Directions:

1. Set your instant pot on Sauté mode, add oil and heat
2. Add onion, stir and fry for 2 minutes.
3. Add tomatoes, noodles, salt, pepper and water, set the pot on Simmer and cook for 10 minutes.
4. Add tuna and artichokes, stir, cover and cook on High for 5 minutes.
5. Release pressure, divide tuna and noodles on plates, sprinkle cheese and parsley on top and serve.

(**Calories** 300|**Fat** 4 g| **Protein** 29 g| **Fiber** 9 g| **Carbohydrates** 23 g)

Cheesy Mushroom Tuna

(**Prep Time:** 5 MIN| **Cook Time:** 5 MIN| **Serve:** 4)

Ingredients:

14 ounces canned tuna, drained
16 ounces egg noodles
28 ounces cream of mushroom
1 cup peas, frozen
3 cups water
4 ounces cheddar cheese, grated
¼ cup breadcrumbs

Directions:

1. Add pasta and water to your instant pot.
2. Also add tuna, peas and cream, stir, cover, cook on High for 4 minutes and release pressure.
3. Add cheese and stir until it melts.
4. Transfer everything to a baking dish, spread breadcrumbs over the top and place in preheated broiler for 3 minutes to brown.
5. Divide among plates and serve.

(**Calories** 270|**Fat** 12 g| **Protein** 15 g| **Fiber** 0.5 g| **Carbohydrates** 20 g)

Asian Roasted Mackerel

(**Prep Time:** 10 MIN| **Cook Time:** 6 MIN| **Serve:** 4)

Ingredients:

18 ounces mackerel, cut into pieces
3 garlic cloves, minced
8 shallots, chopped
1 tsp dried shrimp powder
1 tsp turmeric powder
1 tbsp chili paste
2 lemongrass sticks, cut into halves
1 small piece of ginger, chopped
6 stalks laska leaves
3 ½ ounces water
5 tbsp vegetable oil
1 1/3 tbsp tamarind paste mixed with 3 ½ ounces water
Salt to taste
1 tbsp sugar

Directions:

1. In your blender, mix garlic with shallots, chili paste, turmeric powder and shrimp powder and blend well.
2. Set your instant pot on Sauté mode, add oil and heat
3. Add fish pieces, spices paste, ginger, lemongrass and laska leaves and cook for 1 minute.
4. Add tamarind mixture, water, salt and sugar, stir, cover and cook on High for 5 minutes.
5. Release the pressure, uncover and serve your spicy mackerel.

(**Calories** 189|**Fat** 11 g| **Protein** 20 g| **Fiber** 0 g| **Carbohydrates** 1 g)

Crumbed Mackerel with Lemon

(**Prep Time:** 10 MIN| **Cook Time:** 10 MIN| **Serve:** 4)

Ingredients:

4 mackerels
3 ounces breadcrumbs
Juice and rind from 1 lemon
1 tbsp chives, finely chopped
Salt and black pepper to taste
1 egg, whisked
1 tbsp butter
1 tbsp vegetable oil
2 tbsp margarine
10 ounces water
3 lemon wedges

Directions:

1. In a bowl, mix breadcrumbs with lemon juice, lemon rind, salt, pepper, egg and chives and stir very well.
2. Coat mackerel with this mixture.
3. Set your instant pot on Sauté mode, add oil and butter and heat.
4. Add fish, brown on all sides and transfer to a plate.
5. Clean the pot and add the water.
6. Grease a heat proof dish with the margarine and place in the pot.
7. Add fish, cover and cook on High for 6 minutes.
8. Release the pressure. Divide mackerel onto plates and serve with lemon wedges.

(**Calories** 140|**Fat** 7.8 g| **Protein** 13 g| **Fiber** 0 g| **Carbohydrates** 1 g)

Steamed Garlic Mussels

(**Prep Time:** 10 MIN| **Cook Time:** 5 MIN| **Serve:** 4)

Ingredients:

2 pounds mussels, cleaned and scrubbed
1 radicchio, cut into thin strips
1 white onion, chopped
1 pound baby spinach
½ cup dry white wine
1 garlic clove, crushed
½ cup water
A drizzle of extra virgin olive oil

Directions:

1. Arrange baby spinach and radicchio on appetizer plates.
2. Set instant pot on Sauté mode, add oil and heat
3. Add garlic and onion, stir and fry for 4 minutes.
4. Add wine and stir for a further minute.
5. Place mussels in the steamer basket of the pot, cover and cook on Low for 1 minute.
6. Release the pressure and divide mussels on top of spinach and radicchio.
7. Spoon cooking liquid over mussels and serve.

(**Calories** 50|**Fat** 1 g| **Protein** 1.1 g| **Fiber** 1 g| **Carbohydrates** 0.3 g)

Mussels Neapolitan

(**Prep Time:** 10 MIN| **Cook Time:** 50 MIN| **Serve:** 3)

Ingredients:

28 ounces canned tomatoes, crushed
½ cup white onion, chopped
2 jalapeno peppers, chopped
¼ cup dry white wine
¼ cup extra virgin olive oil
¼ cup balsamic vinegar
2 pounds mussels, cleaned and scrubbed
2 tbsp red pepper flakes
2 garlic cloves, minced
Salt to taste
½ cup basil, chopped
Lemon wedges for serving

Directions:

1. Set your instant pot on Sauté mode, add tomatoes, onion, jalapenos, wine, oil, vinegar, garlic and pepper flakes and bring to the boil.
2. Add mussels, stir, cover and cook on Low for 4 minutes.
3. Release pressure, uncover, discard unopened mussels, add salt and basil, stir, dish into bowls and serve with lemon wedges.

(**Calories** 50|**Fat** 0.2 g| **Protein** 1.5 g| **Fiber** 0.2 g| **Carbohydrates** 1 g)

Mussels and Spicy Sauce

(**Prep Time:** 10 MIN| **Cook Time:** 4 MIN| **Serve:** 4)

Ingredients:

2 pounds mussels, scrubbed and debearded
2 tbsp extra virgin olive oil
1 yellow onion, chopped
½ tsp red pepper flakes
14 ounces tomatoes, chopped
2 tsp garlic, minced
½ cup chicken stock
2 tsp oregano, dried

Directions:

1. Set your instant pot on Sauté mode, add oil and heat
2. Add onions, stir and fry for 3 minutes.
3. Add pepper flakes and garlic, stir and cook for 1 minute.
4. Add stock, oregano and tomatoes and stir well.
5. Add mussels, stir, cover and cook on Low for 2 minutes.
6. Release the pressure quickly, discard unopened mussels, divide into bowls and serve.

(**Calories** 60|**Fat** 0.2 g| **Protein** 1.3 g| **Fiber** 0.2 g| **Carbohydrates** 1 g)

Mussels and Spicy Sausage

(Prep Time: 5 MIN| Cook Time: 5 MIN| Serve: 4)

Ingredients:

2 pounds mussels, scrubbed and debearded
12 ounces amber beer
1 tbsp extra virgin olive oil
1 yellow onion, chopped
8 ounces spicy sausage
1 tbsp paprika

Directions:

1. Set your instant pot on Sauté mode, add oil and heat
2. Add onion, stir and fry for 2 minutes.
3. Add sausages and cook for 4 minutes.
4. Add paprika, beer and mussels, stir, cover and cook on Low for 2 minutes.
5. Release the pressure, uncover, discard unopened mussels, transfer to bowls and serve.

(**Calories** 100|**Fat** 4 g| **Protein** 14 g| **Fiber** 1 g| **Carbohydrates** 3 g)

Cioppino Deluxe

(**Prep Time:** 10 MIN| **Cook Time:** 15 MIN| **Serve:** 4)

Ingredients:

12 shell clams
12 mussels
1 ½ pounds big shrimp, peeled and deveined
1 ½ pounds fish fillets, cut into medium pieces
1 cup butter
2 yellow onions, chopped
3 garlic cloves, minced
½ cup parsley, chopped
20 ounces canned tomatoes, chopped
8 ounces clam juice
1 ½ cups white wine
2 bay leaves
½ tsp marjoram, dried
1 tbsp basil, dried
Salt and black pepper to taste

Directions:

1. Set your instant pot on Sauté mode, add butter and melt it.
2. Add onion and garlic, stir and cook for 2 minutes.
3. Add clam juice, tomatoes, wine, parsley, basil, bay leaves, marjoram, salt and pepper, stir, cover and cook on High for 10 minutes.
4. Release the pressure and switch pot to Sauté mode again.
5. Add clams and mussels, stir and cook for 8 minutes.
6. Discard unopened mussels and clams, add fish and shrimp, stir and cook for 4 minutes.
7. Divide in bowls and serve.

(Calories 300|Fat 12 g| **Protein** 20 g| Fiber 12 g| Carbohydrates 10 g)

Boozy Chorizo Clams

(**Prep Time:** 10 MIN| **Cook Time:** 15 MIN| **Serve:** 4)

Ingredients:

15 small clams
30 mussels, scrubbed and debearded
2 chorizo links, sliced
1 pound baby red potatoes
1 yellow onion, chopped
10 ounces beer
2 tbsp parsley, chopped
1 tsp extra virgin olive oil
Lemon wedges for serving

Directions:

1. Set your instant pot on Sauté mode, add oil and heat
2. Add chorizo and onions, stir and fry for 4 minutes.
3. Add clams, mussels, potatoes and beer, stir, cover and cook on High for 10 minutes.
4. Release the pressure, uncover and add parsley, stir before dividing into bowls and serve with lemon wedges on the side.

(**Calories** 203|**Fat** 3 g| **Protein** 20 g| Fiber 8 g| **Carbohydrates** 10 g)

Stuffed Clams

(**Prep Time:** 10 MIN| **Cook Time:** 5 MIN| **Serve:** 4)

Ingredients:

24 clams, shucked
3 garlic cloves, minced
4 tbsp butter
¼ cup parsley, chopped
¼ cup parmesan cheese, grated
1 tsp oregano, dried
1 cup breadcrumbs
2 cups water
Lemon wedges

Directions:

1. In a bowl, mix breadcrumbs with parmesan, oregano, parsley, butter and garlic and stir.
2. Place 1 tbsp of this mix in exposed clams.
3. Place the clams in the steamer basket of the pot, add 2 cups water in the pot, cover and cook on High for 4 minutes.
4. Release the pressure, uncover, divide among plates and serve with lemon wedges.

(**Calories** 80|**Fat** 5 g| **Protein** 3 g| **Fiber** 0 g| **Carbohydrates** 6 g)

Crab in a Jiffy

(**Prep Time**: 5 MIN| **Cook Time**: 3 MIN| **Serve**: 4)

Ingredients:

4 pounds king crab legs, broken in half
3 lemon wedges
¼ cup butter
1 cup water

Directions:

1. Put crab legs in the steamer basket of the pot.
2. Add water to the pot, cover and cook on High for 3 minutes.
3. Release the pressure, uncover, transfer crab legs to a bowl, add butter and serve with lemon wedges on the side.

(**Calories** 50|**Fat** 0.2 g| **Protein** 7 g| **Fiber** 0.2 g| **Carbohydrates** 0 g)

Shrimp Teriyaki

(**Prep Time**: 10 MIN| **Cook Time**: 4 MIN| **Serve**: 4)

Ingredients:

1 pound shrimp, peeled and deveined
2 tbsp soy sauce
½ pound pea pods
3 tbsp vinegar
¾ cup pineapple juice
1 cup chicken stock
3 tbsp sugar

Directions:

1. Put shrimp and pea pods in your instant pot.
2. In a bowl, mix soy sauce with vinegar, pineapple juice, stock and sugar and stir well.
3. Pour this into the pot, stir, cover and cook on High for 3 minutes.
4. Release the pressure, uncover, divide among plates and serve.

(**Calories** 200|**Fat** 4.2 g| **Protein** 38 g| **Fiber** 0.7 g| **Carbohydrates** 13 g)

Saffron Shrimp Delight

(**Prep Time:** 10 MIN| **Cook Time:** 5 MIN| **Serve:** 4)

Ingredients:

1 ½ pounds shrimp, peeled and deveined
2 tbsp extra virgin olive oil
1 cup yellow onion, chopped
2 tbsp parsley, chopped
4 garlic cloves, minced
2 tsp hot paprika
½ cup fish stock
¼ cup dry white wine
1 cup tomato sauce
A pinch of saffron
A pinch of sugar
1 tsp hot pepper, crushed
¼ tsp thyme dried
1 bay leaf
Salt and black pepper to taste

Directions:

1. Set your instant pot on Sauté mode, add oil and heat up.
2. Add shrimp, cook for 1 minute and transfer to a platter.
3. Add onion, stir and fry for 2 minutes,.
4. Add parsley, garlic, paprika and wine, stir and cook for a further 2 minutes.
5. Add stock, tomato sauce, red pepper, sugar, saffron, thyme, bay leaf, salt and pepper.
6. Cover and cook on High for 4 minutes.
7. Release the pressure, uncover, add shrimp, cover again and cook on High for 2 minutes.
8. Release pressure, remove lid and divide shrimp and sauce into bowls and serve.

(**Calories** 566|**Fat** 20 g| **Protein** 40 g| **Fiber** 8 g| **Carbohydrates** 30 g)

Shrimp Paella

(**Prep Time:** 10 MIN| **Cook Time:** 5 MIN| **Serve:** 4)

Ingredients:

20 shrimp, deveined
1 cup jasmine rice
¼ cup butter
Salt and black pepper to taste
¼ cup parsley, chopped
A pinch of red pepper, crushed
A pinch of saffron
Juice of 1 lemon
1 ½ cups water
4 garlic cloves, minced
Melted butter for serving
Hard cheese, grated for serving
Parsley, chopped for serving

Directions:

1. Put shrimp in your instant pot.
2. Add rice, butter, salt, pepper, parsley, red pepper, saffron, lemon juice, water and garlic.
3. Stir, cover and cook on High for 5 minutes.
4. Release pressure, take shrimps out and peel them
5. Return to pot, stir well and divide into bowls.
6. Add melted butter, cheese and parsley on top and serve.

(**Calories** 320|**Fat** 4 g| **Protein** 22 g| **Fiber** 1.4 g| **Carbohydrates** 12 g)

Red-Hot Shrimp Curry

(**Prep Time:** 10 MIN| **Cook Time:** 30 MIN| **Serve:** 4)

Ingredients:

1 pound big shrimp, peeled and deveined
1/3 cup butter
2 bay leaves
1 cinnamon stick
10 cloves
3 cardamom pods
2 red onions, chopped
14 red chilies, dried
3 green chilies, chopped
½ cup cashews
1 tbsp garlic paste
1 tbsp ginger paste
4 tomatoes, chopped
Salt to taste
1 tsp sugar
1 tsp fenugreek leaves, dried
½ cup cream

Directions:

1. Set your instant pot on Sauté mode, add butter and melt it.
2. Add bay leaves, cardamom, cinnamon stick and onion, stir and fry for 3 minutes.
3. Add red chilies, green chilies, cashews, tomatoes, garlic paste and ginger paste and stir.
4. Add salt, stir, cover and cook on High for 15 minutes.
5. Release the pressure, transfer the mixture to your blender and pulse well.
6. Strain into a pan and heat it up over medium high heat.
7. Add shrimp, stir, cover and cook for 12 minutes.
8. Add fenugreek, cream and sugar, stir, cook for 2 minutes, take off heat and serve your curry in bowls for an Indian style feast!

(**Calories** 299|**Fat** 9 g| **Protein** 27 g| **Fiber** 3 g| **Carbohydrates** 26 g)

Mild Shrimp Curry

(**Prep Time:** 10 MIN| **Cook Time:** 6 MIN| **Serve:** 4)

Ingredients:

1 pound shrimp, peeled and deveined
1 cup bouillon
4 lemon slices
Salt and black pepper to taste
½ tsp curry powder
¼ cup mushrooms, sliced
¼ cup yellow onion, chopped
2 tbsp shortening
½ cup raisins
3 tbsp flour
1 cup milk

Directions:

1. Set your instant pot on Sauté mode, add shortenings and heat up.
2. Add onion and mushroom, stir and cook for 2 minutes.
3. Add salt, pepper, curry powder, lemon, bouillon, raisins and shrimp.
4. Stir, cover and cook on High for 2 minutes.
5. Meanwhile, in a bowl mix flour with milk and whisk well.
6. Release the pressure from the pot, uncover and add flour and milk mixture, stir well and cook until curry thickens on Simmer mode.
7. Divide in bowls and serve.

(**Calories** 300|**Fat** 7 g| **Protein** 29 g| **Fiber** 2.5 g| **Carbohydrates** 34 g)

Quick Shrimp Creole

(Prep Time: 10 MIN| Cook Time: 5 MIN| Serve: 4)

Ingredients:

1 cup cooked shrimp
1 ½ cups already cooked, rice
½ tsp sugar
2 tsp vinegar
1 cup tomato juice
Salt to taste
1 tsp chili powder
1 yellow onion, chopped
1 cup celery, chopped
2 tbsp shortening

Directions:

1. Set the pot on Sauté mode, add shortening and heat
2. Add onion and celery and fry for 2 minutes.
3. Add salt, chili powder, tomato juice, vinegar, sugar, shrimp and rice.
4. Stir, cover and cook on High for 3 minutes.
5. Release the pressure, uncover pot, divide among plates and enjoy!

(Calories 294|Fat 9 g| Protein 24 g| Fiber 1.5 g| Carbohydrates 27 g)

Shrimp and Parmesan Pasta

(**Prep Time:** 10 MIN| **Cook Time:** 4 MIN| **Serve:** 4)

Ingredients:

1 pound shrimp, cooked, peeled and deveined
2 tbsp extra virgin olive oil
1 garlic clove, minced
10 ounces canned tomatoes, chopped
1/3 cup tomato paste
¼ tsp oregano, dried
1 tbsp parsley, finely chopped
1/3 cup water
1 cup parmesan, grated
Cooked spaghetti for serving

Directions:

1. Set your instant pot on Sauté mode, add oil and heat up.
2. Add garlic, stir and brown for 2 minutes.
3. Add shrimp, tomato paste, tomatoes, water, oregano and parsley, stir, cover and cook on High for 3 minutes.
4. Release pressure, divide among plates and serve on your favorite spaghetti.
5. Sprinkle parmesan generously on each serving.

(**Calories** 288|**Fat** 20 g| **Protein** 23 g| Fiber 0 g| Carbohydrates 0.01 g)

Shrimp Risotto

(**Prep Time:** 10 MIN| **Cook Time:** 20 MIN| **Serve:** 4)

Ingredients:

4 tbsp butter
2 garlic cloves, minced
1 yellow onion, chopped
1 ½ cups Arborio rice
2 tbsp dry white wine
4 ½ cups chicken stock
Salt and black pepper to taste
1 pound shrimp, peeled and deveined
¾ cup parmesan, grated
¼ cup tarragon and parsley, chopped

Directions:

1. Set your instant pot on Sauté mode, add 2 tbsp butter and melt.
2. Add garlic and onion, stir and fry for 4 minutes.
3. Add rice, stir and cook for a further minute.
4. Add wine and cook 30 seconds more.
5. Add 3 cups stock, salt and pepper, stir, cover and cook on High for 9 minutes.
6. Release the pressure, uncover pot, add shrimp and the rest of the stock, set pot on Sauté mode again and cook for 5 minutes stirring from time to time.
7. Add cheese, the rest of the butter, tarragon and parsley, stir and allow to sit covered until cheese is melted. Then dish onto plates and enjoy!

(**Calories** 400|**Fat** 8 g| **Protein** 29 g| **Fiber** 4 g| **Carbohydrates** 15 g)

Seafood Gumbo

(Prep Time: 10 MIN| Cook Time: 25 MIN| Serve: 10)

Ingredients:
¾ cup vegetable oil
1 ¼ cups flour
1 cup white onions, chopped
½ cup celery, chopped
1 cup green bell pepper, chopped
4 garlic cloves, chopped
2 tbsp peanut oil
6 plum tomatoes, chopped
A pinch of cayenne pepper
3 bay leaves
½ tsp onion powder
½ tsp garlic powder
1 tsp thyme, dried
1 tsp celery seeds
1 tsp sweet paprika
1 pound sausage, sliced
2 quarts chicken stock
24 shrimp, peeled and deveined
24 crawfish tails
24 oysters
½ pound crab meat
Salt and black pepper to taste

Directions:
1. Heat up a pan with the vegetable oil over medium heat, add flour and stir for 3-4 minutes.
2. Set your instant pot on Sauté mode, add peanut oil and heat
3. Add celery, peppers, onions and garlic, stir and fry for 10 minutes.
4. Add sausage, tomatoes, stock, bay leaves, cayenne, onion and garlic powder, thyme, paprika and celery seeds, and cook for 3 minutes.
5. Add flour mixture you've made earlier, stir until it combines and thickens.
6. Add shrimp, crawfish, crab, oysters, salt and pepper, stir, cover and cook on High for 15 minutes. Release the pressure, uncover, divide gumbo in bowls and serve.

(**Calories** 800|**Fat** 58 g| **Protein** 36 g| **Fiber** 3 g| **Carbohydrates** 35 g)

Greek Herbed Octopus

(**Prep Time:** 10 MIN| **Cook Time:** 16 MIN| **Serve:** 6)

Ingredients:

1 octopus, cleaned and prepared
2 rosemary springs
2 tsp oregano, dried
½ yellow onion, roughly chopped
4 thyme springs
½ lemon
1 tsp black peppercorns
3 tbsp extra virgin olive oil

For the marinade:
¼ cup extra virgin olive oil
Juice from ½ lemon
4 garlic cloves, minced
2 thyme springs
1 rosemary spring
Salt and black pepper to taste

Directions:

1. Put the octopus in your instant pot.
2. Add oregano, 2 rosemary springs, 4 thyme springs, onion, lemon, 3 tbsp olive oil, peppercorns and salt.
3. Stir, cover and cook on Low for 10 minutes.
4. Release the pressure, uncover pot, transfer octopus on a cutting board, cut tentacles into small segments and place them in a bowl.
5. Add ¼ cup olive oil, lemon juice, garlic, 1 rosemary sprig, 2 thyme springs, salt and pepper, toss to coat and leave to marinate for 1 hour.
6. Heat up your grill over medium heat, add octopus, grill for 3 minutes on each side and divide among plates.
7. Drizzle the marinade over octopus and serve.

(**C**alories 161|**F**at 1 g| **P**rotein 9 g| **F**iber 0 g| **C**arbohydrates 1 g)

Stuffed Squid

(**Prep Time:** 10 MIN| **Cook Time:** 20 MIN| **Serve:** 4)

Ingredients:

4 squid
1 cup sticky rice
14 ounces dashi stock
2 tbsp sake
4 tbsp soy sauce
1 tbsp mirin
2 tbsp sugar

Directions:

1. Chop tentacles from 1 squid and mix with the rice.
2. Fill each squid with rice and seal ends with toothpicks.
3. Place squid in your instant pot, add stock, soy sauce, sake, sugar and mirin.
4. Cover and cook on High for 15 minutes.
5. Release the pressure, uncover pot, divide stuffed squid on appetizer plates and serve.

(**C**alories 148|**F**at 2.4 g| **P**rotein 11 g| Fiber 1.1 g| **C**arbohydrates 7 g)

Squid Masala

(**Prep Time:** 10 MIN| **Cook Time:** 15 MIN| **Serve:** 4)

Ingredients:

17 ounces squid
1 ½ tbsp red chili powder
Salt and black pepper to taste
¼ tsp turmeric powder
2 cups water
5 pieces coconut
4 garlic cloves, minced
½ tsp cumin seeds
3 tbsp extra virgin olive oil
¼ tsp mustard seeds
1 inch ginger pieces, chopped

Directions:

1. Put squid in your instant pot.
2. Add chili powder, turmeric, salt, pepper and water, stir, cover and cook on High for 15 minutes.
3. Meanwhile, in your blender, mix coconut with ginger, garlic and cumin and blend well.
4. Heat up a pan with the oil over medium high heat, add mustard seeds and toast for 2-3 minutes.
5. Release the pressure from the pot and transfer squid and water to the pan.
6. Stir and mix with coconut blend.
7. Cook until everything thickens, divide among bowls and serve.

(**Calories** 255|**Fat** 0 g| **Protein** 9 g| **Fiber** 1 g| **Carbohydrates** 7 g)

Italian Braised Squid

(Prep Time: 10 MIN| Cook Time: 20 MIN| Serve: 4)

Ingredients:

1 pound squid, cleaned and cut
1 pound fresh peas
½ pound canned tomatoes, crushed
1 yellow onion, chopped
A splash of white wine
A drizzle of olive oil
Salt and black pepper to taste

Directions:

1. Set your instant pot on Sauté mode, add some oil and heat
2. Add onion and fry for 3 minutes.
3. Add squid, stir and cook for 3 more minutes.
4. Add wine, tomatoes and peas, stir, cover and cook for 20 minutes.
5. Release the pressure, uncover pot, add salt and pepper to taste, stir and enjoy your brightly colored meal.

(**Calories** 145|**Fat** 1 g| **Protein** 12 g| Fiber 0 g| **Carbohydrates** 7 g)

Meat Recipes

Pomegranate Molasses Roasted Chuck

(Prep Time: 10 MIN| Cook Time: 45 MIN| Serve: 10)

Ingredients:

3 lbs chuck steak, boneless
2 tsp salt
1 ½ tsp freshly grounded black pepper
1 ¼ tsp garlic powder
1 tbsp pomegranate molasses
2 tbsp balsamic vinegar
1 onion, finely chopped
2 cups regular water
½ tsp xanthan gum (you can use 1 tsp of Agar Agar if unavailable)
1/3 cup fresh parsley, finely chopped

Directions:
1. On a cutting board, slice the meat in half and season each half, on both sides with salt, pepper and garlic powder.
2. Place the Instant Pot over heat and set on "Sauté" mode.
3. Place the seasoned meat into the pot and cook until browned on each side.
4. Once the meat has browned, start adding the rest of the ingredients. Add the pomegranate molasses, balsamic vinegar, onion and half the water.
5. Cover the pot and set the timer on 35 minutes.
6. When the time is finished, manually release the pressure by pressing "venting".
7. Remove the lid once all the pressure has been released. Transfer the meat to a cutting board and remove any fat or refuse. Cut the meat into large slices.
8. Simmer the sauce that was left in the pot by setting the pot on "sauté". Allow it to simmer for 10 minutes until the liquid has reduced.
9. Stir in the xanthan gum and return the meat into the pot and stir.
10. Turn off the heat and transfer the meat onto serving plate. Drizzle the sauce over the meat and garnish with parsley. Serve hot.

(Calories 466|Fat 32.4g| Protein 37 g| Carbohydrates 3.5 g)

Spicy Minced Lamb with Peas and Tomato Sauce

(Prep Time: 15 MIN| Cook Time: 40 MIN| Serve: 6)

Ingredients:
2 lbs ground lamb
3 tbsp ghee
1 onion, finely chopped
5 cloves garlic, crushed
1 tsp ground ginger
1 Serrano pepper, chopped
2 tsp ground coriander
1 tsp red pepper flakes
1 tsp Kosher salt
½ tsp turmeric powder
¾ tsp freshly ground black pepper
½ tsp chat masala
¾ tsp ground cumin
¼ tsp cayenne powder
2 cardamom pods, shell removed
1 can diced tomatoes
1 can peas
Fresh cilantro, finely chopped

Directions:
1. Place the Instant Pot over medium heat and set on "Sauté". Add the ghee and onion. Stir until the onion is in tender.
2. Stir in the ginger, garlic and the spices. Stir for 3 minutes and then add the minced meat.
3. Stir the meat until browned and covered well with the spices.
4. Add in the tomatoes and peas and cover the pot. Set on "Keep Warm" then choose "Bean/Chili" option.
5. When the time is finished, release the pressure from the pot. Set back on 'Sauté' and allow the liquid to simmer for 10 minutes until reduced.
6. Transfer the meat into serving bowl and sprinkle fresh cilantro and serve hot.

(Calories 242|Fat 12.4g| Protein 24 g| Carbohydrates 10.3g)

Roasted Lamb Shanks with Vegetables

(Prep Time: 15 MIN| Cook Time: 50 MIN| Serve: 4)

Ingredients:

4 lbs lamb shanks
2 tsp salt
1 tsp freshly ground black pepper
3 tbsp ghee
3 carrots, diced
3 celery stalks, sliced
1 large onion, diced
2 tbsp tomato paste
4 cloves garlic, minced
1 can diced tomatoes
1 1/3 cup bone broth
2 tsp fish sauce (optional)
1 ½ tbsp balsamic vinegar
½ cup fresh parsley, finely chopped

Directions:
1. Season the lamb with salt and pepper from both sides.
2. Place the Instant Pot over medium heat and set on "Sauté" , stir in the ghee until melted and add the meat. Stir until browned for a few minutes.
3. Transfer the meat to a plate and add the vegetables to the pot and sauté for a few minutes. Season with some salt and pepper.
4. Add the tomato paste and garlic and stir for a minute. Return the meat to the pot and add the diced tomatoes.
5. Pour in the broth, fish sauce and vinegar.
6. Cover the pot and press "Cancel/Keep Warm". Manually set the timer for 45 minutes. Lower the heat after the first 5 minutes.
7. When the time is finished, release the pressure.
8. Transfer the meat onto serving platter and pour the remaining sauce over the meat. Garnish with fresh parsley and serve hot.

(Calories 422|Fat 19.6| Protein 48.5 g| Carbohydrates 35.8g)

Classic Meatloaf stuffed with Mozzarella

(Prep Time: 15 MIN| Cook Time: 30 MIN| Serve: 8)

Ingredients:

3 lbs minced beef
2 cups bread crumbs
4 eggs
1 tsp salt
1 tsp freshly ground black pepper
1 tsp garlic powder
4 oz mozzarella cheese, sliced
¼ cup fresh basil, finely chopped
1 cup beef broth
¼ cup light brown sugar
½ cup ketchup
2 tbsp Dijon mustard
1 tbsp Worcestershire sauce

Directions:
1. In a large bowl combine the meat with the breadcrumbs. Add the eggs and season with salt, pepper and garlic powder. It is best to use your hands to mix the ingredients to insure that they are fully incorporated.
2. In another bowl, whisk together brown sugar, ketchup, mustard & Worcestershire sauce.
3. Place Instant Pot over medium heat, place the rack provided with the pot inside and pour in the broth.
4. Cut a large piece of aluminum foil and place half of the meatloaf mixture. Flatten it out a little bit. Line the mozzarella slices over meatloaf, sprinkle the basil. Place the other half of the meatloaf and press the sides to seal.
5. Carefully place the wrapped meatloaf inside the pot, on the rack.
6. Using a spoon, spread half of the brown sugar mixture on the meatloaf.
7. Cover the pot and manually set the timer on 30 minutes. Once the time is finished, manually release the pressure and remove the lid.
8. Take the meatloaf out of the pot and allow it to cool a little but before serving.

(Calories 537|Fat 17.1| Protein 63.1 g| Carbohydrates 29.5g)

Baracoa-Style Shredded Beef

(Prep Time: 15 MIN| Cook Time: 60 MIN| Serve: 12)

Ingredients:

3 lbs minced beef
2 cups bread crumbs
4 eggs
1 tsp salt
1 tsp freshly ground black pepper
1 tsp garlic powder
4 oz mozzarella cheese, sliced
¼ cup fresh basil, finely chopped
1 cup beef broth
¼ cup light brown sugar
½ cup ketchup
2 tbsp Dijon mustard
1 tbsp Worcestershire sauce

Directions:
1. Trim any excess fat off the meat then cut into 4 large pieces. Season with salt and pepper on both sides.
2. Place the Instant Pot over medium heat, and one tablespoon of olive oil. Cook the meat until browned for a few minutes. You can add the meat into the pot in two batches.
3. Meanwhile, in a food processor, blend together the onion, vinegar, lime juice, garlic, peppers, broth, cumin, cloves and tomato paste until smooth and no lumps are found.
4. Pour in the blended mixture over the meet and add the bay leaves.
5. Cover the pot and set on "Beef/Stew" for an hour.
6. Once the time is finished, manually release the pressure and uncover the pot.
7. Transfer the meat onto a cutting board, using two forks start shredding the meat.
8. Discard the bay leaves and return the shredded meat into the pot. Cover the pot and allow the meat to sit for 10 minutes.
9. Serve the shredded meat as a filling for tortilla wraps, tacos or sandwiches with your favorite sauce.

(Calories 435|Fat 31.9| Protein 31.4 g| Carbohydrates 4.5g)

Beef Shawarma with Tahini Sauce

(Prep Time: 15 MIN| Cook Time: 60 MIN| Serve: 8)

Ingredients:
3 lbs beef chuck roast
4 clove garlic, crushed
1 tsp salt
½ tsp freshly ground black pepper
½ tsp ground ginger
½ tsp all spice
¼ tsp ground cinnamon
¼ tsp ground nutmeg
1 tsp red pepper flakes
½ lemon juice
2 tbsp balsamic vinegar
2 tbsp extra-virgin olive oil
1 cup beef broth
1 onion, cut into rings
Tahini sauce, to serve
Pita bread, to serve

Directions:
1. Trim the excess fat off the chuck roast and sear the meat lengthwise. Make about 4 cuts. Place the crushed garlic cloves into each cut.
2. In a bowl mix together all the spices together. Add the balsamic vinegar and one tablespoon of the olive oil.
3. Rub the spices mixture on the meat, make sure you cover the entire surface area.
4. Place the meat into a shallow dish and cover with cling film. place the meat in the fridge for at least 8 hours or overnight.
5. Once the meat has rested in the fridge, place the Instant Pot over medium heat and set on "Sauté". Add the remaining olive oil and grill the meat for 8 minutes until browned on both sides. Pour in the broth and cover the pot.
6. Set on "Beef/Stew" and allow it to cook for an hour.
7. Once the time is finished, release the pressure and remove the lid. Stir in the onion rings. Allow the meat to sit in the pot, with the lid off for 5 minutes.
8. Transfer the meat into a cutting board and start slicing or shredding it into small pieces.
9. To serve, spread some tahini sauce into each pita bread, fill with shawarma and wrap. Enjoy these Arabian wraps with some French fries or pickles.

(Calories 740|Fat 56.2| Protein 47.4 g| Carbohydrates 7.8g)

Red Pepper Flakes Beef Ribs with Rice

(Prep Time: 15 MIN| Cook Time: 30 MIN| Serve: 6)

Ingredients:
3 lbs beef short ribs, boneless
2 tbsp red pepper flakes
2 tsp salt
2 tbsp butter
1 onion, finely chopped
2 tbsp tomato paste
5 garlic cloves, minced
2/3 cup roasted tomato salsa (available in supermarkets)
2/3 cup beef broth
1 tsp fish sauce
½ tsp freshly ground black pepper
1 small bunch fresh cilantro, finely chopped

Directions:
1. On a cutting board, cut the meat into cubes or slices. Place the meat into a bowl and add in the red pepper flakes and salt.
2. Place the Instant Pot over medium heat, set on "Sauté" and melt the butter. Stir in the onion, keep stirring until it becomes translucent.
3. Add the tomato paste, garlic and salsa. Stir for a minute.
4. Drop the meat into the pot, and pour in the broth and fish sauce and stir.
5. Cover the pot and set on "Keep Warm" and "Meat/Stew". You only need to cook it for 30 minutes.
6. Once the time is finished, allow the pressure to be released naturally.
7. Meanwhile cook the rice according to the instructions on the package.
8. To serve, place the rice into serving bowl and top with meat, drizzle with the meat sauce and garnish with fresh cilantro.

(Calories 537|Fat 24.8| Protein 67.3 g| Carbohydrates 7.2g)

Simple Corned Beef

(**P**rep Time: 10 MIN| **C**ook Time: 60 MIN| **S**erve: 6)

Ingredients:

4 pounds beef brisket
2 oranges, sliced
2 garlic cloves, minced
2 yellow onions, thinly sliced
11 ounces celery, thinly sliced
1 tbsp dill, dried
3 bay leaves
4 cinnamon sticks, cut into halves
Salt and black pepper to taste
17 ounces water

Directions:

1. Put the beef in a bowl, add some water to cover, leave aside to soak for a few hours, drain and transfer to your instant pot.
2. Add celery, orange slices, onions, garlic, bay leaves, dill, cinnamon, dill, salt and pepper and 17 ounces water.
3. Stir, cover and cook on High for 50 minutes.
4. Release the pressure, leave beef aside to cool down for 5 minutes, transfer to a cutting board, slice and divide among plates.
5. Drizzle the juice and veggies from the pot over beef and serve.

(Calories 251|**F**at 3.14 g| **P**rotein 7 g| Fiber 0 g| **C**arbohydrates 1 g)

Beef Bourguignon

(**Prep Time:** 15 MIN| **Cook Time:** 30 MIN| **Serve:** 6)

Ingredients:

5 pounds round steak, cut into small cubes
2 carrots, sliced
½ cup beef stock
1 cup dry red wine
3 bacon slices, chopped
8 ounces mushrooms, cut into quarters
2 tbsp white flour
12 pearl onions
2 garlic cloves, minced
¼ tsp basil, dried
Salt and black pepper to taste

Directions:

1. Set your instant pot on Sauté mode, add bacon and brown it for 2 minutes.
2. Add beef pieces, stir and brown for 5 minutes.
3. Add flour and stir very well.
4. Add salt, pepper, wine, stock, onions, garlic and basil, stir, cover and cook on High for 20 minutes.
5. Release the pressure quickly, uncover your pot, add mushrooms and carrots, cover again and cook on High for 5 minutes more.
6. Release the pressure again, spoon beef bourguignon onto plates and serve.

(**Calories** 442|**Fat** 17.2 g| **Protein** 39 g| **Fiber** 3 g| **Carbohydrates** 16 g)

Asian Beef Curry

(**Prep Time:** 10 MIN| **Cook Time:** 20 MIN| **Serve:** 4)

Ingredients:

2 pounds beef steak, cubed
2 tbsp extra virgin olive oil
3 potatoes, diced
1 tbsp wine mustard
2 and ½ tbsp curry powder
2 yellow onions, chopped
2 garlic cloves, minced
10 ounces canned coconut milk
2 tbsp tomato sauce
Salt and black pepper to taste

Directions:

1. Set your instant pot on Sauté mode, add the oil and heat
2. Add onions and garlic, stir and cook for 4 minutes.
3. Add potatoes and mustard, stir and cook for 1 minute.
4. Add beef, stir and brown on all sides.
5. Add curry powder, salt and pepper, stir and cook for 2 minutes.
6. Add coconut milk and tomato sauce, cover and cook on High for 10 minutes.
7. Release the pressure, serve and enjoy.

(**Calories** 434|**Fat** 20 g| **Protein** 27.5 g| **Fiber** 2.9 g| **Carbohydrates** 14 g)

Beef Stroganoff

(**Prep Time:** 10 MIN| **Cook Time:** 25 MIN| **Serve:** 4)

Ingredients:

5 pounds beef, cut into small cubes
1 yellow onion, chopped
2 and ½ tbsp vegetable oil
1 and ½ tbsp white flour
2 garlic cloves, minced
4 ounces mushrooms, sliced
1 ½ tbsp tomato paste
Salt and black pepper to taste
3 tbsp Worcestershire sauce
13 ounces beef stock
8 ounces sour cream
Cooked egg noodles, for serving

Directions:

1. Put beef, salt, pepper and flour in a bowl and toss to coat.
2. Set your instant pot on Sauté mode, add oil and heat
3. Add meat and brown it on all sides.
4. Add onion, garlic, mushrooms, Worcestershire sauce, stock and tomato paste, stir well, cover and cook on High for 20 minutes.
5. Release the pressure, uncover, add sour cream, more salt and pepper, stir well and serve on top of egg noodles.

(**Calories** 335|**Fat** 18.4 g| **Protein** 20.1 g| **Fiber** 1.3 g| **Carbohydrates** 22.5 g)

Beef Chili

(**Prep Time:** 10 MIN| **Cook Time:** 40 MIN| **Serve:** 6)

Ingredients:

1 ½ pounds beef, ground
1 sweet onion, chopped
Salt and black pepper to taste
16 ounces mixed beans, soaked overnight and drained
28 ounces canned tomatoes, chopped
17 ounces beef stock
12 ounces pale ale
6 garlic cloves, chopped
7 jalapeno peppers, diced
2 tbsp vegetable oil
4 carrots, chopped
3 tbsp chili powder
1 bay leaf
1 tsp chipotle powder

Directions:

1. Set your instant pot on Sauté mode, add half of the oil and heat
2. Add beef, stir, brown for 8 minutes and transfer to a bowl.
3. Add the rest of the oil to the pot and heat
4. Add carrots, onion, jalapenos and garlic, stir and Sauté for 4 minutes.
5. Add ale and tomatoes and stir.
6. Also add beans, bay leaf, stock, chili powder, chipotle powder, salt and pepper and the beef, stir, cover and cook on High for 25 minutes.
7. Release the pressure naturally, uncover, stir chili, transfer to bowls and serve.

(**Calories** 272|**Fat** 5 g| **Protein** 25 g| **Fiber** 0 g| **Carbohydrates** 32 g)

Bordeaux Pot Roast

(**Prep Time:** 10 MIN| **Cook Time:** 1 HOUR| **Serve:** 6)

Ingredients:

3 pounds beef roast
Salt and black pepper to taste
17 ounces beef stock
3 ounces red wine
½ tsp chicken salt
½ tsp smoked paprika
1 yellow onion, chopped
4 garlic cloves, minced
3 carrots, chopped
5 potatoes, chopped

Directions:

1. In a bowl, mix salt, pepper, chicken salt and paprika and stir.
2. Rub beef with this mixture and put roast in your instant pot.
3. Add onion, garlic, stock and wine, toss to coat, cover and cook on High for 50 minutes.
4. Release the pressure quickly, uncover, add carrots and potatoes, cover again and cook on High for 10 minutes.
5. Release the pressure again, uncover, transfer roast to a platter, drizzle cooking juices all over and serve with veggies on the side.

(**Calories** 290|**Fat** 20 g| **Protein** 25 g| Fiber 0 g| **Carbohydrates** 2 g)

Beef Hot Pot

(**Prep Time:** 10 MIN| **Cook Time:** 30 MIN| **Serve:** 4)

Ingredients:

2 tbsp extra virgin olive oil
1 ½ pounds beef stew meat, cubed
4 tbsp white flour
1 yellow onion, chopped
2 tbsp red wine
2 garlic cloves, minced
2 cups water
2 cups beef stock
Salt and black pepper to taste
1 bay leaf
½ tsp thyme, dried
2 celery stalks, chopped
2 carrots, chopped
4 potatoes, chopped
½ bunch parsley, chopped

Directions:
1. Season beef with salt and pepper and mix with half of the flour.
2. Set your instant pot on Sauté mode, add oil and heat
3. Add beef, brown for 2 minutes and transfer to a bowl.
4. Add onion to your pot, stir and fry for 3 minutes.
5. Add garlic, stir and cook for 1 minute.
6. Add wine, stir well and cook for 15 seconds.
7. Add the rest of the flour and stir well for 2 minutes to avoid lumps forming.
8. Return meat to pot, add stock, water, bay leaf and thyme, stir, cover and cook on High for 12 minutes.
9. Release the pressure quickly, add carrots, celery and potatoes, stir and cover pot again and cook on High for 5 minutes.
10. Release the pressure naturally for 10 minutes and serve with parsley sprinkled on top.

(**Calories** 221|**Fat** 5.3 g| **Protein** 22.7 g| **Fiber** 1 g| **Carbohydrates** 20.2 g)

Veal and Mushroom Symphony

(**Prep Time:** 10 MIN| **Cook Time:** 35 MIN| **Serve:** 4)

Ingredients:

3.5 ounces button mushrooms, sliced
3.5 ounces shiitake mushrooms, sliced
2 pounds veal shoulder, cut into medium chunks
17 ounces potatoes, chopped
16 ounces shallots, chopped
9 ounces beef stock
2 ounces white wine
1 tbsp white flour
2 garlic cloves, minced
2 tbsp chives, chopped
1 tsp sage, dried
1/8 tsp thyme, dried
Salt and black pepper to taste
3 ½ tbsp extra virgin olive oil

Directions:

1. Set your instant pot on Sauté mode, add 1 ½ tbsp oil and heat
2. Add veal, season with salt and pepper, stir, brown for 5 minutes and transfer to a bowl.
3. Add the rest of the oil to the pot and heat
4. Add all mushrooms and fry for 3 minutes.
5. Add garlic, stir for 1 minute and transfer everything to a bowl.
6. Add wine and flour to the pot, stir and cook for a further minute.
7. Add stock, sage, thyme and return meat to pot as well.
8. Stir, cover and cook on High for 20 minutes.
9. Release pressure, uncover, return mushrooms and garlic to the pot.
10. Also add potatoes and shallots, stir, cover and cook on High for 4 minutes.
11. Release the pressure again, uncover your instant pot, add more salt and pepper if needed, divide in bowls and serve with chive garnish.

(**Calories** 395|**Fat** 18 g| **Protein** 47.8 g| **Fiber** 1.4 g| **Carbohydrates** 7.1 g)

Beef and Pasta Casserole

(**Prep Time:** 10 MIN| **Cook Time:** 20 MIN| **Serve:** 4)

Ingredients:

17 ounces pasta
1 pound beef, ground
13 ounces mozzarella cheese, shredded
16 ounces tomato puree
1 celery stalk, chopped
1 yellow onion, chopped
1 carrot, chopped
1 tbsp red wine
2 tbsp butter
Salt and black pepper to taste

Directions:

1. Set your instant pot on Sauté mode, add the butter and melt.
2. Add carrot, onion and celery and fry for 5 minutes.
3. Add beef, salt and pepper and cook for 10 more minutes.
4. Add wine, while stirring and cook for a further minute.
5. Add pasta, tomato puree and water to cover pasta, stir, cover and cook on High for 6 minutes.
6. Release the pressure, uncover, add cheese, stir well to melt cheese and enjoy.

(**Calories** 182|**Fat** 1 g| **Protein** 12 g| **Fiber** 1.4 g| **Carbohydrates** 31 g)

Chinese Beef and Broccoli

(Prep Time: 10 MIN| Cook Time: 10 MIN| Serve: 4)

Ingredients:

3 pounds chuck roast, cut into thin strips
1 tbsp peanut oil
1 yellow onion, chopped
½ cup beef stock
1 pound broccoli florets
2 tsp toasted sesame oil
2 tbsp potato starch

<u>For the marinade:</u>
½ cup soy sauce
½ cup black soy sauce
1 tbsp sesame oil
2 tbsp fish sauce
5 garlic cloves, minced
3 red peppers, dried and crushed
½ tsp Chinese five spice
White rice, already cooked for servings
Toasted sesame seeds for serving

Directions:

1. In a bowl, mix black soy sauce with soy sauce, fish sauce, 1 tbsp sesame oil, 5 garlic cloves, five spice and crushed red peppers and stir well.
2. Add beef strips, toss to coat and marinade for 10 minutes.
3. Set your instant pot on Sauté mode, add peanut oil and heat
4. Add onions, stir and fry for 4 minutes.
5. Add beef and marinade, stir and cook for 2 minutes.
6. Add stock, stir, cover and cook on High for 5 minutes.
7. Release the pressure naturally for 10 minutes, uncover, add cornstarch after you've mixed it to a smooth paste with ¼ cup liquid from the pot, add broccoli to the steamer basket, cover pot again and cook for 3 minutes on High.

8. Release the pressure again and dish up beef into bowls on top of rice, add broccoli on the side, drizzle toasted sesame oil over contents of bowls, sprinkle sesame seeds and enjoy this delicious Chinese meal.

(Calories 338| Fat 18 g| **P**rotein 20 g| Fiber 5 g| Carbohydrates 50 g)

Brisket and Cabbage Hodgepodge

(**P**rep Time: 10 MIN| **C**ook Time: 1 HOUR 20 MIN| **S**erve: 6)

Ingredients:

2 ½ pounds beef brisket
4 cups water
2 bay leaves
3 garlic cloves, chopped
4 carrots, chopped
1 cabbage heat, cut into 6 wedges
6 potatoes, cut into quarters
Salt and black pepper to taste
3 turnips, cut into quarters
Horseradish sauce for serving

Directions:

1. Put beef brisket and water in your instant pot, add salt, pepper, garlic and bay leaves, cover and cook on High for 1 hour and 15 minutes.
2. Release the pressure quickly, uncover, add carrots, cabbage, potatoes and turnips, stir, cover again and cook on High for 6 minutes.
3. Release the pressure naturally, uncover your pot and serve this delicious meal with horseradish sauce.

(Calories 340| Fat 24 g| **P**rotein 26 g| Fiber 1 g| Carbohydrates 14 g)

Merlot Lamb Shanks

(**Prep Time:** 10 MIN| **Cook Time:** 45 MIN| **Serve:** 4)

Ingredients:

4 lamb shanks
2 tbsp extra virgin olive oil
2 tbsp white flour
1 yellow onion, finely chopped
3 carrots, roughly chopped
2 garlic cloves, minced
2 tbsp tomato paste
1 tsp oregano, dried
1 tomato, roughly chopped
2 tbsp water
4 ounces red Merlot wine
Salt and black pepper to taste
1 beef bouillon cube

Directions:

1. In a bowl, mix flour with salt and pepper.
2. Add lamb shanks and toss to coat.
3. Set your instant pot on Sauté mode, add oil and heat
4. Add lamb, brown on all sides and transfer to a bowl.
5. Add onion, oregano, carrots and garlic to the pot, stir and cook for 5 minutes.
6. Add tomato, tomato paste, water, wine and bouillon cube, stir and bring to a boil.
7. Return lamb to pot, cover and cook on High for 25 minutes.
8. Release the pressure and put one shank on each plate, pour cooking sauce over and enjoy with seasonal vegetables!

(**Calories** 430|**Fat** 17 g| **Protein** 50 g| **Fiber** 2.5 g| **Carbohydrates** 11.3 g)

Mediterranean Lamb

(**Prep Time:** 15 MIN| **Cook Time:** 1 HOUR| **Serve:** 4)

Ingredients:

6 pounds lamb leg, boneless
2 tbsp extra virgin olive oil
Salt and black pepper to taste
1 bay leaf
1 tsp marjoram
1 tsp sage, dried
1 tsp ginger, grated
3 garlic cloves, minced
1 tsp thyme, dried
2 cups veggie stock
3 pounds potatoes, chopped
3 tbsp arrowroot powder mixed with 1/3 cup water

Directions:

1. Set your instant pot on Sauté mode, add the oil and heat
2. Add lamb leg and brown on all sides.
3. Add salt, pepper, bay leaf, marjoram, sage, ginger, garlic, thyme and stock, stir, cover and cook on High for 50 minutes.
4. Release the pressure quickly and add potatoes, arrowroot mix, more salt and pepper if needed, stir, cover again and cook on High for 10 minutes.
5. Release the pressure again, uncover, divide Mediterranean lamb onto serving plates and enjoy.

(**Calories** 238|**Fat** 5 g| **Protein** 7.3 g| **Fiber** 4 g| **Carbohydrates** 17 g)

Creamy Lamb Curry

(**Prep Time:** 10 MIN| **Cook Time:** 25 MIN| **Serve:** 6)

Ingredients:

1 ½ pounds lamb shoulder, cut into medium chunks
2 ounces coconut milk
3 ounces dry white wine
3 tbsp pure cream
3 tbsp curry powder
2 tbsp vegetable oil
3 tbsp water
1 yellow onion, chopped
1 tbsp parsley, chopped
Salt and black pepper to taste

Directions:

1. In a bowl, mix half of the curry powder with salt, pepper and coconut milk and stir well.
2. Set your instant pot on Sauté mode, add oil and heat
3. Add onion, stir and fry for 4 minutes.
4. Add the rest of the curry powder, stir and cook for 1 minute.
5. Add lamb pieces, brown them for 3 minutes and mix with water, salt, pepper and wine.
6. Stir, cover and cook on High for 20 minutes.
7. Release the pressure quickly, set pot to Simmer mode, add coconut milk mixture, stir and boil for 5 minutes.
8. Divide among serving plates, sprinkle parsley on top and serve.

(**Calories** 378|**Fat** 8 g| **Protein** 22 g| **Fiber** 3 g| **Carbohydrates** 18 g)

Lamb and Vegetable Hotpot

(**Prep Time:** 15 MIN| **Cook Time:** 35 MIN| **Serve:** 6)

Ingredients:

3 pounds lamb chops
Salt and black pepper to taste
2 tbsp flour
2 tbsp extra virgin olive oil
2 yellow onions, chopped
3 ounces red wine
2 garlic cloves, crushed
2 carrots, sliced
2 celery sticks, chopped
2 tbsp tomato sauce
2 bay leaves
1 cup green peas
14 ounces canned tomatoes, chopped
4 ounces green beans
2 tbsp parsley, finely chopped
Beef stock for the pot

Directions:

1. Put flour in a bowl and mix with salt and pepper.
2. Add lamb chops and toss to coat.
3. Set your instant pot on Sauté mode, add the oil and heat
4. Add lamb, stir, brown for 3 minutes on all sides and transfer to a plate.
5. Add garlic and onion and stir for 2 minutes.
6. Add wine and cook a further 2 minutes.
7. Add bay leaves, carrots, celery and return lamb to pot.
8. Also add tomato sauce, tomatoes, green beans and peas and stir.
9. Add stock to cover ingredients, cover and cook on High for 20 minutes.
10. Release the pressure, uncover, add parsley, more salt and pepper if needed.

(**Calories** 435|**Fat** 31 g| **Protein** 22 g| **Fiber** 4 g| **Carbohydrates** 6 g)

Moroccan Lamb

(**Prep Time:** 10 MIN| **Cook Time:** 25 MIN| **Serve:** 8)

Ingredients:

2 ½ pounds lamb shoulder, chopped
3 tbsp honey
3 ounces almonds, peeled and chopped
9 ounces prunes, pitted
8 ounces vegetable stock
2 yellow onions, chopped
2 garlic cloves, minced
1 bay leaf
Salt and black pepper to tastes
1 cinnamon stick
1 tsp cumin powder
1 tsp turmeric powder
1 tsp ginger powder
1 tsp cinnamon powder
Sesame seeds for servings
3 tbsp extra virgin olive oil

Directions:

1. In a bowl, mix cinnamon powder with ginger, cumin, turmeric, garlic and 2 tbsp olive oil and stir well.
2. Add meat and toss to coat.
3. Put prunes in a bowl, cover them with hot water and leave aside.
4. Set your instant pot on Sauté mode, add the rest of the oil and heat
5. Add onions, stir, cook for 3 minutes, transfer to a bowl and leave aside.
6. Add meat to your pot and brown it for 10 minutes.
7. Add stock, cinnamon stick, bay leaf and return onions, stir, cover and cook on High for 25 minutes.
8. Release the pressure naturally, uncover, add drained prunes, salt, pepper, honey and stir.
9. Set the pot on Simmer mode, cook mixture for 5 minutes and discard bay leaf and cinnamon stick.
10. Divide among plates and scatter almonds and sesame seeds on top.

(**Calories** 434|**Fat** 21 g| **Protein** 20 g| **Fiber** 4 g| **Carbohydrates** 41 g)

Lamb Ragout

(**Prep Time:** 15 MIN| **Cook Time:** 1 HOUR| **Serve:** 8)

Ingredients:

1 ½ pounds mutton, bone-in
2 carrots, sliced
½ pound mushrooms, sliced
4 tomatoes, chopped
1 small yellow onion, chopped
6 garlic cloves, minced
2 tbsp tomato paste
1 tsp vegetable oil
Salt and black pepper to taste
1 tsp oregano, dried
A handful parsley, finely chopped

Directions:

1. Set your instant pot on Sauté mode, add oil and heat
2. Add meat and brown it on all sides.
3. Add tomato paste, tomatoes, onion, garlic, mushrooms, oregano, carrots and water to cover.
4. Add salt, pepper, stir, cover and cook on High for 1 hour.
5. Release the pressure, take meat out of the pot and discard bones before shredding.
6. Return meat to pot, add parsley and stir.
7. Add more salt and pepper if needed and serve right away.

(**Calories** 360|**Fat** 14 g| **Protein** 30 g| **Fiber** 3 g| **Carbohydrates** 15.1 g)

Mexican Style Lamb

(**Prep** Time: 10 MIN| **Cook** Time: 50 MIN| **Serve**: 4)

Ingredients:

3 pounds lamb shoulder, cubed
19 ounces enchilada sauce
3 garlic cloves, minced
1 yellow onion, chopped
2 tbsp extra virgin olive oil
Salt to taste
½ bunch cilantro, finely chopped
Corn tortillas, warm for serving
Lime wedges for serving
Refried beans for serving

Directions:

1. Put enchilada sauce in a bowl, add lamb meat and marinade for 24 hours.
2. Set your instant pot on Sauté mode, add the oil and heat
3. Add onions and garlic and fry for 5 minutes.
4. Add lamb, salt and its marinade, stir, bring to a boil, cover and cook on High for 45 minutes.
5. Release the pressure, take meat and put on a cutting board and leave to cool down for a few minutes.
6. Shred meat and put in a bowl.
7. Pour cooking sauce over it and stir.
8. Portion out meat onto tortillas, sprinkle cilantro on each, add beans, squeeze lime juice over, roll and serve.

(**Calories** 484|**Fat** 19 g| **Protein** 44 g| **Fiber** 9 g| **Carbohydrates** 28 g)

Goat and Tomato Pot

(**Prep Time:** 10 MIN| **Cook Time:** 1 HOUR| **Serve:** 4)

Ingredients:

17 ounces goat meat, cubed
1 carrot, chopped
1 celery rib, chopped
4 ounces tomato paste
1 yellow onion, chopped
3 garlic cloves, crushed
A dash of sherry wine
½ cup water
Salt and black pepper to taste
1 cup chicken stock
2 tbsp extra virgin olive oil
1 tbsp cumin seeds, ground
A pinch of rosemary, dried
2 roasted tomatoes, chopped

Directions:

1. Set your instant pot on Sauté mode, add 1 tbsp oil and heat
2. Add goat meat, salt and pepper and brown for a few minutes on each side.
3. Add cumin seeds, rosemary, stir, cook for 2 minutes and transfer to a bowl.
4. Add the rest of the oil to the pot and heat
5. Add onion, garlic, salt and pepper, stir and cook for 1 minute.
6. Add carrot and celery, stir and cook 2 minutes.
7. Add sherry wine, stock, water, goat meat, tomato paste, more salt and pepper, stir, cover and cook on High for 40 minutes.
8. Release the pressure naturally, uncover, add tomatoes, stir, divide among plates and serve.

(**Calories** 340|**Fat** 3.8 g| **Protein** 12.6 g| **Fiber** 4.1 g| **Carbohydrates** 30 g)

Spicy Taco Meat

(Prep Time: 10 MIN| Cook Time: 35 MIN| Serve: 6)

Ingredients:

2 lbs ground beef
1/2 tbsp chili powder
1/4 Tsp chipotle powder
1 tsp cayenne
1/2 Tsp cumin
1/2 Tsp smoked paprika
1/2 Tsp turmeric
2 tsp oregano
2 large bell peppers, diced
1 large onion, diced
4 tbsp olive oil
3 garlic cloves, minced
1/4 Tsp black pepper
1 tsp salt

Directions:

1. Add all ingredients except meat into the instant pot.
2. Select sauté and stir fry for 5 minutes.
3. Add ground beef and stir until lightly brown.
4. Seal pot with lid and cook on HIGH pressure for 30 minutes.
5. Allow to releasing steam its own then open.
6. Select sauté function and stir for 10 minutes.
7. Garnish with fresh chopped cilantro and serve.

(Calories 414|Fat 21.6 g| Protein 46.9 g| Carbohydrates 7.2 g)

Spicy Beef Barbacoa

(**Prep Time:** 15 MIN| **Cook Time:** 60 MIN| **Serve:** 8)

Ingredients:

3 lbs beef bottom round roast, trimmed and cut into 3" pieces
2 bay leaves
1 tsp olive oil
1 cup beef stock
1/4 Tsp ground cloves
1/2 tbsp ground oregano
1/2 tbsp ground cumin
4 tbsp adobo sauce
1 tbsp fresh lime juice
1 small onion, chopped
4 garlic cloves
1/4 Tsp black pepper
2 1/2 Tsp kosher salt

Directions:

1. Add garlic, cloves, adobo sauce, oregano, cumin, lime juice, onion, and stock in a blender and blend until smooth.
2. Season meat with pepper and salt.
3. Select sauté function of the instant pot.
4. Once the pot is hot then add oil and meat in batches and brown the meat, about 5 minutes.
5. Add bay leaves and blender sauce and stir well.
6. Seal pot with lid and select MANUAL button and set the timer for 60 minutes.
7. Once cooking is finish then removes meat from pot and place in a dish.
8. Using fork shred the meat and pour pot liquid over shredded meat.
9. Serve warm and enjoy.

(Calories 327|Fat 11.8 g| Protein 47.9 g| Carbohydrates 4.3 g)

Pork Carnitas

(**Prep Time:** 10 MIN| **Cook Time:** 55 MIN| **Serve:** 10)

Ingredients:

2 1/2 lbs pork shoulder blade roast, boneless and trimmed
1 tsp garlic powder
2 bay leaves
2 chipotle peppers
3/4 cup beef stock
1/2 Tsp dry oregano
1 tsp cumin
1/4 Tsp black pepper
2 tsp kosher salt

Directions:

1. Season pork with pepper and salt.
2. In a large pan, brown the pork over high heat, about 5 minutes.
3. Remove pork from pan and set aside to cool.
4. Season pork with garlic powder, oregano, and cumin.
5. Pour broth in pot. Add bay leaves and chipotle. Stir well.
6. Place pork in the pot.
7. Seal pot with lid and cook on HIGH pressure for 50 minutes.
8. Allow releasing pressure by its own then open.
9. Remove bay leaves and using fork shred the pork.
10. Stir shredded pork well in pot liquid and serve.

(Calories 270|Fat 16.3 g| Protein 28 g| Carbohydrates 1.2 g)

Sweet and Savory Pork Chops

(**Prep Time:** 10 MIN| **Cook Time:** 20 MIN| **Serve:** 4)

Ingredients:

2 lbs pork chops, boneless
1/2 Tsp ground cloves
1/4 Tsp ground cinnamon
1 tsp fresh ginger, minced
1 1/2 tbsp Dijon mustard
4 tbsp honey
1/4 Tsp black pepper
1/4 Tsp salt

Directions:

1. Season pork chops with pepper and salt.
2. In a large pan, brown the pork chops on both the sides, about 5 minutes.
3. Remove pork chops from heat and set aside to cool.
4. In a bowl, combine together honey, cloves, cinnamon, ginger, and Dijon.
5. Place pork chops in instant pot and pour honey mixture over the pork.
6. Seal pot with lid and select MANUAL and set the timer for 15 minutes.
7. Allow to release pressure by its own then open and serve.

(Calories 797|Fat 56.7 g| Protein 51.4 g| Carbohydrates 18.3 g)

Easy Ranch Season Pork Chops

(**Prep Time:** 5 MIN| **Cook Time:** 5 MIN| **Serve:** 6)

Ingredients:

6 pork chops, boneless
1 cup chicken stock
1 packet ranch seasoning
8 tbsp butter
1 tbsp olive oil
Pepper
Salt

Directions:

1. Season pork chops with pepper and salt.
2. Heat olive oil in large pan over medium heat adds pork chops on hot pan and brown them on both the sides, about 5 minutes.
3. Remove pan from heat and set aside to cool.
4. Place pork chops in instant pot.
5. Sprinkle ranch seasoning over the pork chops.
6. Add butter and stock over the pork.
7. Seal pot with lid and select MANUAL button and set the timer for 5 minutes.
8. Allow to release pressure by its own then open and serve.

(Calories 415|Fat 37.7 g| Protein 18.3 g| Carbohydrates 0.1 g)

Asian Pork

(**Prep Time:** 5 MIN| **Cook Time:** 65 MIN| **Serve:** 4)

Ingredients:

2 lbs pork roast
3 tbsp brown sugar
2 tbsp soy sauce, low sodium
1 tbsp sesame seeds, toasted
1/2 cup water
1 tbsp sesame oil
1/4 Tsp salt

Directions:

1. Heat sesame oil in a pan over high heat.
2. Season pork with salt.
3. Place pork on hot pan and brown pork on both the sides, about 5 minutes.
4. Remove pan from heat and set aside to cool.
5. Place pork into the instant pot.
6. In a bowl, combine together brown sugar, soy sauce, and water.
7. Pour brown sugar mixture over pork.
8. Seal pot with lid and cook on HIGH pressure for 60 minutes.
9. Allow releasing pressure by its own then open.
10. Sprinkle toasted sesame seeds over pork and serve.

(Calories 542|Fat 25.9 g| Protein 65.6 g| Carbohydrates 7.8 g)

BBQ Ribs

(Prep Time: 3 MIN| Cook Time: 25 MIN| Serve: 4)

Ingredients:

3 lbs pork ribs rack
1 cup BBQ sauce
1 cup water
1 tsp garlic powder
1 tsp onion powder
1 tsp chipotle powder

Directions:

1. Pour water into the instant pot and place trivet into the pot.
2. In a small bowl, mix together garlic powder, onion powder, and chipotle powder.
3. Rub bowl mixture over ribs and place ribs on a trivet.
4. Seal pot with lid and cook on MANUAL HIGH pressure for 25 minutes.
5. Allow releasing steam on its own then open.
6. Remove ribs from pot and place on foil and coat with BBQ sauce.
7. Place ribs under the broiler until caramelized.
8. Cut ribs and serve.

(Calories 988|Fat 54.6 g| Protein 94.3 g| Carbohydrates 24.4 g)

Mustard Infused Meatloaf

(**Prep Time:** 10 MIN| **Cook Time:** 35 MIN| **Serve:** 4)

Ingredients:

1 lb ground beef
1/2 Tsp garlic powder
1/2 Tsp thyme, dried
2 tsp parsley, dried
1 tbsp Dijon mustard
1 large egg
1/2 cup ketchup
1 medium onion, chopped
1 apple, chopped
1 cup bread crumbs
1/4 Tsp pepper
1/4 Tsp salt

Directions:

1. Take one loaf pan which fits into your instant pot and sprays with cooking spray.
2. In a bowl, combine together all ingredients and pour into the prepared loaf pan.
3. Pour 1 cup water into the instant pot then place a trivet in the pot.
4. Place loaf pan on a trivet.
5. Seal pot with lid and select MANUAL button and set the timer for 35 minutes.
6. Release steam quickly and open.
7. Cut meatloaf into the slices and serve.

(Calories 409|Fat 10.1 g| Protein 40.8 g| Carbohydrates 38 g)

Tasty Beef Curry

(**Prep Time:** 10 MIN| **Cook Time:** 37 MIN| **Serve:** 4)

Ingredients:

1 lb beef stew meat, cut into chunks
1/4 Tsp paprika
1/2 Tsp oregano
2 tbsp curry powder
1/2 cup vegetable broth
1 cup coconut milk
4 garlic cloves, diced
4 carrots, cut into chunks
4 medium potatoes, cut into chunks
1 onion, cut into chunks
2 tbsp olive oil
1/2 Tsp black pepper
1/2 Tsp salt

Directions:

1. Add olive oil in instant pot and select sauté button.
2. Once the oil is hot then add onion and garlic and stir for 2 minutes.
3. Add meat chunks into the pot and brown them on both the sides, about 5 minutes.
4. Add all remaining ingredients into the pot and stir well.
5. Seal pot with lid and select meat/ stew function, it takes 30 minutes.
6. Allow releasing steam on its own then open.
7. Stir well and serve with rice.

(Calories 613|Fat 29.3 g| Protein 41.4 g| Carbohydrates 48.6 g)

Delicious Lamb Curry

(**Prep Time:** 10 MIN| **Cook Time:** 35 MIN| **Serve:** 4)

Ingredients:

1 lb ground lamb
10 oz can tomato sauce
2 potatoes, chopped
2 carrots, chopped
1 cup peas
1/2 Tsp ground turmeric
1/4 Tsp cayenne
1/2 Tsp cumin powder
1 tsp curry powder
1 tsp paprika
1 tsp ground coriander
4 tomatoes, chopped
2 Serrano peppers, minced
1 tsp fresh ginger, minced
3 garlic cloves, minced
1 onion, diced
2 tbsp vegetable oil
1/4 Tsp black pepper
1 tsp salt

Directions:

1. Add oil in instant pot and select sauté.
2. Once the oil is hot then add onion and stir onion until brown.
3. Add Serrano pepper, garlic, and ginger and stir for 1 minute.
4. Add tomatoes and stir for 5 minutes.
5. Add all spices and stir for a minute.
6. Add ground lamb and stir fry until lightly brown.
7. Add tomato sauce, potatoes, carrots, and peas and mix well.
8. Seal pot with lid and select chili setting, it takes 30 minutes.
9. Allow to release steam on its own then open and stir well.
10. Serve with plain rice and enjoy.

(Calories 448|Fat 16.1 g| Protein 38.6 g| Carbohydrates 38.4 g)

Gluten Free Beef Rice

(**Prep Time:** 5 MIN| **Cook Time:** 10 MIN| **Serve:** 4)

Ingredients:

1/2 lb ground beef
2 cups cabbage, shredded
3/4 cup rice, rinsed and drained
3/4 cup chicken broth
2 garlic cloves, minced
1 onion, diced
1/2 tbsp olive oil
1/2 Tsp salt

Directions:

1. Add oil in instant pot and select sauté.
2. Once the oil is hot then add garlic and stir for 30 seconds.
3. Add onion and meat and stir for minutes.
4. Add cabbage, rice, stock, and salt and stir well.
5. Seal pot with lid and cook on HIGH pressure for 5 minutes.
6. Allow releasing steam on its own then open.
7. Stir well and serve.

(Calories 276|Fat 5.9 g| Protein 21.4 g| Carbohydrates 33 g)

Lentil Beef Stew

(**Prep Time:** 10 MIN| **Cook Time:** 20 MIN| **Serve:** 4)

Ingredients:

1 lb beef, cut into chunks
2 tbsp curry powder
28 oz can tomatoes, diced
4 cups chicken stock
4 garlic cloves, minced
2 carrots, diced
3 potatoes, peeled and diced
1 onion, diced
1 cup lentils, dry
Pepper
Salt

Directions:

1. Add all ingredients into the instant pot and stir well.
2. Seal pot with lid and select MANUAL button and set the timer for 20 minutes.
3. Allow to release steam on its own then open and stir well.
4. Serve warm and enjoy.

(Calories 581|Fat 8.8 g| Protein 53.1 g| Carbohydrates 73.2 g)

Classic Garlic Herb Pot Roast

(**Prep Time:** 10 MIN| **Cook Time:** 55 MIN| **Serve:** 6)

Ingredients:

3 lbs beef chuck roast
5 large carrots, peeled
2 cups chicken stock
1 onion, diced
2 tbsp butter
1 tbsp Italian seasoning
2 garlic cloves, minced
1 tsp black pepper
1 tsp salt

Directions:

1. Place beef chunks in a large dish and sprinkle with spices.
2. Add butter in instant pot and select sauté.
3. Add onion in a pot and stir fry until brown, about 5 minutes.
4. Add roast chunks over the onions then pour chicken stock.
5. Seal pot with lid and select MANUAL button and set the timer for 40 minutes.
6. Release steam quickly than open lid carefully.
7. Add carrots and stir well.
8. Again Seal pot with lid and select MANUAL button and set the timer for another 10 minutes.
9. Release steam quickly than open the lid.
10. Stir well and serve.

(Calories 902|Fat 67.9 g| Protein 60.4 g| Carbohydrates 8.7 g)

Apple Pork Tenderloin

(**Prep Time:** 10 MIN| **Cook Time:** 26 MIN| **Serve:** 4)

Ingredients:

1 pork tenderloin
1/2 cup brown sugar
2 cups apple cider
1 large onion, chopped
2 apples, cored and chopped
2 tbsp olive oil
Pepper
Salt

Directions:

1. Add olive oil in instant pot and select sauté mode.
2. Add pork tenderloin in a pot and brown them on both the sides, about 2 minutes on each side.
3. Transfer pork tenderloin on the dish.
4. Add apple cider, onion, and apples in a pot and stir well.
5. Season tenderloin with pepper and salt and rub 4 tbsp brown sugar over tenderloin.
6. Return tenderloin to the pot and add remaining sugar.
7. Seal pot with lid and select MANUAL HIGH pressure for 22 minutes.
8. Allow releasing steam on its own then open.
9. Serve and enjoy.

(Calories 422|Fat 11.4 g| Protein 30.5 g| Carbohydrates 51.2 g)

Jalapeno Beef

(**P**rep Time: 10 MIN| **C**ook Time: 15 MIN| **S**erve: 6)

Ingredients:

2 lbs flank steak, sliced into thin slices
5 green onion, chopped
1 tbsp cornstarch
1 jalapeno peppers, seeded and sliced
2 tbsp olive oil
2 garlic cloves, minced
1/2 cup water
1 cup soy sauce, low sodium
1/2 cup brown sugar

Directions:

1. Add sliced steak, jalapenos, and garlic in instant pot and select sauté and sauté for 5 minutes.
2. Add water, soy sauce, and brown sugar. Stir well.
3. Seal pot with lid and cook on MANUAL HIGH pressure for 10 minutes.
4. Release steam quickly than open.
5. Remove half cup broth from pot and mix with cornstarch.
6. Return broth mixture to the pot and stir well and select sauté for 2 minutes.
7. Garnish with green onions and serve.

(Calories 413|Fat 17.3 g| Protein 45.1 g| Carbohydrates 17.7 g)

Spicy Beef with Tomato Sauce

(**Prep Time:** 10 MIN| **Cook Time:** 1 hrs 20 MIN| **Serve:** 4)

Ingredients:

2 lbs chuck roast, cut in half
1 tbsp olive oil
1 tsp garlic powder
2 tsp cumin
2 tsp chili powder
1 tbsp lime juice
1/4 cup fresh cilantro
1/2 cup chicken broth
2 tbsp chipotle sauce
8 oz tomato sauce
1/2 Tsp pepper
1 tsp salt

Directions:

1. Season roast with garlic powder, pepper, cumin, chili powder, and salt.
2. Add oil in instant pot and select sauté.
3. Once the oil is hot then place seasoned roast in pot and sauté for 5 minutes on each side.
4. Now add remaining ingredients and stir well.
5. Seal pot with lid and select MANUAL button and set the timer for 70 minutes.
6. Allow releasing steam on its own then open.
7. Using fork shred the beef and serves.

(Calories 557|Fat 23.1 g| Protein 76.8 g| Carbohydrates 6.6 g)

Spicy Goat and Potatoes

(Prep Time: 10 MIN| Cook Time: 50 MIN| Serve: 5)

Ingredients:

2 ½ pounds goat meat, cut into small cubes
Salt and black pepper to taste
5 tbsp vegetable oil
3 tsp turmeric powder
3 potatoes, cut into halves
1 tsp sugar
4 cloves
3 cardamom pods
3 onions, chopped
2 inch cinnamon stick
Small piece of ginger, grated
2 tomatoes, chopped
4 garlic cloves, minced
2 green chilies, chopped
¾ tsp chili powder
2 ½ cups water
1 tsp coriander, chopped

Directions:

1. Put goat cubes in a bowl, add salt, pepper & turmeric, toss to coat and leave aside for 10 minutes.
2. Set your instant pot on Sauté mode, add the oil and half of the sugar, stir and heat up.
3. Add potatoes, fry them a bit and transfer to a bowl.
4. Add cloves, cinnamon stick and cardamom to pot and stir.
5. Also add ginger, onion, chilies and garlic, stir and cook for 3 minutes.
6. Add tomatoes and chili powder, stir and cook for 5 minutes.
7. Add meat, stir and cook for 10 more minutes.
8. Add 2 cups water, stir, cover and cook on High for 15 minutes.
9. Release the pressure, uncover, add more salt and pepper, the rest of the sugar, potatoes and ½ cup water, cover and cook on High for 5 minutes.
10. Release the pressure again, uncover and serve with sprinkle coriander on top.

(Calories 300|Fat 17 g| Protein 30 g| Fiber 1 g| Carbohydrates 5 g)

Apple Cider Pork

(**Prep Time:** 10 MIN| **Cook Time:** 25 MIN| **Serve:** 4)

Ingredients:

2 pounds pork loin
2 cups apple cider
2 tbsp extra virgin olive oil
Salt and black pepper to taste
1 yellow onion, chopped
2 apples, chopped
1 tbsp dry onion, minced

Directions:

1. Set your instant pot on Sauté mode, add the oil and heat
2. Add pork loin, salt, pepper and dried onion, stir and brown meat on all sides and transfer to a plate.
3. Add onion to pot, stir and cook for 2 minutes.
4. Return meat to pot, add cider, apples, more salt and pepper, stir, cover and cook on High for 20 minutes.
5. Release the pressure, uncover, transfer pork to a cutting board, slice it and divide among plates.
6. Add sauce and mixture from the pot on the side and serve.

(**Calories** 450|**Fat** 22 g| **Protein** 37.2 g| **Fiber** 2.2 g| **Carbohydrates** 29 g)

Creamy Mushroom Pork Chops

(**Prep Time:** 10 MIN| **Cook Time:** 20 MIN| **Serve:** 4)

Ingredients:

4 pork chops, boneless
1 cup water
2 tbsp extra virgin olive oil
2 tsp chicken bouillon powder
10 ounces canned cream of mushroom soup
1 cup sour cream
Salt and black pepper to taste
½ small bunch parsley, chopped

Directions:

1. Set your instant pot on Sauté mode, add oil and heat
2. Add pork chops, salt and pepper, brown them on all sides, transfer to a plate and set aside.
3. Add water and chicken bouillon powder to the pot and stir well.
4. Return pork chops, stir, cover and cook on High for 9 minutes.
5. Release the pressure naturally, transfer pork chops to a platter and keep warm.
6. Set the pot on Simmer mode and heat up the cooking liquid.
7. Add mushroom soup, stir, cook for 2 minutes and take off heat.
8. Add parsley and sour cream, stir and pour over pork chops.

(**Calories** 284|**Fat** 16 g| **Protein** 23.2 g| **Fiber** 1 g| **Carbohydrates** 10.5 g)

Tangy Pulled Pork

(**P**rep Time: 10 MIN| **C**ook Time: 1 HOUR 20 MIN| **S**erve: 6)

Ingredients:

3 pounds pork shoulder, halves
11 ounces beer
8 ounces water
3 ounces sugar
Salt to taste
2 tsp dried mustard
2 tsp smoked paprika

For the sauce:
4 ounces hot water
12 ounces apple cider vinegar
2 tbsp brown sugar
Salt and black pepper to taste
A pinch of cayenne pepper
2 tsp dry mustard

Directions:

1. In a bowl, mix 3 ounces sugar with smoked paprika, 2 tsp dry mustard and salt to taste.
2. Rub pork meat with this mix and put pieces in your instant pot.
3. Add beer and 3 ounces water, stir, cover and cook on High for 75 minutes.
4. Release the pressure quickly, uncover pot and transfer pork to a cutting board, shred with 2 forks and set aside.
5. Discard half of the cooking liquid from the pot.
6. In a bowl, mix brown sugar with 4 ounces hot water, vinegar, cayenne, salt, pepper and 2 tsp dry mustard and stir well.
7. Pour this over cooking sauce from the pot, stir, cover and cook on High for 3 minutes.
8. Release the pressure, dish pork onto serving plates, drizzle the sauce all over and enjoy!

(**C**alories 440|**F**at 12 g| **P**rotein 32 g| **F**iber 4 g| **C**arbohydrates 40 g)

Chinese BBQ Pork

(**Prep Time:** 10 MIN| **Cook Time:** 50 MIN| **Serve:** 86)

Ingredients:

2 pounds pork belly
4 tbsp soy sauce
2 tbsp dry sherry
1 quart chicken stock
8 tbsp Char Siu sauce
2 tsp sesame oil
2 tbsp honey
1 tsp peanut oil

Directions:

1. Set your instant pot on Simmer mode, add sherry, stock, soy sauce and half of Char Siu sauce, stir and cook for 8 minutes.
2. Add pork, stir, cover and set on High for 30 minutes.
3. Release the pressure naturally, transfer pork to a cutting board, leave to cool down and chop in small pieces.
4. Heat up a pan with the peanut oil over medium high heat, add pork, stir and cook for a few minutes.
5. Meanwhile, in a bowl, mix sesame oil with the rest of the Char Siu sauce and honey.
6. Brush pork from the pan with this mix, stir and cook for 10 minutes.
7. Heat up another pan over medium high heat, add cooking liquid from the instant pot and bring to a boil.
8. Simmer for 3 minutes and remove from heat.
9. Divide pork on plates, drizzle the delicious sticky sauce over it and serve.

(**C**alories 400|**F**at 23 g| **P**rotein 41 g| **F**iber 1 g| **C**arbohydrates 15 g)

Hot Pepper Pork Chops

(**Prep Time:** 4 HOURS| **Cook Time:** 25 MIN| **Serve:** 6)

Ingredients:

2 cups water
1/3 cup brown sugar
1/3 cup salt
2 cups ice
2 hot peppers, crushed
1 tbsp peppercorns
4 garlic cloves, crushed
2 bay leaves
2 pounds pork chops
2 cups brown rice
1 cup onion, chopped
3 tbsp butter
2 ½ cups beef stock
Salt and black pepper to taste

Directions:

1. Heat up a pan over medium high heat with the water inside.
2. Add salt and brown sugar, stir until it dissolves, take off heat and add ice.
3. Add hot peppers, garlic, peppercorns and bay leaves and stir.
4. Add pork chops, toss to coat, cover and marinate in the fridge for 4 hours.
5. Rinse pork chops and pat dry them with paper towels.
6. Set your instant pot on Sauté mode, add butter and melt.
7. Add pork chops, brown them on all sides, transfer to a plate and keep warm.
8. Add onion to your instant pot and cook for 2 minutes.
9. Add rice, stir and cook for 1 minute.
10. Add stock, pork chops, cover and cook on High for 22 minutes.
11. Release the pressure naturally for 10 minutes, uncover, add salt and pepper to taste, dish up pork chops and rice on plates and enjoy!

(**Calories** 430|**Fat** 12.3 g| **Protein** 30 g| **Fiber** 4.3 g| **Carbohydrates** 53 g)

Pork Chops and Creamy Garlic Potatoes

(**Prep Time:** 15 MIN| **Cook Time:** 20 MIN| **Serve:** 6)

Ingredients:

6 pork chops, boneless
2 pounds potatoes, cut into chunks
2 cups chicken stock
3 garlic cloves, chopped
1 yellow onion, cut into chunks
1 bunch mixed rosemary, sage, oregano and thyme
Salt and black pepper to taste
2 tbsp butter
1 tsp smoked paprika
2 tbsp white flour

Directions:

1. Put the potatoes in your instant pot and add garlic and half of the onion, herbs and stock.
2. Place pork chops on top of mixture, add salt, pepper and smoked paprika.
3. Cover and cook on High for 15 minutes.
4. Meanwhile, heat up a pan over medium heat, add butter and heat
5. Add flour, stir very well, cook for 2 minutes and take off heat.
6. Release the pressure quickly, transfer pork to a platter and discard herbs.
7. Transfer potatoes to a bowl, add some of the cooking liquid, add salt, pepper and beat using your hand mixer until creamy and smooth.
8. Set your instant pot on Simmer mode and cook the cooking liquid for 2 minutes.
9. Add butter and flour mixture and stir until it thickens.
10. Place pork chops on plates, add creamy mashed potatoes on the side and drizzle the gravy all over. Yummy!

(**Calories** 510|**Fat** 22 g| **Protein** 30.2 g| **Fiber** 5.7 g| **Carbohydrates** 47 g)

Hot Sweet Ribs

(**P**rep Time: 2 HOURS| **C**ook Time: 20 MIN| **S**erve: 8)

Ingredients:

5 pounds country style ribs, boneless

For the brine:
½ cup brown sugar
½ cup salt
4 cups water
2 tbsp liquid smoke
3 garlic cloves, crushed

For the ribs:
2 tbsp butter
½ tbsp water
1 cup onion, chopped
1 pound apples, peeled and sliced
½ tsp cinnamon
1 tsp chili powder
A pinch of cayenne pepper

For the sauce:
1 tbsp liquid smoke
2 tbsp yellow mustard
2 tbsp Dijon mustard
2 tbsp brown sugar
1 tsp hot chili sauce
1 tbsp Worcestershire sauce
1 tbsp soy sauce
¼ cup honey
2 tbsp water
2 tbsp cornstarch

Directions:

1. In a bowl, mix 4 cups water with ½ cup salt, ½ cup sugar, 2 tbsp liquid smoke and garlic.

2. Stir, add pork ribs and marinate in the fridge for 2 hours.
3. Set your instant pot on Sauté mode, add 2 tbsp butter and melt.
4. Add ribs, brown them on all sides and transfer to a plate.
5. Add onions and ½ tbsp water, stir and cook for 2 minutes.
6. Add cinnamon, cayenne, chili powder and apples.
7. Return ribs, cover and cook on High for 15 minutes.
8. Release the pressure quickly, transfer ribs to a plate and keep warm.
9. Puree onions and apples using a hand blender and set the pot on Sauté mode again.
10. Add mustard, Dijon mustard, 1 tbsp liquid smoke, 2 tbsp sugar, Worcestershire sauce, hot chili sauce, soy sauce and honey to the apple mixture and stir well.
11. Add cornstarch mixed with 2 tbsp water, stir to avoid lumps forming and cook for 2 minutes.
12. Dish up ribs onto plates, drizzle the gravy all over and attack them with gusto!

(Calories 470|Fat 34 g| Protein 29 g| Fiber 3 g| Carbohydrates 11 g)

Simple Beef Tacos

(Prep Time: 5 MIN| Cook Time: 2 hrs| Serve: 6)

Ingredients:

3 lbs beef roast
4 tbsp taco seasoning
2/3 cup chicken stock

Directions:

1. Place beef roast in instant pot.
2. Pour stock over the roast and sprinkle roast with taco seasoning.
3. Seal pot with lid and select MANUAL button and set the timer for 120 minutes.
4. Allow releasing steam on its own then open.
5. Using a fork and shred the roast and serve.

(Calories 427|Fat 14.2 g| Protein 68.9 g| Carbohydrates 1.1 g)

Pulled Pork Tamales

(**Prep Time**: 10 MIN| **Cook Time**: 1 HOUR 35 MIN| **Serve**: 24 pieces)

Ingredients:

8 ounces dried corn husks, soaked for 1 day and drained
4 cups water
3 pounds pork shoulder, boneless and chopped
1 yellow onion, chopped
2 garlic cloves, crushed
1 tbsp chipotle chili powder
2 tbsp chili powder
Salt and black pepper to taste
1 tsp cumin
4 cups masa
¼ cup corn oil
¼ cup shortening
1 tsp baking powder

Directions:

1. In your instant pot, mix 2 cups water with salt, pepper, onion, garlic, chipotle powder, chili powder and cumin.
2. Add pork, stir, cover and cook on High for 75 minutes.
3. Release the pressure naturally for 10 minutes, uncover, transfer meat to a cutting board and shred it with 2 forks.
4. Put pork in a bowl, add 1 tbsp of cooking liquid, more salt and pepper, stir and set aside.
5. In a bowl, mix masa with salt, pepper, baking powder, shortening, oil & stir using a mixer.
6. Add cooking liquid from the instant pot and blend again well.
7. Add 2 cups of water to your instant pot and place the steamer basket inside.
8. Unfold 2 corn husks, place them on a work surface, add ¼ cup masa mixture near the top of the husk, press into a square and leave 2 inches at the bottom.
9. Add 1 tbsp pork in the center of the masa, wrap the husk around the dough and place standing up in the steamer basket.
10. Repeat with the rest of the husks, cover and cook on High for 20 minutes.
11. Release the pressure for 15 minutes, uncover, transfer tamales to plates and serve.

(**C**alories 150|**F**at 7.2 g| **P**rotein 7 g| **F**iber 2 g| **C**arbohydrates 11 g)

Mexican Pork Tostadas
(Prep Time: 10 MIN| Cook Time: 30 MIN| Serve: 4)

Ingredients:

4 pounds pork shoulder, boneless and cubed
Salt and black pepper to taste
2 cups Coca Cola
1/3 cup brown sugar
½ cup picante sauce
2 tsp chili powder
2 tbsp tomato paste
¼ tsp cumin
1 cup enchilada sauce
Corn tortillas
Mexican cheese, shredded for serving
Shredded lettuce, for serving
Salsa
Guacamole for serving

Directions:

1. In your instant pot, mix 1 cup Coca Cola with picante sauce, salsa, sugar, tomato paste, chili powder and cumin and stir.
2. Add pork pieces, stir, cover and cook for 25 minutes.
3. Release the pressure for 15 minutes, uncover, drain juice from the pot, transfer meat to a cutting board and shred it.
4. Return meat to instant pot, add the rest of the Coke and enchilada sauce, stir, set the pot on Sauté mode and heat everything up.
5. Brown tortillas in the oven at 350 degrees F for 5 minutes and place them on a working surface.
6. Add lettuce leaves, cheese and guacamole, fold and serve for a delicious feast.

(**Calories** 160|**Fat** 3 g| **Protein** 9 g| **Fiber** 3 g| **Carbohydrates** 13 g)

Meatball Delight

(**Prep** Time: 10 MIN| **Cook** Time: 10 MIN| **Serve:** 8)

Ingredients:

1 ½ pounds ground pork meat
2 tbsp parsley, chopped
1 egg
2 bread slices, soaked in water
2 garlic cloves, minced
Salt and black pepper to taste
¾ cup beef stock
½ tsp nutmeg
¼ cup flour
1 tsp Worcestershire sauce
½ tsp paprika
2 tbsp extra virgin olive oil
2 carrots, chopped
¾ cup fresh peas
2 potatoes, cubed
1 bay leaf
¼ cup white wine

Directions:

1. In a bowl, mix ground meat with soaked bread, egg, salt, pepper, parsley, paprika, garlic and nutmeg and stir well.
2. Add 1 tbsp stock and Worcestershire sauce and stir again
3. Shape meatballs and dust them with flour
4. Set your instant pot on Sauté mode, add oil and heat
5. Add meatballs and brown them on all sides.
6. Add carrots, peas, potatoes, bay leaf, stock and wine, cover and cook on High for 6 minutes.
7. Release the pressure, uncover, discard bay leaf, divide meatballs mix into bowls and serve.

(Calories 400|Fat 13 g| **Protein** 17 g| **Fiber** 7 g| **Carbohydrates** 24 g)

Italian Meatballs

(**Prep Time:** 10 MIN| **Cook Time:** 10 MIN| **Serve:** 6)

Ingredients:

1 onion, chopped
1/3 cup parmesan, grated
½ cup bread crumbs
½ tsp oregano, dried
Salt and black pepper to taste
½ cup milk
1 pound ground meat
1 tbsp extra virgin olive oil
1 egg, whisked
1 carrot, chopped
½ celery stalk, chopped
2 and ¾ cups tomato puree
2 cups water

Directions:

1. In a bowl, mix bread crumbs with cheese, half of the onion, oregano, salt and pepper and stir.
2. Add milk and meat and mix well.
3. Add the egg and stir again to blend fully.
4. Set your instant pot on Sauté mode, add oil and heat
5. Add onion, stir and fry for 3 minutes.
6. Add celery and carrot, tomato puree, water and salt and stir again.
7. Shape meatballs with your hands and add them to the pot, toss them to coat, cover and cook on High for 5 minutes.
8. Release the pressure naturally for 10 minutes and serve with your favorite spaghetti.

(**Calories** 150|**Fat** 3 g| **Protein** 8 g| **Fiber** 1 g| **Carbohydrates** 4 g)

Soups & Stew Recipes

Onion Soup with Gruyere Cheese

(**Prep Time:** 5 MIN| **Cook Time:** 15 MIN| **Serve:** 4)

Ingredients:

5 yellow onions, sliced
1/3 cup unsalted butter
1 tbsp extra-virgin olive oil
6 cups vegetable stock
3 bay leaves
1 tsp salt
½ tsp freshly ground black pepper
1 tsp oregano
5 slices of French baguette
6 slices Gruyere cheese

Directions:

1. Start by slicing the onions into medium slices.
2. Place the Instant pot over medium heat, melt the butter.
3. Add the sliced onions and olive oil and stir for 3 minutes.
4. Pour the vegetable stock and add the bay leaves. Season with salt, pepper and oregano.
5. Cover the pot and set the timer on 10 minutes. Once the time has finished allow the pressure to be released automatically.
6. Set on "Keep Warm" until serving time.
7. To serve, pour into bowls and serve with baguette and cheese slices.

(Calories 350|Fat 22.4g| Protein 13.1 g| Carbohydrates 25.6 g)

Lobster Whip Cream Bisque

(**Prep Time:** 5 MIN| **Cook Time:** 5 MIN| **Serve:** 4)

Ingredients:

2 tbsp unsalted butter
2 onion, finely chopped
2 cloves garlic, crushed
2 large carrots, cubed
3 celery stalks, chopped
2 cans diced tomatoes
4 cups chicken stock
2 tsp Old Bay Seasonings
2 tsp dill
½ tsp freshly ground black pepper
1 tbsp paprika
5 frozen Lobster tails, thawed
2 cups heavy whip cream

Directions:

1. Peel the onion and finely chop it. Place the Instant pot over medium heat, melt the butter.
2. Stir in the onions and cook until translucent. Add the garlic and stir for 2 more minutes.
3. Add the tomatoes, cubed carrots and chopped celery.
4. Pour in the chicken stock and season with Old Bay Seasonings, dill, black pepper and paprika.
5. Place the lobster tails into the pot and cover. Set the timer for 5 minutes. Once the time is finished allow the pressure to be released automatically.
6. Uncover the pot and using a handheld blender, puree the lobster soup until smooth.
7. Add the whip cream and stir. Serve hot.

(Calories 422|Fat 27.5g| Protein 23.2 g| Carbohydrates 16.2 g)

Hot Broccoli Cheddar Soup

(**Prep Time:** 8 MIN| **Cook Time:** 20 MIN| **Serve:** 4)

Ingredients:

½ onion, finely chopped

3 cups broccoli florets

2 large carrots, grated

4 cups chicken stock

3 cups heavy cream

1 cup Cheddar cheese, shredded

3 tbsp hot sauce

Directions:
1. Place the Instant Pot over medium heat and set on "Sauté" mode. Stir in the onion until translucent.
2. Add the broccoli, carrots and chicken stock.
3. Cover the pot and set on 15 minutes. Once the time is done, carefully release the pressure.
4. Remove the lid and pour in the cream and simmer for 5 minutes.
5. When you are ready to serve, add the cheese and hot sauce.

(Calories 479|Fat 43.5g| Protein 12 g| Carbohydrates 13.1 g)

Chicken Broth Noodle Soup

(**Prep Time:** 10 MIN| **Cook Time:** 25 MIN| **Serve:** 4)

Ingredients:
2 tbsp extra-virgin olive oil
½ onion, finely chopped
4 cloves garlic, minced
6 carrots, peeled and sliced
3 celery sticks, sliced
1 whole chicken, insides removed
3 tbsp soy sauce
7 cups water
1 tsp salt, to taste
½ tsp freshly ground pepper
1 package egg noodles
1/3 cup fresh parsley, finely chopped

Directions:
1. Place the Instant Pot over medium heat and set on "Sauté" mode. Add the olive oil and stir in the onions until translucent.
2. Add the garlic along with the sliced carrots and celery.
3. Place the chicken into the pot and pour in the water and soy sauce.
4. Season with salt and black pepper, to taste.
5. Set the Instant Pot on "High Pressure" and timer for 20 minutes.
6. When the time is finished, carefully release the pressure from the pot.
7. Open the pot and take out the chicken and using a fork, shred the chicken. Discard the bones.
8. Return the pot over medium heat and bring to a simmer. Allow it to boil and add the noodles and cook for 5 minutes.
9. Return the shredded chicken into the pot and add parsley.

(Calories 497|Fat 19.2g| Protein 46.4 g| Carbohydrates 33.7 g)

Pea Ham Soup

(**Prep Time:** 10 MIN| **Cook Time:** 22 MIN| **Serve:** 4)

Ingredients:

3 tbsp extra-virgin olive oil
1 small onion, finely chopped
1 cup ham, chopped into bite-size pieces
2 ½ cup dry split peas
1 large carrot, chopped
3 celery stalks, sliced
5 cup vegetable stock
1 tsp salt
1 tsp garlic powder

Directions:

1. Place the Instant Pot over medium heat and add the olive oil. Stir in the onions and ham for 5 minutes.
2. Add the peas, carrots, celery and vegetable stock.
3. Season with salt and garlic powder.
4. Cover the lid and set for 18 minutes on high pressure. Once the time is finished, carefully release the pressure.
5. Uncover the lid and stir. Pour into serving bowls and serve hot.

(Calories 591|Fat 15g| Protein 36.9 g| Carbohydrates 81 g)

Toscana Coconut Soup

(**Prep Time:** 10 MIN| **Cook Time:** 20 MIN| **Serve:** 4)

Ingredients:
2 tbsp avocado oil
1 onion, diced
4 cloves garlic, minced
2 lbs turkey sausage
4 potatoes, peeled
6 cups chicken stock
1 tbsp dried basil
½ dried cumin
3 cups fresh kale, chopped
¾ cup full fat coconut milk
1 tsp red pepper flakes
1 tsp salt
½ tsp freshly ground black pepper

Directions:
1. Place the Instant pot over medium heat and add the avocado oil. Dice the onion and mince the garlic.
2. Fry the onions for 3 minutes and then add the garlic.
3. Add the sausage and cook until browned.
4. Pour in the chicken stock and chop the potatoes into chunks.
5. Add the potato along with the dried basil and fennel. Cover the pot and set the timer for 13 minutes.
6. Once the time is finished, carefully release the pressure.
7. Uncover the pot and add in the kale and stir until it wilts. Pour in the coconut milk and add spices.
8. Serve warm with some toasted bread.

(Calories 413|Fat 17.8g| Protein 16.7 g| Carbohydrates 50.8 g)

Hearty Vegetable Stew

(**Prep Time:** 10 MIN| **Cook Time:** 20 MIN| **Serve:** 4)

Ingredients:
1 small onion, finely chopped
2 celery stalks, chopped
2 carrot, diced
3 garlic cloves, crushed
½ tbsp rosemary
1/3 tsp sage
½ tbsp Italian Seasoning
1 can Portobello mushrooms
1 can white button mushrooms
5 tbsp chicken stock
1/2 cup red wine
1 can tomatoes, diced
1 can organic tomato sauce
3 ½ cup vegetable stock
1 cup frozen green beans, thawed
1 large potato, diced
2 tsp balsamic vinegar
Pinch of salt, to taste
Pinch of freshly ground black pepper
1 cup frozen peas, thawed

Directions:
1. Place the Instant pot over medium heat and add the onion with half the celery and carrots. Stir until the onion is translucent.
2. Add the garlic and stir for 2 more minutes.
3. Add the rosemary, sage and seasonings. Stir in the mushrooms and chicken stock and cook until liquid has evaporated.
4. Pour in the red wine and stir in the tomatoes, sauce and vegetable stock.
5. Add the beans, potatoes and peas, season with salt and pepper and add balsamic vinegar.
6. Cover the pot and set the timer for 15 minutes.
7. Once the time is finished, carefully release the pressure and uncover the pot.
8. Divide into serving bowls and serve hot.

(Calories 222|Fat 12g| Protein 9.3 g| Carbohydrates 41 g)

Simple Vegetable Beef Soup

(**Prep Time:** 5 MIN| **Cook Time:** 4 MIN| **Serve:** 6)

Ingredients:

2 lbs ground beef
2 cup beef stock
3 cans tomatoes, diced
1 cup corn
2 cups mix vegetables
2 cups fresh lima beans
1 small onion, diced
Pepper
Salt

Directions:
1. Add onion and ground beef in instant pot and select sauté.
2. Sauté onion until soften.
3. Add all remaining ingredients into the pot and stir well.
4. Seal pot with lid and select MANUAL button and set the timer for 4 minutes.
5. Allow to release steam on its own then open and stir well.
6. Serve hot and enjoy.

(Calories 424|Fat 10.5 g| Protein 53.5 g| Carbohydrates 26.9 g)

Healthy Vegetable Steak Soup

(Prep Time: 5 MIN| Cook Time: 20 MIN| Serve: 4)

Ingredients:

1 lb steak, trimmed and diced
2 cups water
2 cups chicken stock
1 cup tomatoes, crushed
1 bay leaf
1/2 tbsp thyme
1 1/2 tbsp oregano
2 tbsp garlic powder
8 oz mushrooms, sliced
1 large bell pepper, diced
1 large celery stalk, diced
3 medium carrots, diced
1 onion, diced
1 tbsp salt

Directions:
1. Select sauté mode on instant pot.
2. Add steak meat into the pot and sauté until brown.
3. Add carrots, pepper, celery, and onion and cook until softened.
4. Add mushrooms and cook until softened.
5. Add spices, stock, water, and salt and stir well.
6. Seal pot with lid and select SOUP setting for 15 minutes.
7. Release steam quickly and stir well.
8. Serve hot and enjoy.

(Calories 313|Fat 6.6 g| Protein 45.5 g| Carbohydrates 18.1 g)

Beef Mushroom Stew

(**Prep Time:** 10 MIN| **Cook Time:** 30 MIN| **Serve:** 4)

Ingredients:
2 lbs beef
1 tsp salt, to taste
½ tsp freshly ground black pepper
2 tbsp all-purpose flour
3 tbsp unsalted butter
3 cups beef stock
2 tsp soy sauce
2 tsp Worcestershire sauce
1 tbsp light brown sugar
3 garlic cloves, crushed
3 tbsp tomato paste
½ tbsp rosemary
½ tbsp dried thyme
14 oz bag frozen pearl onions
8 oz mushrooms
2 large carrots, diced
3 large potatoes, peeled and diced

Directions:
1. Ina bowl, combine the flour with the salt and pepper. Flip the meat into the flour mixture until evenly coated.
2. Place the Instant Pot over medium heat and add the butter. Place the meat in the pot and cook until browned on both sides.
3. Pour in the beef stock, add in the soy sauce, Worcestershire sauce and sugar.
4. Stir in the garlic, tomato paste and season with rosemary and thyme.
5. Add the carrots and potatoes and stir.
6. Cover the pot and set the timer on 30 minutes. Once the time is finished allow the pressure to be released manually.
7. Wash and quarter the mushrooms.
8. Uncover the pot and adjust the seasonings of the stew and serve hot.

(Calories 654|Fat 15.9g| Protein 62 g| Carbohydrates 64.7 g)

Chicken and Corn Chowder

(**Prep Time:** 10 MIN| **Cook Time:** 17 MIN| **Serve:** 4)

Ingredients:

4 chicken breasts, skinless and boneless
2 tbsp extra virgin olive oil
1 onion, chopped
3 garlic cloves, minced
16 ounces jarred chunky salsa
29 ounces canned tomatoes, peeled and chopped
29 ounces canned chicken stock
Salt and black pepper to taste
2 tbsp parsley, dried
1 tsp garlic powder
1 tbsp onion powder
1 tbsp chili powder
15 ounces frozen corn
32 ounces canned black beans, drained

Directions:

1. Set your instant pot on Sauté mode, add oil and heat
2. Add onion, stir and cook 5 minutes, then add garlic, stir and cook for 1 minute more.
3. Add chicken breasts, salsa, tomatoes, stock, salt, pepper, parsley, garlic powder, onion and chili powder, stir, cover and cook on High for 8 minutes.
4. Release the pressure for 10 minutes, uncover pot and transfer chicken breasts to a cutting board, shred with 2 forks and return to pot.
5. Add beans and corn, set the pot on Simmer mode and cook for 2-3 minutes more.
6. Divide into soup bowls and serve.

(**Calories** 210|**Fat** 4.4 g| **Protein** 26 g| Fiber 4.3 g| Carbohydrates18 g)

Butternut and Chicken Soup

(**Prep** Time: 10 MIN| **Cook** Time: 16 MIN| **Serve:** 6)

Ingredients:

1 ½ pounds butternut squash, baked, peeled and cubed
½ cup green onions, chopped
3 tbsp butter
½ cup carrots, chopped
½ cup celery, chopped
29 ounces canned chicken stock
1 garlic clove, minced
½ tsp Italian seasoning
15 ounces canned tomatoes and their juice, chopped
Salt and black pepper to taste
1/8 tsp red pepper flakes, dried
1 cup orzo, already cooked
1/8 tsp nutmeg, grated
1 ½ cup half and half
1 cup chicken meat, already cooked and shredded
Some green onions, chopped for serving

Directions:

1. Set your instant pot on Sauté mode, add butter and melt.
2. Add celery, carrots and onions, stir and cook for 3 minutes.
3. Also add garlic, stir and cook for 1 minute more.
4. Add squash, tomatoes, stock, Italian seasoning, salt, pepper, pepper flakes and nutmeg.
5. Stir, cover and cook on High for 10 minutes.
6. Release the pressure fast, uncover and puree everything with your immersion blender.
7. Set the pot on Simmer mode, add half and half, orzo and chicken, stir and simmer for 3 minutes.
8. Divide soup into bowls, sprinkle green onions on top and serve.

(**Calories** 130|**Fat** 2.3 g| **Protein** 6 g| **Fiber** 0.4 g| **Carbohydrates** 18 g)

Cheesy Potato Soup

(**Prep Time:** 10 MIN| **Cook Time:** 10 MIN| **Serve:** 6)

Ingredients:

6 cups potatoes, cubed
2 tbsp butter
½ cup yellow onion, chopped
28 ounces canned chicken stock
Salt and black pepper to taste
2 tbsp parsley, dried
1/8 red pepper flakes
2 tbsp cornstarch
2 tbsp water
3 ounces cream cheese, cubed
2 cups half and half
1 cup cheddar cheese, shredded
1 cup corn
6 bacon slices, cooked and crumbled

Directions:

1. Set your instant pot on Sauté mode, add butter and melt. Add onion, stir and cook 5 minutes
2. Add half of the stock, salt, pepper, pepper flakes and parsley and stir.
3. Put potatoes in the steamer basket, cover and cook on High for 4 minutes.
4. Release the pressure fast, uncover pot and transfer potatoes to a bowl.
5. In another bowl, mix cornstarch with water and stir well.
6. Set the pot to Simmer mode, add cornstarch, cream cheese and shredded cheese and stir well to melt cheese and avoid lumps forming.
7. Also add the rest of the stock, corn, bacon, potatoes, half and half.
8. Stir, bring to a simmer, ladle into bowls and enjoy!

(**Calories** 188|**Fat** 7.14 g| **Protein** 9 g| **Fiber** 1.5 g| **Carbohydrates** 22 g)

Split Pea Soup

(**Prep Time:** 10 MIN| **Cook Time:** 20 MIN| **Serve:** 6)

Ingredients:

2 tbsp butter
1 pound chicken sausage, ground
1 yellow onion, chopped
½ cup carrots, chopped
½ cup celery, chopped
2 garlic cloves, minced
29 ounces chicken stock
Salt and black pepper to taste
2 cups water
16 ounces split peas, rinsed
½ cup half and half
¼ tsp red pepper flakes, dried

Directions:

1. Set the pot on Sauté mode, add sausage, brown it on all sides and transfer to a plate.
2. Add butter to your instant pot and melt.
3. Add celery, onions and carrots, stir and cook 4 minutes.
4. Add garlic, stir and cook for a further minute.
5. Add water, stock, peas and pepper flakes, stir, cover and cook on High for 10 minutes.
6. Release the pressure, puree the mix using an immersion blender and set the pot on Simmer mode.
7. Add sausage, salt, pepper and half and half, stir, bring to a simmer and ladle into soup bowls.

(**Calories** 30|**Fat** 11 g| **Protein** 20 g| **Fiber** 12 g| **Carbohydrates** 14 g)

Hearty Beef and Beans Soup

(Prep Time: 10 MIN| Cook Time: 15 MIN| Serve: 6)

Ingredients:
1 pound beef meat, ground
3 garlic cloves, minced
1 yellow onion, chopped
1 tbsp vegetable oil
1 celery rib, chopped
28 ounces canned beef stock
14 ounces canned tomatoes, crushed
½ cup white rice
12 ounces spicy V8 juice
15 ounces canned garbanzo beans, rinsed
1 potato, cubed
Salt and black pepper to taste
½ cup frozen peas
2 carrots, thinly sliced

Directions:

1. Set your instant pot on Sauté mode, add beef, stir, cook until it browns and transfer to a plate.
2. Add the oil to your pot and heat. Add celery and onion, stir and cook for 5 minutes.
3. Add garlic, stir and cook for 1 minute more.
4. Add V8 juice, stock, tomatoes, rice, beans, carrots, potatoes, beef, salt and pepper, stir, cover and cook on High for 5 minutes.
5. Release the pressure, uncover pot and set it on Simmer mode.
6. Add more salt and pepper if needed and peas, stir, bring to a simmer, transfer to bowls and serve hot.

(Calories 230|Fat 7 g| **P**rotein 3 g| Fiber 4 g| **C**arbohydrates 10 g)

Old-Fashioned Chicken Noodle Soup

(**Prep Time:** 10 MIN| **Cook Time:** 12 MIN| **S**erve: 6)

Ingredients:

1 yellow onion, chopped
1 tbsp butter
1 celery rib, chopped
4 carrots, sliced
Salt and black pepper to taste
6 cups chicken stock
2 cups chicken, already cooked and shredded
Egg noodles, already cooked

Directions:

1. Set your instant pot on Sauté mode, add butter and heat
2. Add onion, stir and fry for 2 minutes.
3. Add celery and carrots, stir and cook for 5 minutes.
4. Add chicken, stock, stir, cover pot and cook on High for 5 minutes.
5. Release the pressure, uncover pot, add salt and pepper to taste.
6. Divide noodles into soup bowls, ladle soup over them and serve.

(**Calories** 100|**Fat** 1 g| **Protein** 7 g| Fiber 1 g| **C**arbohydrates 4 g)

Chicken and Wild Rice Soup

(**Prep Time:** 10 MIN| **Cook Time:** 15 MIN| **Serve:** 6)

Ingredients:

1 cup yellow onion, chopped
2 tbsp butter
1 cup celery, chopped
1 cup carrots, chopped
28 ounces chicken stock
2 chicken breasts, skinless and boneless and chopped
6 ounces wild rice
A pinch of red pepper flakes
Salt and black pepper to taste
1 tbsp parsley, dried
2 tbsp cornstarch mixed with 2 tbsp water
1 cup milk
1 cup half and half
4 ounces cream cheese, cubed

Directions:

1. Set your instant pot on Sauté mode, add butter and melt.
2. Add carrot, onion and celery and fry for 5 minutes.
3. Add rice, chicken, stock, parsley, salt and pepper, stir, cover and cook on High for 5 minutes.
4. Release the pressure, uncover, add cornstarch mixed with water, stir to avoid lumps and set the pot on Simmer mode.
5. Add cheese, milk and half and half, stir until the cheese is melted, heat up and serve.

(**C**alories 200|**F**at 7 g| **P**rotein 5 g| Fiber 1 g| Carbohydrates 19 g)

Creamy Tomato Soup

(**Prep Time**: 10 MIN| **Cook Time**: 6 MIN| **Serve**: 8)

Ingredients:

1 yellow onion, chopped
3 tbsp butter
1 carrot, chopped
2 celery stalks, chopped
2 garlic cloves, minced
29 ounces canned chicken stock
Salt and black pepper to taste
¼ cup basil, chopped
3 pounds tomatoes, peeled, cored and cut into quarters
1 tbsp tomato paste
1 cup half and half
½ cup parmesan cheese, shredded

Directions:

1. Set your instant pot on Sauté mode, add butter and melt, add onion, carrots and celery, stir and fry for 3 minutes.
2. Add garlic, stir and cook for 1 minute more.
3. Add tomatoes, tomato paste, stock, basil, salt and pepper, stir, cover and cook on High for 5 minutes.
4. Release the pressure, uncover pot and puree soup using and immersion blender.
5. Add half and half and cheese, stir until melted, set the pot on Simmer mode and heat soup up before eating.

(**C**alories 280|**F**at 8 g| **P**rotein 24 g| **F**iber 4 g| **C**arbohydrates 32 g)

Vegetable Lamb Stew

(**Prep Time:** 10 MIN| **Cook Time:** 35 MIN| **Serve:** 4)

Ingredients:

2 lbs lamb stew meat, cut into pieces
3 tbsp water
5 garlic cloves, sliced
1 bay leaf
1 rosemary sprig
1 large onion, sliced
3 carrots, peel and cut into circles
1 acorn squash, peel, seed and cubed
1/4 Tsp salt

Directions:

1. Add all ingredients into the instant pot and stir well.
2. Seal pot with lid and select soup/ stew function, it takes 35 minutes.
3. Quick release steam then open.
4. Stir well and serve.

(Calories 504|Fat 16.8 g| Protein 65.6 g| Carbohydrates 20.5 g)

Creamy Zuppa Toscana

(**Prep Time:** 10 MIN| **Cook Time:** 17 MIN| **Serve:** 8)

Ingredients:

1 pound chicken sausage, ground
6 bacon slices, chopped
3 garlic cloves, minced
1 cup yellow onion, chopped
1 tbsp butter
40 ounces chicken stock
Salt and black pepper to taste
A pinch of red pepper flakes
3 potatoes, cubed
3 tbsp cornstarch
12 ounces evaporated milk
1 cup parmesan, shredded
2 cup spinach, chopped

Directions:

1. Set your instant pot on Sauté mode, add bacon and cook until it's crispy, then transfer to a plate.
2. Add sausage to the pot, cook until it browns on all sides and also transfer to a plate.
3. Add butter to the pot and melt, add onion and cook for 5 minutes, add garlic, stir and cook for a further minute.
4. Add 1/3 of the stock, salt, pepper and pepper flakes and stir.
5. Place potatoes in the steamer basket of the pot, cover and cook on High for 4 minutes.
6. Release the pressure fast, uncover and transfer potatoes to a bowl.
7. Add the rest of the stock to the pot, cornstarch mixed with some evaporated milk and the rest of the evaporated milk, stir and set the pot on Simmer mode.
8. Add parmesan, sausage, bacon, potatoes, spinach, more salt and pepper if needed, serve and enjoy!

(**Calories** 170|**Fat** 4 g| **Protein** 10 g| **Fiber** 2 g| **Carbohydrates** 24 g)

Minestrone Soup

(**Prep Time:** 10 MIN| **Cook Time:** 15 MIN| **Serve:** 8)

Ingredients:

1 tbsp extra virgin olive oil
1 celery stalk, chopped
2 carrots, chopped
1 onion, chopped
1 cup corn kernels
1 zucchini, chopped
3 pounds tomatoes, peeled and chopped
4 garlic cloves, minced
29 ounces canned chicken stock
1 cup uncooked pasta
Salt and black pepper to taste
1 tsp Italian seasoning
2 cups baby spinach
15 ounces canned kidney beans
1 cup asiago cheese, grated
2 tbsp basil, chopped

Directions:

1. Set your instant pot on Sauté mode, ad oil and heat, then add onion and cook for 5 minutes.
2. Add carrots, garlic, celery, corn and zucchini, stir for a further 5 minutes.
3. Add tomatoes, stock, Italian seasoning, pasta, salt and pepper, stir, cover and cook on High for 4 minutes.
4. Release the pressure fast, uncover, add beans, basil and spinach.
5. Add more salt and pepper if needed, divide into bowls, sprinkle cheese on top and enjoy!

(**Calories** 110|**Fat** 2 g| **Protein** 5 g| **Fiber** 4 g| **Carbohydrates** 18 g)

Carrot and Ginger Soup

(**Prep Time:** 10 MIN| **Cook Time:** 16 MIN| **Serve:** 4)

Ingredients:

1 tbsp vegetable oil
1 onion, chopped
1 tbsp butter
1 garlic clove, minced
1 pound carrots, chopped
1 small ginger piece, grated
Salt and black pepper to taste
¼ tsp brown sugar
2 cups chicken stock
1 tbsp Sriracha
14 ounces canned coconut milk
Cilantro leaves, chopped for serving

Directions:

1. Set your instant pot on Sauté mode, add butter and oil and fry onion for 3 minutes.
2. Add ginger and garlic, stir and cook another minute.
3. Then add sugar, carrots, salt and pepper and cook 2 more minutes.
4. Add Sriracha sauce, coconut milk, stock, stir, cover and cook on High for 6 minutes.
5. Release the pressure for 10 minutes, uncover, blend soup with an immersion blender, add more salt and pepper if needed and serve bowls with cilantro garnish.

(**Calories** 60|**Fat** 1 g| **Protein** 2 g| Fiber 3.1 g| **Carbohydrates** 12 g)

Country Ham and Bean Soup

(**Prep Time:** 10 MIN| **Cook Time:** 15 MIN| **Serve:** 8)

Ingredients:

1 pound white beans, soaked for 1 hour and drained
1 carrot, chopped
1 tbsp extra virgin olive oil
1 yellow onion, chopped
3 garlic cloves, minced
1 tomato, peeled and chopped
1 pound ham, chopped
Salt and black pepper to taste
4 cups water
4 cups veggie stock
1 tsp mint, dried
1 tsp paprika
1 tsp thyme, dried

Directions:

1. Set your instant pot on Sauté mode, add oil and then add carrot, onion, garlic, tomato, stir and cook for 5 minutes.
2. Add beans, ham, salt, pepper, water, stock, mint, paprika and thyme, stir, cover and cook on High for 15 minutes.
3. Release the pressure for 10 minutes, uncover, divide into soup bowls and enjoy!

(**Calories** 177|**Fat** 2 g| **Protein** 14 g| **Fiber** 1 g| **Carbohydrates** 26 g)

Lentil and Spinach Soup

(**Prep Time:** 10 MIN| **Cook Time:** 30 MIN| **Serve:** 4)

Ingredients:

2 celery stalks, chopped
1 tbsp olive oil
1 small onion, chopped
2 carrots, chopped
½ pound chicken sausage, ground
3 ½ cups beef stock
2 tsp garlic, minced
1 cup lentils
15 ounces canned tomatoes, chopped
Salt and black pepper to taste
2 cups spinach

Directions:

1. Set your instant pot on Sauté mode, add oil and fry celery, onion, carrots, for 4 minutes.
2. Add chicken sausage and cook 5 more minutes.
3. Add stock, garlic, lentils, tomatoes, salt, pepper and spinach, stir, cover and cook on High for 25 minutes.
4. Release the pressure fast, uncover, ladle into soup bowls and enjoy!

(**Calories** 175|**Fat** 1 g| **Protein** 2 g| **Fiber** 1 g| **Carbohydrates** 2 g)

Cream of Asparagus Soup

(Prep Time: 10 MIN| Cook Time: 25 MIN| Serve: 4)

Ingredients:

2 pounds green asparagus, trimmed, tips cut off and cut into medium pieces
3 tbsp butter
1 yellow onion, chopped
6 cups chicken stock
¼ tsp lemon juice
½ cup crème fraiche
Salt and white pepper to taste

Directions:

1. Set your instant pot on Sauté mode, add butter, melt and add asparagus, salt and pepper, stir and cook for 5 minutes.
2. Add 5 cups stock, cover pot and cook on Low for 15 minutes.
3. Release the pressure, uncover pot and transfer soup to your blender.
4. Pulse very well and return to pot.
5. Set the pot on Simmer mode, add crème fraiche, the rest of the stock, salt and pepper and lemon juice, bring to a boil, divide into soup bowls for a delicious creamy feast!

(Calories 80|Fat 8 g| Protein 6.3 g| Fiber 1 g| Carbohydrates 16 g)

Creamed Artichoke Soup

(**Prep Time:** 10 MIN| **Cook Time:** 20 MIN| **Serve:** 4)

Ingredients:

5 artichoke hearts, washed and trimmed
1 leek, sliced
5 tbsp butter
6 garlic cloves, minced
½ cup shallots, chopped
8 ounces gold potatoes, chopped
12 cups chicken stock
1 bay leaf
4 parsley springs
2 thyme springs
¼ tsp black peppercorns, crushed
Salt to taste
¼ cup cream

Directions:

1. Set your instant pot on Sauté mode, add butter and melt.
2. Add artichoke hearts, shallots, leek and garlic, stir and brown for 3-4 minutes.
3. Add potatoes, stock, bay leaf, thyme, parsley, peppercorns and salt, stir, cover and cook on High for 15 minutes.
4. Release the pressure, uncover pot, discard herbs, blend well using an immersion blender, add cream and salt to taste, stir well and ladle into bowls for a creamy, warming soup.

(**Calories** 95|**Fat** 2 g| **Protein** 4 g| **Fiber** 4 g| **Carbohydrates** 15 g)

Cream of Broccoli Soup

(**Prep Time:** 10 MIN| **Cook Time:** 10 MIN| **Serve:** 4)

Ingredients:

1 yellow onion, chopped
3 carrots, chopped
1 potato, chopped
1 broccoli head, florets separated and chopped
1 tbsp olive oil
2 cups chicken stock
5 garlic cloves, minced
Salt and black pepper to taste
2 tbsp cream
Cheddar cheese, grated for serving
1 tbsp chives, chopped

Directions:

1. Set your instant pot on Sauté mode, add oil and fry onion and garlic for 2 minutes.
2. Add broccoli, carrots, potato, stock, salt and pepper, stir, cover and cook on High for 5 minutes.
3. Release the pressure, uncover pot, set it on Simmer mode, add cream, cheese and chives, stir until the cheese has melted and ;ladle into bowls for a steamy winter treat.

(**C**alories 180|**F**at 11 g| **P**rotein 6 g| **F**iber 3 g| **C**arbohydrates 14 g)

Curried Celery Soup

(**Prep Time:** 10 MIN| **Cook Time:** 17 MIN| **Serve:** 2)

Ingredients:

1 yellow onion, chopped
7 celery stalks, chopped
3 potatoes, chopped
1 tsp extra virgin olive oil
Salt and black pepper to taste
4 cups veggie stock
1 tbsp curry powder
1 tsp celery seeds
A handful parsley, chopped for serving

Directions:

1. Set your instant pot on Sauté mode, add oil and fry onion, celery seeds and curry powder for 1 minute.
2. Add celery and potatoes and cook for 5 more minutes.
3. Add stock, salt, pepper stir, cover and cook on High for 10 minutes.
4. Release the pressure, uncover pot, blend well using an immersion blender, add parsley, stir and ladle into bowls for a light, piquant meal

(**Calories** 90|**Fat** 4 g| **Protein** 2 g| **Fiber** 4 g| **Carbohydrates** 8.5 g)

Cheeky Chestnut Soup

(**Prep Time:** 10 MIN| **Cook Time:** 25 MIN| **Serve:** 4)

Ingredients:

1 pound canned chestnuts, drained and rinsed
1 celery stalk, chopped
4 tbsp butter
1 yellow onion, chopped
1 sage sprig, chopped
Salt and white pepper to taste
1 bay leaf
1 potato, chopped
4 cups chicken stock
2 tbsp rum
A pinch of nutmeg
Whole cream for serving
Sage leaves, chopped for serving

Directions:

1. Set your instant pot on Sauté mode, add butter and melt it.
2. Add onion, sage, celery, salt and pepper, stir and fry for 5 minutes.
3. Add chestnuts, potato, bay leaf and stock, stir, cover and cook on Low for 20 minutes.
4. Release the pressure, uncover pot, add nutmeg and rum, discard bay leaf and blend soup using an immersion blender.
5. Divide your delicious soup into bowls, add cream and sprinkle chopped sage leaves to garnish.

(**Calories** 230|**Fat** 13 g| **Protein** 2.1 g| **Fiber** 2 g| **Carbohydrates** 22 g)

Cauliflower and Cream Cheese Soup

(**Prep Time:** 10 MIN| **Cook Time:** 10 MIN| **Serve:** 6)

Ingredients:

1 small onion, chopped
1 cauliflower head, florets separated and chopped
2 tbsp butter
3 cups chicken stock
Salt and black pepper to taste
1 tsp garlic powder
4 ounces cream cheese, cubed
1 cup cheddar cheese, grated
½ cup half and half

Directions:

1. Set your instant pot on Sauté mode, add butter and fry onion for 3 minutes.
2. Add cauliflower, stock, salt, pepper and garlic powder, stir, cover and cook on High for 5 minutes.
3. Release the pressure, uncover pot, blend everything using an immersion blender, add more salt and pepper if needed, cubed cream cheese, grated cheese and half and half.
4. Stir, set the pot on Simmer mode and heat 2 minutes, before ladling into soup bowls and devouring!

(**Calories** 78|**Fat** 1.2 g| **Protein** 3 g| Fiber 1 g| Carbohydrates 10 g)

Turkey and Sweet Potato Soup

(Prep Time: 10 MIN| Cook Time: 12 MIN| Serve: 4)

Ingredients:

1 pound Italian turkey sausage, chopped
1 yellow onion, chopped
2 celery stalks, chopped
2 carrots, chopped
1 big sweet potato, cubed
5 cups turkey stock
2 garlic cloves, minced
1 tsp red pepper flakes
1 tsp basil, dried
1 tsp oregano, dried
Salt and black pepper to taste
1 tsp thyme, dried
5 ounces spinach, chopped
2 bay leaves

Directions:

1. Set your instant pot on Sauté mode, add sausage, brown it and transfer to a plate.
2. Add onion, celery and carrots, stir and cook for 2 minutes, before adding potato and cooking for 2 minutes.
3. Add stock, garlic, red pepper, salt, pepper, basil, oregano, thyme, spinach and bay leaves,
4. Stir, cover and cook on High for 4 minutes.
5. Release the pressure, uncover pot, discard bay leaves and serve this chunky, delicious soup into bowls.

(Calories 190|Fat 12 g| Protein 5 g| Fiber 1 g| Carbohydrates 2 g)

Chicken Chili Soup

(**P**rep Time: 10 MIN| **C**ook Time: 30 MIN| **S**erve: 4)

Ingredients:

1 white onion, chopped
2 tbsp olive oil
1 jalapeno pepper, chopped
4 garlic cloves, minced
2 tsp oregano, dried
1 tsp cumin
½ tsp red pepper flakes, crushed
3 cups chicken stock
1 pound chicken breast, skinless and boneless
30 ounces canned cannellini beans, drained
Salt and black pepper to taste
Cilantro, chopped for serving
Tortilla chips, for serving
Lime wedges for serving

Directions:

1. Set your instant pot on Sauté mode, add oil and heat.
2. Add jalapeno and onion, stir and cook for 3 minutes.
3. Add garlic, stir and cook for 1 minute. Then add oregano, cumin, pepper flakes, stock, chicken, beans, salt and pepper, stir, cover and cook on Low for 30 minutes.
4. Release the pressure, uncover pot, shred meat with 2 forks, add more salt and pepper, stir and divide into soup bowls.
5. Serve with cilantro on top and tortilla chips and lime wedges on the side. Yum!

(**C**alories 200|**F**at 8 g| **P**rotein 19 g| Fiber 6 g| **C**arbohydrates 17 g)

Broccoli and Bacon Soup

(Prep Time: 10 MIN| Cook Time: 10 MIN| Serve: 6)

Ingredients:

4 bacon slices, chopped
1 tsp olive oil
2 small broccoli heads, chopped
1 leek, chopped
1 celery rib, chopped
2 cups spinach, chopped
4 tbsp basmati rice
1 tbsp parmesan, grated
1 quart veggie stock
Salt and black pepper to taste

Directions:

1. Set your instant pot on Sauté mode, add oil and bacon, cook until it's crispy, transfer to a plate and set aside.
2. Add broccoli, leek, celery, spinach, rice, salt, pepper and veggie stock, stir, cover and cook on High for 6 minutes.
3. Release the pressure, uncover, add more salt and pepper if needed, add bacon, divide into soup bowls and serve with parmesan on top.

(**Calories** 151|**Fat** 2.2 g| **Protein** 10 g| **Fiber** 7 g| **Carbohydrates** 26 g)

Chorizo, Chicken and Kale Soup

(**Prep Time**: 10 MIN| **Cook Time**: 10 MIN| **Serve**: 8)

Ingredients:

9 ounces chorizo, casings removed
2 tbsp olive oil
4 chicken thighs, chopped
Salt and black pepper to taste
4 garlic cloves, minced
2 yellow onions, chopped
4 cups chicken stock
15 ounces canned tomatoes, chopped
3 potatoes, chopped
2 bay leaves
5 ounces baby kale
14 ounces garbanzo beans, drained

Directions:

1. Set your instant pot on Sauté mode, add oil and when hot, add chorizo, chicken and onion, stir and cook 5 minutes.
2. Add garlic, stir and cook for a further minute.
3. Add stock, tomatoes and bay leaves, kale and potatoes, salt and pepper, stir, cover and cook on High for 4 minutes.
4. Release the pressure, uncover pot, add beans, more salt and pepper if needed, stir, divide into bowls and enjoy!

(**Calories** 200|**Fat** 9 g| **Protein** 11 g| **Fiber** 2 g| **Carbohydrates** 19 g)

Endive and Ginger Soup

(**Prep Time:** 10 MIN| **Cook Time:** 25 MIN| **Serve:** 4)

Ingredients:

1 tbsp canola oil
2 tsp sesame oil
2 scallions, chopped
3 garlic cloves chopped
1 tbsp ginger, grated
1 tsp chili sauce
½ cup uncooked rice
6 cups veggie stock
1 ½ tbsp soy sauce
3 endives, trimmed and roughly chopped
Salt and white pepper to taste

Directions:

1. Set your instant pot on Sauté mode, add canola and sesame oil and heat
2. Add scallions and garlic and fry for 4 minutes.
3. Add chili sauce and ginger, stock and soy sauce, stir and cook for 3 minutes.
4. Add rice, stir, cover and cook on High for 15 minutes.
5. Release the pressure, uncover pot, add salt, pepper and endives, stir, cover again and cook on High for 5 minutes.
6. Release the pressure again, uncover pot and ladle into bowls and serve.

(**Calories** 207|**Fat** 9 g| **Protein** 11.5 g| **Fiber** 12 g| **Carbohydrates** 12 g)

Chicken Enchilada Soup

(**Prep Time:** 10 MIN| **Cook Time:** 30 MIN| **Serve:** 4)

Ingredients:

2 chicken breasts, boneless and skinless and chopped
1 ¼ cup jarred red enchilada sauce
3 cups chicken stock
14 ounces canned tomatoes, chopped
28 ounces canned black beans, drained
15 ounces canned corn, drained
Salt and black pepper to taste
4 ounces canned green chilies, chopped
2 garlic cloves, minced
1 cup white onion, chopped
½ cup quinoa
1 tsp cumin, ground
1 tsp oregano

For serving:
Chopped cilantro
Chopped avocado
Chopped red onion
Shredded cheddar cheese

Directions:

1. In your instant pot, mix chicken with enchilada sauce, stock, tomatoes, black beans, corn, green chilies, salt, pepper, garlic, onion, quinoa, cumin and oregano, stir, cover and cook on Medium heat for 25 minutes.
2. Release the pressure, uncover pot, divide soup into bowls and serve with chopped cilantro, avocado and red onion on top and with shredded cheese sprinkled all over. Enjoy!

(**Calories** 400|**Fat** 23 g| **Protein** 27 g| **Fiber** 3 g| **Carbohydrates** 23 g)

Hearty Beef and Barley Soup

(Prep Time: 10 MIN| Cook Time: 1 HOUR 10 MIN| Serve: 4)

Ingredients:

1 ½ pounds beef stew meat, chopped
2 tbsp vegetable oil
Salt and black pepper to taste
10 baby bell mushrooms, cut into quarters
3 cups mixed onion, carrots and celery
8 garlic cloves, minced
6 cups beef stock
2 bay leaves
1 cup water
½ tsp thyme, dried
1 potato, chopped
2/3 cup barley

Directions:

1. Set your instant pot on Sauté mode, add oil, heat and add meat, salt and pepper, stir, cook for 3 minutes and transfer to a plate.
2. Add mushrooms, stir, brown them for 2 minutes and transfer to the plate.
3. Add mixed veggies to the pot, stir and cook for 4 minutes.
4. Return meat, mushrooms to the pot and stir everything.
5. Also add bay leaves, thyme, water, stock, salt and pepper, stir, cover and cook on High for 16 minutes.
6. Release the pressure, uncover pot, add potatoes and barley, stir, cover and cook on Low for 1 hour.
7. Release the pressure again, stir soup, divide it into bowls and serve.

(Calories 120|Fat 3 g| **Protein** 5 g| Fiber 2 g| Carbohydrates 11 g)

Pork and Mixed Vegetable Stew

(**P**rep Time: 10 MIN| **C**ook Time: 30 MIN| **S**erve: 4)

Ingredients:

1 ½ pounds pork shoulder, cubed
1 yellow onion, chopped
3 tbsp extra virgin olive oil
1 red bell pepper, chopped
2 garlic cloves, chopped
1 rutabaga, cubed
Salt and black pepper to taste
8 baby potatoes
4 carrots, cut into big chunks
½ cup chicken stock
14 ounces canned tomatoes, chopped

Directions:

1. Set your instant pot on Sauté mode, add 2 tbsp oil and once hot, add pork and salt and pepper, brown on all sides and transfer to a bowls.
2. Add onions, garlic, bell pepper and the rest of the oil to the pot, stir and cook for 3 minutes.
3. Return pork to pot, add carrots, potatoes, rutabaga, salt, pepper, tomatoes and stock, stir, cover and cook on Medium for 20 minutes.
4. Release the pressure, uncover pot, stir stew one more time and then ladle into bowls and serve.

(**C**alories 272|**F**at 6 g| **P**rotein 24 g| **F**iber 3 g| **C**arbohydrates 2 g)

Colombian Chicken Stew

(**Prep Time:** 10 MIN| **Cook Time:** 25 MIN| **Serve:** 4)

Ingredients:

4 gold potatoes, cut into medium chunks
1 yellow onion, thinly sliced
4 big tomatoes, cut into medium chunks
1 chicken, cut into 8 pieces
Salt and black pepper to taste
2 bay leaves
Salt and black pepper to taste

Directions:

1. In your instant pot, mix potatoes with onion, chicken, tomato, bay leaves, salt and pepper, stir well, cover and cook on High for 25 minutes.
2. Release the pressure naturally, uncover, adjust seasoning and discard bay leaves. Serve in bowls for a comforting feast.

(**Calories** 270|**Fat** 12 g| **Protein** 14 g| **Fiber** 1 g| **Carbohydrates** 23 g)

Chicken and Potato Hot Pot

(**Prep Time:** 10 MIN| **Cook Time:** 1 HOUR 15 MIN| **Serve:** 6)

Ingredients:

6 chicken thighs
1 tsp vegetable oil
Salt and black pepper to taste
1 yellow onion, chopped
¼ pound baby carrots, sliced
1 celery stalk, chopped
½ tsp thyme, dried
2 tbsp tomato paste
½ cup white wine
2 cups chicken stock
15 ounces canned tomatoes, chopped
¾ pound baby carrots
1 ½ pounds new potatoes

Directions:

1. Set your instant pot on Sauté mode, add oil, heat and brown seasoned chicken for 4 minutes on each side and transfer to a plate.
2. Add celery, onion, tomato paste, carrots, thyme, salt and pepper, stir and cook for 5 minutes.
3. Add wine, bring to a boil and simmer for 3 minutes.
4. Add stock, return chicken pieces and add tomatoes. Put potatoes in the steamer basket of your pot.
5. Cover pot and cook on High for 30 minutes.
6. Release the pressure, uncover pot, take potatoes out of the pot and put them in a bowl.
7. Transfer chicken pieces to a cutting board, leave aside to cool down for a few minutes, discard bones, shred the meat with forks and return it to the stew.
8. Add more salt and pepper if needed and serve hot.

(**Calories** 271|**Fat** 2 g| **Protein** 15 g| **Fiber** 4 g| **Carbohydrates** 18 g)

Simple Fish Chowder

(**Prep** Time: 10 MIN| **Cook** Time: 10 MIN| **Serve**: 4)

Ingredients:

1 yellow onion, chopped
2 celery ribs, chopped
¾ cup bacon, chopped
1 carrot, chopped
2 garlic cloves, chopped
3 cups potatoes, cubed
4 cups chicken stock
1 pound haddock fillets
2 tbsp butter
1 cup frozen corn
Salt and white pepper to taste
1 tbsp potato starch
2 cups heavy cream

Directions:

1. Set your instant pot on Sauté mode, add butter and fry bacon until it's crispy.
2. Add garlic, celery and onion, stir and cook for 3 minutes.
3. Add the rest of the ingredients excluding cream and potato starch, cover and cook on High for 5 minutes.
4. Release the pressure naturally, uncover pot, add heavy cream mixed with potato starch, stir well, set the pot on Simmer mode and cook chowder for 3 minutes.
5. Divide the lovely thick mixture into bowls and enjoy!

(**C**alories 195|**F**at 4.4 g| **P**rotein 17 g| Fiber 2 g| Carbohydrates 21 g)

Italian Chickpea Stew

(**Prep Time:** 10 MIN| **Cook Time:** 25 MIN| **Serve:** 4)

Ingredients:

1 yellow onion, chopped
2 carrots, chopped
1 garlic head, halved
1 pound chickpeas, drained
22 ounces canned tomatoes, chopped
22 ounces water
1 tsp oregano, dried
3 bay leaves
2 tbsp olive oil
Salt and black pepper to taste
½ tsp red pepper flakes
A drizzle of olive oil for serving
2 tbsp parmesan cheese, grated

Directions:

1. Put onion, carrots, garlic, chickpeas, tomatoes, water, oregano, bay leaves, 2 tbsp olive oil, salt and pepper in your instant pot.
2. Cover, cook on High for 25 minutes and release pressure.
3. Ladle into bowls, add parmesan, pepper flakes and a drizzle of oil on top. Delicious!

(**C**alories 164|**F**at 2 g| **P**rotein 8.2 g| Fiber 9 g| **C**arbohydrates 28 g)

Moroccan Sweet Potato Stew

(**Prep Time:** 10 MIN| **Cook Time:** 20 MIN| **Serve:** 4)

Ingredients:

1 big onion, chopped
1 sweet potato, cubed
3 garlic cloves, chopped
1 celery stalk, chopped
2 carrots, chopped
1 cup green lentils
½ cup red lentils
2 cups veggie stock
¼ cup raisins
14 ounces canned tomatoes, chopped
Salt and black pepper to taste

For the spice blend:
1 tsp cumin
1 tsp turmeric
½ tsp cinnamon
1 tsp paprika
2 tsp coriander
¼ tsp ginger, grated
A pinch of cloves
A pinch of chili flakes

Directions:

1. Set your instant pot on Sauté mode, add onions and brown them for 2 minutes adding some of the stock from time to time.
2. Add garlic and cook for a further minute. Then add carrots, raisins, celery and sweet potatoes and cook, stirring for 1 more minute.
3. Add red and green lentils, stock, tomatoes, salt, pepper and the spice blend, cover and cook on High for 15 minutes.
4. Release the pressure, uncover pot, add more salt and pepper if needed, ladle into bowls and enjoy this delicious spicy feast!

(**Calories** 150|**Fat** 9 g| **Protein** 4 g| **Fiber** 3 g| **Carbohydrates** 25 g)

Spinach Stew with Turmeric

(**Prep Time:** 10 MIN| **Cook Time:** 30 MIN| **Serve:** 4)

Ingredients:

1 small yellow onion, chopped
2 tbsp olive oil
1 celery stalk, chopped
2 carrots, chopped
4 garlic cloves, minced
1 tsp turmeric
2 tsp cumin
1 tsp thyme
Salt and black pepper to taste
1 cup brown lentils, rinsed
6 cups baby spinach
4 cups veggie stock

Directions:

1. Set your instant pot on Sauté mode, add oil and fry onions, celery and carrots for 5 minutes.
2. Add garlic, turmeric, cumin, thyme, salt and pepper, stir and cook for 1 minute more.
3. Add stock and lentils, stir, cover and cook on High for 12 minutes.
4. Release the pressure for 10 minutes, uncover pot and add spinach. Adjust seasoning, divide into bowls and enjoy this vitamin-packed stew.

(**Calories** 100|**Fat** 2 g| **Protein** 7 g| Fiber 5 g| Carbohydrates 16 g)

Turkey Stew with Cranberry Sauce

(**Prep Time:** 10 MIN| **Cook Time:** 35 MIN| **Serve:** 4)

Ingredients:

1 tbsp avocado oil
1 yellow onion, chopped
3 celery stalks, chopped
2 carrots, chopped
Salt and black pepper to taste
2 cups potatoes, chopped
3 cups turkey meat, already cooked and shredded
15 ounces canned tomatoes, chopped
5 cups turkey stock
1 tbsp cranberry sauce
1 tsp dried garlic, minced

Directions:

1. Set your instant pot on Sauté mode, add oil and fry carrots, celery and onions for 3 minutes.
2. Add potatoes, tomatoes, stock, garlic, meat and cranberry sauce, stir, cover and cook on Low for 30 minutes.
3. Release the pressure, uncover and add salt and pepper to taste, stir and ladle into bowls and enjoy!

(**Calories** 210|**Fat** 4 g| **Protein** 28 g| **Fiber** 0 g| **Carbohydrates** 15 g)

Mushroom and Beef Stew

(**Prep Time:** 10 MIN| **Cook Time:** 25 MIN| **Serve:** 6)

Ingredients:

1 tbsp olive oil
1 red onion, chopped
2 pounds beef chuck, cubed
1 tsp rosemary, chopped
1 celery stalk, chopped
½ cup red wine
1 cup beef stock
Salt and black pepper to taste
1 ounce dried porcini mushrooms, chopped
2 carrots, chopped
2 tbsp flour
2 tbsp butter

Directions:

1. Set your instant pot on Sauté mode, add oil and brown beef for 5 minutes.
2. Add onion, celery, rosemary, salt, pepper, wine and stock and stir.
3. Add carrots and mushrooms, cover pot and cook on High for 15 minutes.
4. Release the pressure, uncover pot and set it on Simmer mode.
5. Meanwhile, heat up a pan over medium high heat, add butter and melt it.
6. Add flour and 6 tbsp of cooking liquid from the stew and stir well as it thickens.
7. Pour this over stew, stir, cook for 5 minutes, divide into bowls and enjoy this rich delicious stew!

(**Calories** 322|**Fat** 18 g| **Protein** 24 g| **Fiber** 3 g| **Carbohydrates** 12 g)

Oxtail and Red Wine Stew

(**Prep Time:** 10 MIN| **Cook Time:** 40 MIN| **Serve:** 4)

Ingredients:

5 pounds oxtail
1 yellow onion, chopped
Salt and black pepper to taste
3 carrots, chopped
3 celery stalks, chopped
1 garlic clove, chopped
1 parsley bunch, chopped
2 cups red wine, chopped
1 cup tomatoes, chopped
1 cup water
Sugar to taste
Mashed potato to serve

Directions:

1. In your instant pot, mix oxtail with salt, pepper, onion, carrots, celery, garlic, tomatoes, red wine, parsley, water and sugar, stir, cover and cook on Medium for 40 minutes.
2. Release the pressure, uncover pot and adjust seasoning, divide oxtail stew into bowls over mashed potato and tuck in!

(**Calories** 312|**Fat** 12 g| **Protein** 14 g| **Fiber** 14 g| **Carbohydrates** 15 g)

Tuscan Lamb Stew

(**Prep Time:** 10 MIN| **Cook Time:** 30 MIN| **Serve:** 4)

Ingredients:

2 pounds lamb shoulder, cubed
¼ cup red wine vinegar
1 tbsp garlic, minced
14 ounces canned tomatoes, chopped
2 yellow onions, chopped
1 tbsp olive oil
2 tbsp tomato paste
1 tsp oregano, dried
1 tsp basil, dried
Salt and black pepper to taste
2 bay leaves
1 red bell pepper, chopped
1 green bell pepper, chopped
1/3 cup parsley, chopped

Directions:

1. Set the pot on Sauté mode, add oil and fry onions and garlic for 2 minutes.
2. Add vinegar and cook for a further 2 minutes.
3. Add lamb, tomatoes, tomato paste, oregano, basil, salt, pepper and bay leaves, stir, cover pot and cook on High for 12 minutes.
4. Release the pressure for 10 minutes, uncover pot, discard bay leaves, add green and red pepper, more salt and pepper if needed, stir, cover and cook on High for 8 more minutes.
5. Release the pressure again, uncover, add parsley and serve this protein-rich stew in bowls.

(**Calories** 700|**Fat** 52 g| **Protein** 40 g| **Fiber** 4.4 g| **Carbohydrates** 17 g)

Beer and Lamb Stew

(**Prep Time:** 10 MIN| **Cook Time:** 15 MIN| **Serve:** 6)

Ingredients:

    2 onions, chopped
    3 pounds lamb shoulder, cut into medium chunks
    2 big potatoes, roughly chopped
    Salt and black pepper to taste
    2 thyme springs, chopped
    6 ounces dark beer
    2 cups water
    2 carrots, chopped
    ¼ cup parsley, minced

Directions:

1. Put onions and lamb in your instant pot.
2. Add salt, pepper, potatoes, thyme, water, beer and carrots, stir, cover and cook on High for 15 minutes.
3. Release the pressure, uncover pot, add parsley, more salt and pepper if needed, stir, divide into bowls and serve.

(**C**alories 236|**F**at 8 g| **P**rotein 19 g| Fiber 2.5 g| **C**arbohydrates 22 g)

German Kielbasa Stew

(**P**rep Time: 10 MIN| **C**ook Time: 10 MIN| **S**erve: 4)

Ingredients:

1 pound Kielbasa, cut into medium pieces
14 ounces canned tomatoes, chopped
2 potatoes, cut into quarters
1 small jar sauerkraut
1 onion, cut into medium chunks

Directions:

1. In your instant pot, add kielbasa, tomatoes, potatoes, sauerkraut and onion, stir, cover and cook on High for 10 minutes.
2. Release pressure, uncover pot, divide stew into bowls and serve.

(**C**alories 140|**F**at 4 g| **P**rotein 12 g| Fiber 2 g| **C**arbohydrates 11 g)

Italian Sausage Stew

(**Prep Time:** 10 MIN| **Cook Time:** 20 MIN| **Serve:** 6)

Ingredients:

1 pound Andouille sausage, crumbled
½ pound cherry tomatoes, cut into halves
1 sweet onion, chopped
1 ½ pounds gold potatoes, cubed
¾ pound collard greens, thinly sliced
1 cup chicken stock
Salt and black pepper to taste
Juice from ½ lemon

Directions:

1. Set your instant pot on Sauté mode, add sausage, stir and fry for 8 minutes.
2. Add onions and tomatoes, stir and cook 4 minutes more.
3. Add potatoes, stock, salt, pepper and collard greens, stir, cover pot and cook on High for 10 minutes.
4. Release the pressure, uncover and add more salt and pepper and lemon juice to taste, stir, ladle into bowls and enjoy!

(**Calories** 230|**Fat** 10 g| **Protein** 28 g| **Fiber** 1 g| **Carbohydrates** 24 g)

Beans & Grain Recipes

Quick Black Beans

(**Prep Time:** 6 MIN| **Cook Time:** 20 MIN| **Serve:** 4)

Ingredients:
2 tbsp extra-virgin olive oil
1 large onion, finely chopped
4 garlic cloves, minced
1 chili, seeds removed and chopped
1 lbs black beans, dry
Pinch of salt, to taste
½ tsp freshly ground black pepper
2 tbsp white vinegar
2 tsp light brown sugar
½ tbsp oregano
1/2 tsp ground cumin
2 bay leaves
3 cups low-sodium chicken stock
4 cups water
Juice of 1 lemon
Fresh cilantro, finely chopped to garnish

Directions:
1. Place the Instant Pot over medium heat and add the olive oil. Stir in the onion and sauté until translucent for about 3 minutes. Add the garlic and stir for a minutes.
2. Stir in the chili and beans. Season with salt and pepper.
3. Add the vinegar, brown sugar, oregano, cumin and bay leaves.
4. Pour in the chicken stock and water.
5. Cover the pot and set the timer on 20 minutes. Once the time is finished, carefully release the pressure and uncover the lid.
6. Add the lemon juice and stir. Serve into bowls and garnish with fresh cilantro.

(Calories 492|Fat 9.4g| Protein 26.2 g| Carbohydrates 79.5 g)

Mexican Charro Beans

(**Prep Time:** 10 MIN| **Cook Time:** 60 MIN| **Serve:** 4)

Ingredients:
2 cups pinto bean, rinsed
1 lbs bacon, coarsely chopped
1 large onion, finely chopped
1 bell pepper, diced
3 jalapenos, seeds removed and diced
4 garlic cloves, crushed
4 tomatoes, diced
1 tsp salt
½ tsp freshly ground black pepper
4 cups chicken stock
1/3 cup fresh cilantro, finely chopped

Directions:
1. Rinse the beans and place on a paper towel to dry.
2. Place the Instant Pot over medium heat and sauté. Add the bacon and stir until browned.
3. Stir in the bell pepper, jalapenos and crushed garlic.
4. Add in the tomatoes and the beans. Season with salt and pepper.
5. Pour in the chicken stock and cover the pot. Set the timer on 60 minutes. When the time is finished, carefully release the pressure and uncover the pot.
6. Transfer the cooked beans to serving bowl and top with fresh cilantro

(Calories 572|Fat 15.5g| Protein 35.3 g| Carbohydrates 73.9 g)

Mashed Beans with Jalapeno

(**Prep Time:** 10 MIN| **Cook Time:** 40 MIN| **Serve:** 4)

Ingredients:
2 lbs dried pinto beans, sorted
1 onion, finely chopped
5 cloves garlic, minced
2 jalapeno, seeds removed and diced
1 tbsp oregano
1 tbsp ground cumin
1 tsp salt
½ tsp freshly ground black pepper
5 cups chicken stock
3 cups water
4 tbsp shortening

Directions:
1. Soak the beans in water while you prepare the rest of the ingredients.
2. Place the Instant Pot over medium heat, add the onion and sauté for 3 minutes. Stir in the garlic and jalapeno.
3. Season with oregano, cumin, salt and pepper.
4. Pour in the chicken stock and water. Rinse the beans and add to the pot.
5. Add the shortening and cover the pot. Press "Bean/Chili" and set the timer for 40 minutes.
6. Once the time is finished, allow the pressure to be released automatically.
7. Uncover the pot and adjust seasonings if desired.
8. Using a handheld blender, puree the beans to your liking and serve warm.

(Calories 656|Fat 15.8g| Protein 32.9 g| Carbohydrates 97.2 g)

Pinto Beans with Garlic Bread

(**Prep Time:** 10 MIN| **Cook Time:** 40 MIN| **Serve:** 4)

Ingredients:

2 lbs pinto beans, rinsed and dry

3 tbsp vegetable base

1 tsp salt, to taste

½ tsp freshly ground black pepper

8 cups water

½ baguette, sliced diagonally

3 tbsp extra-virgin olive oil

3 garlic cloves, minced

Directions:

1. Place the Instant Pot over medium heat, add the beans with the vegetable base. Season with salt and pepper.
2. Pour in the water cover the pot. Set the timer for 40 minutes.
3. Meanwhile preheat your oven to 150 degrees Celsius Fan, and line a baking sheet with parchment paper.
4. Slice the baguette diagonally. Line the slices on the baking sheet.
5. In a small bowl, mix the olive oil with the minced garlic.
6. Brush the bread slices with olive oil and garlic, on both sides.
7. Place the baking sheet in the oven until golden, flip the slices.
8. Serve the beans warm with crispy garlic bread.

(Calories 690|Fat 11.7g| Protein 28.8 g| Carbohydrates 117.3 g)

Quick Lemon Rice

(**Prep Time:** 10 MIN| **Cook Time:** 15 MIN| **Serve:** 4)

Ingredients:

1 ½ cups low sodium vegetable stock

1/2 cup water

3 tbsp vegetable oil

Juice and zest of 1 lemon

2 cups parboiled or long grain rice

1 tsp salt

Fresh cilantro, to garnish

Directions:
1. Place the Instant Pot over medium heat and add all the ingredients in it, except the cilantro.
2. Cover the pot and press "Rice" and set the timer for 15 minutes.
3. Once the time is finished, carefully release the pressure and uncover the lid.
4. Stir the rice and transfer to serving bowl. Garnish with fresh cilantro.
5. Serve warm as a side dish for meat or grains.

(Calories 439|Fat 10.9g| Protein 7 g| Carbohydrates 76.5 g)

Black Bean Avocado Bowl

(**Prep Time:** 10 MIN| **Cook Time:** 15 MIN| **Serve:** 4)

Ingredients:
2 tbsp olive oil
1 red onion, finely chopped
2 green bell pepper , cubed
1 tsp salt
½ tsp freshly ground black pepper
½ tsp ground cumin
2 cup quinoa , presoaked
2 cup salsa
3 cups black beans, cooked
2 cup water
1 ripe avocado, sliced
2 scallion, sliced
Fresh parsley, to garnish
1 lime, cut in wedges

Directions:
1. Place the Instant Pot over medium heat and add the olive oil and onion, sauté for 5 minutes then add the peppers.
2. Season with salt, pepper and cumin and stir for 3 minutes.
3. Add in the presoaked quinoa with the salsa and beans. And stir for minute. Pour in the water and cover the pot. Select "Rice" and set the timer on 10 minutes.
4. Once the time is finished allow the pressure to be release automatically.
5. Transfer the quinoa mixture into serving bowl and top with avocado and scallions. Sprinkle some fresh parsley and serve with lime wedges.

(Calories 635|Fat 22.9g| Protein 22.3 g| Carbohydrates 92.7 g)

Pinto Beans Risotto with Pepper Jack Cheese

(**Prep Time:** 10 MIN| **Cook Time:** 10 MIN| **Serve:** 4)

Ingredients:
2 tbsp extra-virgin olive oil
1 medium onion, finely chopped
2 garlic cloves, crushed
2 cups Arborio rice
4 cups low sodium vegetable stock
1 can cooked beans, pinto is fine
2 chili, diced
1 wrap of chard leaves, chopped
2/3 cup pepper jack cheese, grated
1 tsp salt

Directions:
1. Place the Instant Pot over medium heat and add the olive oil and onion. Sauté the onion until translucent for about 5 minutes.
2. Stir in the garlic and rice. Pour in two thirds of the vegetable stock and cover the pot.
3. Set the timer for 5 minutes then carefully release the pressure once the time is finished.
4. Uncover the pot and add the beans, chili and chard and the rest of the vegetable stock. Season with salt.
5. Cook until the risotto is creamy. Add the pepper jack cheese and remove the pot from the heat.
6. Serve the rice hot with extra cheese if you like.

(Calories 580|Fat 18.8g| Protein 15.7 g| Carbohydrates 85.2 g)

Risotto with Salmon Crumble

(**P**rep Time: 10 MIN| **C**ook Time: 10 MIN| **S**erve: 4)

Ingredients:
2 cups peas
6 smoked bacon, sliced
2 tbsp extra-virgin olive oil
1 medium onion, diced
2 cups Arborio rice
3 ¼ cups vegetable stock
½ cup white vinegar
¼ cup Parmesan cheese, grated
2 salmon fillet, precooked

Directions:
1. Heat the olive oil in the Instant Pot over medium heat and sauté the onion for 3 minutes. Add the bacon slices and stir until crispy.
2. Transfer the bacon slices to a plate and place aside.
3. Add the rice into the pot and stir for a minute. Pour in 3 cups of the vegetable stock and the vinegar.
4. Cover the pot and set the timer for 6 minutes. When the time is finished, carefully release the pressure and uncover the pot.
5. Transfer the rice into serving bowl.
6. In a food processor blend the peas with the cheese. Add the remaining stock and blend for 3 seconds.
7. Add the bacon and the precooked salmon and pulse twice.
8. Top the rice with the bacon crumble mixture and serve warm.

(Calories 539|Fat 27.4g| Protein 40.1 g| Carbohydrates 32.3 g)

Barley Mushroom Risotto

(**Prep Time:** 10 MIN| **Cook Time:** 30 MIN| **Serve:** 4)

Ingredients:

2 cups yellow onions, chopped
1 tbsp olive oil
1 cup pearl barley
1 tsp fennel seeds
2 tbsp black barley
3 cups chicken stock
1/3 cup dry sherry
1 and ½ cups water
1.5 ounce dried mushrooms
Salt and black pepper to taste
¼ cup parmesan, grated

Directions:

1. Set your instant pot on Sauté mode, add oil and fry fennel and onions for 4 minutes.
2. Add barley and black barley, sherry, mushrooms, stock, water, salt and pepper and stir well.
3. Cover, cook on High for 18 minutes, release the pressure, uncover pot and set it on Simmer mode.
4. Add more salt and pepper if needed, stir and cook for 5 more minutes.
5. Divide into bowls, add parmesan on top and serve.

(**Calories** 200|**Fat** 5 g| **Protein** 7.6 g| **Fiber** 6.1 g| **Carbohydrates** 31 g)

Barley and Parmesan Risotto

(**P**rep Time: 10 MIN| **C**ook Time: 25 MIN| **S**erve: 4)

Ingredients:

1 tbsp extra virgin olive oil
1 tbsp butter
1 white onion, chopped
1 garlic clove, minced
1 ½ cups pearl barley, rinsed
1 celery stalk, chopped
1/3 cup mushrooms, chopped
4 cups veggie stock
2 ¼ cups water
Salt and black pepper to taste
3 tbsp parsley, chopped
1 cup parmesan cheese, grated

Directions:

1. Set your instant pot on Sauté mode, add oil and butter and fry onion and garlic for 4 minutes.
2. Add celery and barley and toss to coat.
3. Add mushrooms, water, stock, salt and pepper, stir, cover pot and cook on High for 18 minutes.
4. Release the pressure, uncover pot, add cheese and parsley and more salt and pepper if needed, stir for 2 minutes, divide risotto into bowls and enjoy!

(**C**alories 170|**F**at 6 g| **P**rotein 8 g| Fiber 4.5 g| **C**arbohydrates 30 g)

Cracked Wheat a la Mumbai

(**Prep Time:** 10 MIN| **Cook Time:** 15 MIN| **Serve:** 4)

Ingredients:

½ cup cracked whole wheat
1 ½ cups water
2 tomatoes, chopped
2 small potatoes, cubed
5 cauliflower florets, chopped
Salt and black pepper to taste
¼ tsp mustard seeds
¼ tsp cumin seeds
1 tsp ginger, grated
1 tbsp chana dal
2 garlic cloves, minced
1 yellow onion, chopped
2 curry leaves
3 tbsp vegetable oil
¼ tsp garam masala
A few cilantro leaves, chopped for serving

Directions:

1. Set your instant pot on Sauté mode, add oil and heat cumin and mustard seeds for 1 minute.
2. Add onion, garlic, chana dal, garam masala, ginger and curry leaves, stir and fry for 2 minutes.
3. Add cauliflower, potatoes and tomatoes and cook for a further 4 minutes.
4. Add wheat, salt, pepper and water, stir, cover and cook on High for 5 minutes.
5. Release the pressure, uncover and transfer wheat and veggies to plates, sprinkle cilantro on top and serve.

(**Calories** 145|**Fat** 2 g| **Protein** 7 g| **Fiber** 4 g| **Carbohydrates** 16 g)

Bulgur Pilaf

(**Prep** Time: 10 MIN| **Cook** Time: 21 MIN| **Serve**: 6)

Ingredients:

2 cups red onions, chopped
2 tbsp extra virgin olive oil
Salt and black pepper to taste
2 tsp ginger, grated
¼ cup dill, chopped
1 garlic clove, minced
1 ½ cups bulgur
¼ cup mint, chopped
¼ cup parsley, chopped
3 tbsp lemon juice
½ tsp cumin, ground
½ tsp turmeric, ground
2 cups veggie stock
1 ½ cups carrot, chopped
½ cup walnuts, toasted and chopped

Directions:

1. Set your instant pot on Sauté mode, add oil and heat
2. Add onions and allow them to sweat at a low temperature for 12 minutes.
3. Add garlic, stir and cook for 1 minute.
4. Add cumin, turmeric and bulgur and stir to combine for 1 minute.
5. Add ginger, stock, carrots, salt and pepper, stir, cover and cook on High for 5 minutes.
6. Release the pressure, uncover pot, add mint, dill, parsley, lemon juice and more salt and pepper if needed and stir gently.
7. Divide among plates and serve with walnuts sprinkled on top.

(**Calories** 270|**Fat** 12 g| **Protein** 7 g| **Fiber** 8 g| **Carbohydrates** 38 g)

Israeli Couscous

(**Prep Time:** 10 MIN| **Cook Time:** 8 MIN| **Serve:** 4)

Ingredients:

½ cup red onion, chopped
½ tsp sesame oil
¼ cup red bell pepper, chopped
1 cup couscous, rinsed
1 and ½ cups veggie stock
½ tsp cinnamon, ground
¼ tsp coriander, ground
Salt and black pepper to taste
2 tbsp red wine vinegar

Directions:

1. Set your instant pot on Sauté mode, add oil and fry bell pepper and onion for 5 minutes.
2. Add couscous, coriander, stock, cinnamon, salt, pepper and vinegar, stir, cover and cook on High for 3 minutes.
3. Release the pressure, uncover and spoon couscous into bowls for a delicious vegetarian meal.

(**Calories** 150|**Fat** 1 g| **Protein** 6 g| Fiber 5 g| Carbohydrates 33 g)

Creamy Millet and Peas

(**Prep Time:** 10 MIN| **Cook Time:** 20 MIN| **Serve:** 4)

Ingredients:
1 cup split mung beans
1 bay leaf
1 cup carrot, chopped
1 cup millet, chopped
1 cup celery, chopped
4 cardamom pods
6 cups water
1 ½ cups fresh peas
1 tbsp lime juice
¼ cup cilantro, chopped
1 tbsp ghee
1 tsp coriander seeds, ground
1 tsp fennel seeds, ground
½ tsp cumin seeds, ground
½ tsp turmeric powder
Salt and black pepper to tasted
½ tsp ginger, grated

Directions:
1. Set your instant pot on Sauté mode, add mung beans and cook until they are golden.
2. Add millet, carrot, bay leaf, celery, cardamom, water, salt and pepper, stir, cover and cook on High for 10 minutes.
3. Release pressure, uncover pot and set it on Simmer mode.
4. Heat up a pan with the ghee over medium heat, add coriander, fennel, cumin, turmeric and ginger, stir and cook for 2 minutes.
5. Add this spicy sauce to your instant pot, stir, add more salt and pepper, peas and lime juice, simmer for 5 minutes before serving on plates with cilantro garnish.

(**Calories** 231|**Fat** 2 g| **Protein** 11 g| **Fiber** 8 g| **Carbohydrates** 41 g)

Spicy Oats

(**Prep Time:** 10 MIN| **Cook Time:** 15 MIN| **Serve:** 4)

Ingredients:

1 cup steel-cut oats
1 ½ cups water
1 carrots, chopped
½ green bell pepper, chopped
1 inch ginger, grated
1 Thai green chili, chopped
2 curry leaves
¼ tsp mustard seeds
½ tsp urad dal
A pinch of asafetida powder
1 ½ tbsp canola oil
A pinch of turmeric powder
Salt to taste

Directions:

1. Put oats in your instant pot, add water, cover and cook on High for 7 minutes.
2. Heat up a pan with the oil over medium heat, add mustard seeds, urad dal, asafetida powder, turmeric, chili pepper, curry leaf, ginger, carrot and bell pepper, stir and fry for 5 minutes.
3. Release pressure from the pot, uncover, add oats to the pan, also add salt and fold spice mixture through oats before dishing into bowls and enjoying!

(**Calories** 211|**Fat** 6.3 g| **Protein** 7.5 g| **Fiber** 5.6 g| **Carbohydrates** 32 g)

Olive and Feta Quinoa

(**Prep Time:** 10 MIN| **Cook Time:** 2 MIN| **Serve:** 4)

Ingredients:

1 ½ cups quinoa
1 red bell pepper, chopped
3 celery stalks, chopped
Salt to taste
4 cups spinach
2 tomatoes, chopped
1 ½ cups chicken stock
½ cup black olives, pitted and chopped
½ cup feta cheese, crumbled
1/3 cup jarred pesto
¼ cup almonds, sliced

Directions:

1. In your instant pot, mix quinoa with bell pepper, celery, spinach, stock and salt, stir gently, cover and cook on High for 2 minutes.
2. Release the pressure for 10 minutes, uncover pot and add tomatoes, pesto and olives, stir and spoon onto plates.
3. Add cheese and almonds on top, toss to coat and serve.

(**Calories** 249|**Fat** 7 g| **Protein** 7.4 g| **Fiber** 5.4 g| **Carbohydrates** 20 g)

Mexican Cranberry Beans

(Prep Time: 10 MIN| Cook Time: 20 MIN| Serve: 6)

Ingredients:

1 pound cranberry beans, soaked for 8 hours and drained
3 ¼ cups water
4 garlic cloves, minced
1 yellow onion, chopped
1 ½ tsp cumin
1/3 cup cilantro, chopped
1 tbsp chili powder
1 tsp oregano, dried
Salt and black pepper to taste
Cooker rice for serving

Directions:

1. Put beans in your instant pot, add the water, garlic and onion, cover and cook on High for 20 minutes.
2. Release the pressure, uncover pot and add cumin, cilantro, oregano, chili powder, salt and pepper and stir well.
3. Mash the mixture a bit using a potato masher, serve on rice and enjoy!

(**C**alories 100|**F**at 1 g| **P**rotein 6 g| Fiber 4 g| **C**arbohydrates 10 g)

Cranberry and Kale Pasta

(**Prep Time:** 10 MIN| **Cook Time:** 20 MIN| **Serve:** 8)

Ingredients:

2 cups dried cranberry beans, soaked for 8 hours and drained
7 garlic cloves, minced
6 cups water
2 celery ribs, chopped
1 yellow onion, chopped
1 tsp rosemary, chopped
¼ tsp red pepper flakes
26 ounces canned tomatoes, chopped
3 tsp basil, dried
½ tsp smoked paprika
2 tsp oregano, dried
Salt and black pepper to taste
2 cups small pasta
3 tbsp nutritional yeast
10 ounces kale leaves

Directions:

1. Set your instant pot on Sauté mode, add onion, celery, garlic, pepper flakes, rosemary and a pinch of salt and brown for 2 minutes.
2. Add tomatoes, basil, oregano and paprika and cook for 1 minute.
3. Add beans, 6 cups water, cover pot and cook on High for 10 minutes.
4. Release the pressure, uncover pot, add pasta, yeast, kale, salt and pepper, stir and set the pot on Sauté mode again.
5. Cook for 5 minutes more, before dividing into bowls and serving this nutrition-packed feast.

(Calories 330|Fat 14 g| **Protein** 18 g| **Fiber** 10 g| **Carbohydrates** 32 g)

Shiitake and Cranberry Bean Ensemble

(**Prep Time:** 10 MIN| **Cook Time:** 15 MIN| **Serve:** 6)

Ingredients:

1 ½ cups cranberry beans, soaked for 8 hours and drained
4 inch kombu piece, sliced
4 bacon slices, chopped
Salt and black pepper to taste
8 cups kale, chopped
4 ounces shiitake mushrooms, chopped
½ tsp garlic powder
1 tsp extra virgin olive oil

Directions:

1. Put beans in your instant pot, add 2 inches water, salt, pepper, kombu, cover and cook on High for 8 minutes.
2. Release the pressure and uncover pot, transfer beans and cooking liquid to a pot and set aside.
3. Set your pot on Sauté mode, add oil and heat.
4. Add garlic powder, bacon, mushrooms, salt, pepper and ¾ cup cooking liquid from the pot, stir well and cook for 1 minute.
5. Cover pot, cook on High for 3 minutes and release pressure.
6. Add beans and kale, stir to mix the ingredients evenly and divide into bowls.

(**C**alories 228|**F**at 2 g| **P**rotein 9 g| Fiber 14 g| **C**arbohydrates 41 g)

Cranberry Bean Chili

(**Prep Time:** 10 MIN| **Cook Time:** 40 MIN| **Serve:** 8)

Ingredients:

- 1 pound cranberry beans, soaked in water for 7 hours and drained
- 5 cups water
- 14 ounces canned tomatoes and green chilies, chopped
- ¼ cup millet
- ½ cup bulgur
- 1 ½ tsp cumin, ground
- 2 tbsp tomato paste
- 1 tsp chili powder
- 1 tsp garlic, minced
- ½ tsp liquid smoke
- 1 tsp oregano, dried
- ½ tsp Ancho chili powder
- Salt and black pepper to taste
- Hot sauce for serving
- Pickled jalapenos for serving

Directions:

1. Put beans and 3 cups water in your instant pot, cover and cook on High for 25 minutes.
2. Release the pressure fast and add all the rest of the ingredients, stir, cover and cook on High for 10 minutes more.
3. Release the pressure again, uncover, ladle into bowls and serve with hot sauce on top and pickled jalapenos on the side.

(**Calories** 200|**Fat** 13 g| **Protein** 15 g| **Fiber** 4 g| **Carbohydrates** 14 g)

Indian Lentils

(Prep Time: 10 MIN| Cook Time: 20 MIN| Serve: 4)

Ingredients:

3 tsp butter
1 tsp extra virgin olive oil
1 cup red lentils
1 yellow onion, chopped
2 tsp cumin
¼ tsp coriander
¼ tsp garlic powder
¼ tsp turmeric
¼ tsp Aleppo pepper
¼ tsp red pepper flakes
Salt and black pepper to taste
3 cups chicken stock

Directions:

1. Set your instant pot on Sauté mode, add butter and oil and fry onions for 4 minutes.
2. Add cumin, coriander, garlic powder, turmeric, Aleppo pepper and pepper flakes and cook for 2 minutes.
3. Add lentils and stock, stir, cover and cook on High for 15 minutes.
4. Release the pressure, uncover and ladle into bowls for a spicy winter meal!

(**Calories** 198|**Fat** 6 g| **Protein** 10.4 g| **Fiber** 8.7 g| **Carbohydrates** 26 g)

Chickpea Curry

(**P**rep Time: 10 MIN| **C**ook Time: 21 MIN| **S**erve: 6)

Ingredients:

4 tsp cumin seeds
8 tsp olive oil
4 tsp garlic, minced
1 yellow onion, finely chopped
2 tsp garam masala
2 tsp coriander, ground
2 tsp turmeric, ground
3 cups chickpeas, already cooked, drained and rinsed
28 ounces canned tomatoes, chopped
3 potatoes, cubed
½ cup water
Salt and black pepper to taste
Basmati rice, already cooked for serving
Some cilantro, chopped for serving

Directions:

1. Set your instant pot on Sauté mode, add oil and heat
2. Add cumin seeds and stir for 30 seconds.
3. Add onion, stir and cook for 5 more minutes.
4. Add garlic, garam masala, coriander, turmeric, tomatoes, potatoes, chickpeas, water, salt and pepper, cover and cook on High for 15 minutes.
5. Release the pressure, uncover pot, ladle chickpeas curry on plates and serve with rice on the side and cilantro sprinkled on top.

(**C**alories 384|**F**at 8.3 g| **P**rotein 11.5 g| **F**iber 12 g| **C**arbohydrates 384 g)

Chickpeas and Dumplings

(Prep Time: 10 MIN| Cook Time: 17 MIN| Serve: 4)

Ingredients:

4 carrots, chopped
1 yellow onion, chopped
4 red baby potatoes, chopped
2 garlic cloves, minced
28 ounces veggie stock
1 veggie bouillon cube
2 cans chickpeas
Salt and black pepper to taste
A pinch of cayenne pepper
2 green onions, chopped
2 celery stalks, chopped
1 ¾ tsp baking powder
¾ cup white flour
½ tsp dill, dried
½ cup milk

Directions:

1. Set your instant pot on Sauté mode, add onion and garlic and a splash of stock and cook for 3 minutes.
2. Add potatoes, carrots, chickpeas, stock, bouillon cube, salt, pepper and cayenne pepper, stir, cover and cook on High for 7 minutes.
3. Release the pressure, uncover and add celery and green onions to the pot, stir and set aside.
4. Meanwhile, in a bowl, mix flour with baking powder, a pinch of salt, dill and milk and stir very well.
5. Shape 10 dumplings with your hands, heat up soup on Simmer mode, drop dumplings into pot, cover it and cook on Steam mode for 10 minute.
6. Uncover pot, add more salt and pepper if needed, stir, dish into bowls and enjoy!

(Calories 300|**Fat** 5 g| **Protein** 12 g| Fiber 10 g| **Carbohydrates** 56 g)

Chickpea Pesto

(**Prep Time:** 10 MIN| **Cook Time:** 20 MIN| **Serve:** 4)

Ingredients:

For the pesto:
¼ cup extra virgin olive oil
1 ½ cups basil
1 garlic clove, minced
¼ cup parmesan cheese, grated
1 tbsp pine nuts, roasted

For the chickpeas:
12 ounces chickpeas, soaked for 8 hours
1 yellow onion, chopped
2 tbsp extra virgin olive oil
2 carrots, chopped
14 ounces canned tomatoes
4 cups chicken stock
¼ cup parmesan, grated

Directions:

1. In your blender, mix basil with ¼ cup cheese, 1 garlic clove, pine nuts, ¼ cup oil and some salt and blend very well.
2. Transfer to a bowl and set aside.
3. Set your instant pot on Sauté mode, add 2 tbsp oil and fry onion and some salt for 3 minutes.
4. Add carrots, chickpeas, tomatoes, stock, salt and pepper to taste, stir, cover and cook on High for 10 minutes.
5. Release the pressure fast, uncover pot and transfer chickpea mixture into bowls.
6. Add pesto on top and sprinkle ¼ cup parmesan over before serving.

(**Calories** 100|**Fat** 3.5 g| **Protein** 3.2 g| **Fiber** 3 g| **Carbohydrates** 13 g)

Kidney Bean Etouffee

(Prep Time: 10 MIN| Cook Time: 30 MIN| Serve: 4)

Ingredients:

1 tbsp vegetable oil
2 cups bell pepper, chopped
1 cup yellow onion, chopped
2 tsp garlic, chopped
1 cup water
3 bay leaves
1 cup red kidney beans, soaked for 12 hours and drained
2 tsp smoked paprika
1 ½ thyme, dried
A pinch of cayenne pepper
2 tsp marjoram, dried
1 tsp oregano, dried
14 ounces canned tomatoes, crushed
½ tsp liquid smoke
Salt and black pepper to taste
Cooked rice for serving

Directions:

1. Set your instant pot on Sauté mode, add oil and fry onion for 5 minutes.
2. Add bell pepper and garlic, stir and cook 5 more minutes.
3. Add beans, bay leaves, water, thyme, paprika, cayenne and marjoram, stir, cover and cook on High for 15 minutes.
4. Release the pressure, uncover pot, discard bay leaves, add oregano, tomatoes, liquid smoke, salt and pepper to taste, stir, cover pot again and cook on High for 3 more minutes.
5. Release the pressure naturally, uncover and ladle bean mixture onto plates on top of cooked rice.

(Calories 189|Fat 3 g| Protein 11.3 g| Fiber 10 g| Carbohydrates 32 g)

Rajma Kidney Bean Curry

(**Prep Time:** 10 MIN| **Cook Time:** 1HOUR 10 MIN| **Serve:** 8)

Ingredients:

2 cups red kidney beans, soaked for 8 hours and drained
1 inch piece ginger, chopped
1 yellow onion, chopped
4 garlic cloves, chopped
2 tbsp vegetable oil
2 tsp ghee
2 red chili peppers, dried and crushed
Salt and black pepper to taste
6 cloves
1 tsp cumin seeds
1 tsp turmeric, ground
1 tsp cumin, ground
1 tsp coriander, ground
2 tomatoes chopped
2 cups water
1 tsp sugar
1 tsp red pepper, ground
2 tsp garam masala
¼ cup cilantro, chopped

Directions:

1. Grind ginger, garlic and onion using a mortar and pestle and transfer paste to a bowl.
2. Set your instant pot on Sauté mode, add ghee and oil and fry red chili pepper, cloves and cumin seeds for 3 minutes. Add onion paste, stir and cook for 3 more minutes.
3. Add coriander, cumin and turmeric, stir and cook for 30 seconds.
4. Then add tomatoes and cook 5 minutes.
5. Add beans, 2 cups water, salt, pepper and sugar, stir, cover and cook on High for 40 mins.
6. Switch instant pot to Low and cook for 10 minutes more.
7. Release the pressure, uncover pot, add red pepper, garam masala and cilantro, stir and serve on plates for a very spicy meal.

(**Calories** 224|**Fat** 4 g| **Protein** 12 g| **Fiber** 7 g| **Carbohydrates** 30 g)

Cajun Kidney Beans

(Prep Time: 10 MIN| Cook Time: 25 MIN| Serve: 8)

Ingredients:

1 pound red kidney beans, soaked for 8 hours and drained
2 yellow onions, chopped
8 ounces smoked Cajun Tasso, chopped
1 celery rib, chopped
2 tbsp garlic, minced
1 green bell pepper, chopped
2 tsp thyme, dried
3 tbsp extra virgin olive oil
2 bay leaves
Cajun seasoning to taste
4 green onions, chopped
Hot sauce to taste

Directions:

1. Set your instant pot on Sauté mode, add oil and heat
2. Add Tasso and cook for 5 minutes and transfer to a bowl.
3. Add onions and Cajun seasoning to the pot, stir and cook for 10 minutes.
4. Add garlic and cook 5 minutes.
5. Add bell pepper and celery and cook a further 5 minutes.
6. Add beans, water to cover the ingredients, bay leaves, thyme, cover and cook on High for 15 minutes.
7. Release the pressure fast, uncover and add Tasso and leave aside for 5 minutes.
8. Dish beans and Tasso mixture onto plates, garnish with green onions and serve with hot sauce to taste.

(**Calories** 240|**Fat** 3 g| **Protein** 5 g| **Fiber** 4 g| **Carbohydrates** 16 g)

Black Beans and Chorizo

(**Prep Time:** 10 MIN| **Cook Time:** 45 MIN| **Serve:** 6)

Ingredients:

1 tbsp vegetable oil
6 ounces chorizo, chopped
1 yellow onion, cut into half
1 pound black beans, soaked for 8 hours and drained
6 garlic cloves, minced
2 bay leaves
1 orange, cut into half
2 quarts chicken stock
Salt to taste
Chopped cilantro, chopped for serving

Directions:

1. Set your instant pot on Sauté mode, add oil and fry chorizo for 2 minutes.
2. Add onion, beans, garlic, bay leaves, orange, salt and stock, stir, cover and cook on High for 40 minutes.
3. Release the pressure naturally, uncover your pot, discard bay leaves, onion and orange, add more salt and cilantro, stir, divide into bowls and serve.

(**Calories** 230|**Fat** 7.7 g| **Protein** 12.5 g| Fiber 8 g| **Carbohydrates** 30 g)

Spicy Mexican Black Beans

(**Prep Time:** 10 MIN| **Cook Time:** 35 MIN| **Serve:** 8)

Ingredients:

16 ounces black beans, soaked overnight and drained
2 tbsp chili powder
1 yellow onion, chopped
4 garlic cloves, minced
2 tsp cumin, ground
1 tsp chipotle powder
2 tsp oregano, dried
8 ounces tomato paste
2 quarts water
4 tbsp sunflower oil
Salt to taste

Directions:

1. In your instant pot, mix beans with garlic, onion, chili powder, chipotle powder, cumin, oregano, tomato paste, water, oil and salt, stir, cover and cook on High for 30 minutes.
2. Release the pressure, uncover and set on Simmer mode.
3. Add more salt if needed and cook for 3 minutes. Then divide into bowls and serve.

(**Calories** 180|**Fat** 3 g| **Protein** 10 g| **Fiber** 7 g| **Carbohydrates** 7 g)

Chili Lime Black Beans

(**Prep Time:** 10 MIN| **Cook Time:** 42 MIN| **Serve:** 4)

Ingredients:

2 cups black beans, soaked for 8 hours and drained
2 tbsp red palm oil
1 yellow onion, chopped
Salt to taste
4 garlic cloves, minced
1 tbsp chili powder
1 tsp smoked paprika
3 cups water
Juice from 1 lime

Directions:

1. Set your instant pot on Sauté mode, add oil and cook garlic and onion for 2 minutes.
2. Add beans, chili powder, paprika, salt and water, cover and cook on High for 40 minutes.
3. Release the pressure naturally, uncover and add lime juice and more salt. Dish up into bowls and enjoy!

(**Calories** 200|**Fat** 3 g| **Protein** 7 g| **Fiber** 5 g| **Carbohydrates** 22 g)

White Beans and Shrimp

(**Prep Time:** 10 MIN| **Cook Time:** 35 MIN| **Serve:** 8)

Ingredients:

1 pound white beans, soaked for 8 hours and drained
1 garlic clove, minced
2 yellow onions, chopped
1 green bell pepper, chopped
1 celery rib, chopped
4 parsley springs, chopped
2 cups seafood stock
2 bay leaves
3 tbsp canola oil
Creole seasoning to taste
1 pound shrimp, peeled and deveined
Cooked rice for serving
Hot sauce for serving

Directions:

1. Set your instant pot on Sauté mode, add oil and fry onions with Creole seasoning for 5 minutes.
2. Add garlic and cook 5 minutes more.
3. Then add bell pepper and celery and cook for a further 5 minutes.
4. Add beans, stock and some water to cover all the ingredients.
5. Add bay leaves and parsley, stir, cover and cook on High for 15 minutes.
6. Release the pressure, uncover and add shrimp, cover pot and set aside for 10 minutes.
7. Spoon beans and shrimp on top of cooked rice and serve with hot sauce.

(**Calories** 340|**Fat** 11 g| **Protein** 21 g| **Fiber** 11 g| **Carbohydrates** 38 g)

Grandma's Baked Beans

(**Prep Time:** 10 MIN| **Cook Time:** 55 MIN| **Serve:** 4)

Ingredients:

1 pound white beans, soaked for 8 hours and drained
½ cup molasses
2 garlic cloves, minced
1 yellow onion, chopped
½ cup maple syrup
1 tbsp mustard powder
Salt and black pepper to taste
7 cups water
1/8 cup balsamic vinegar

Directions:

1. Put the beans and 3 cups water in your instant pot, cover and cook on High for 10 minutes.
2. Release pressure naturally, uncover and drain beans and return them to the pot.
3. Add 4 cups water, molasses, garlic, onion, maple syrup, vinegar, salt and pepper, stir, cover and cook on High for 45 minutes.
4. Release the pressure again, uncover and dish into bowls and serve.

(**Calories** 152|**Fat** 5.5 g| **Protein** 5.5 g| **Fiber** 5.4 g| **Carbohydrates** 21 g)

Bengal Mung Beans

(**Prep Time:** 10 MIN| **Cook Time:** 17 MIN| **Serve:** 4)

Ingredients:

¾ cup mung beans, soaked for 15 minutes and drained
1 small red onion, chopped
½ tsp cumin seeds
½ tsp coconut oil
½ cup brown rice, soaked for 15 minutes and drained
28 ounces canned tomatoes, crushed
5 garlic cloves, minced
1 inch ginger piece, chopped
1 tsp coriander, ground
1 tsp turmeric
½ tsp garam masala
A pinch of cayenne
Salt and black pepper to taste
1 tsp lemon juice
4 cups water

Directions:

1. In your food processor, mix tomatoes with onions, ginger, garlic, coriander, turmeric, cayenne, salt, pepper and garam masala and blend well.
2. Set your instant pot on Sauté mode, add oil and fry cumin seeds for 2 minutes.
3. Add tomato mixture, stir and cook for 15 minutes.
4. Add beans, rice, water, salt, pepper and lemon juice, cover and cook on High for 15 minutes.
5. Release the pressure for 10 minutes, uncover and stir again, before dishing into bowls and enjoying!

(**Calories** 180|**Fat** 1 g| **Protein** 7 g| **Fiber** 15 g| **Carbohydrates** 39 g)

Indian Style Mung Feast

(**P**rep Time: 10 MIN| **C**ook Time: 1 HOUR| **S**erve: 4)

Ingredients:

1 cup mung beans, soaked for 6 hours and drained
1 tsp cumin seeds
2 tsp ghee
A pinch of cayenne pepper
2 tsp turmeric
½ tbsp coriander, ground
1 tsp cumin, ground
1 tbsp ginger, grated
1 yellow onion, chopped
1 tomato, chopped
1 ½ cups water
4 jalapeno peppers, chopped
¼ cup cilantro, chopped
Salt and black pepper to taste

Directions:

1. Set your instant pot on Sauté mode, add ghee and fry cumin seeds for 1 minute.
2. Add cayenne, turmeric, coriander, cumin and ginger and cook a further 2 minutes.
3. Add jalapenos and onion, stir and cook for 4 minutes, before adding beans and water, salt and pepper. Then cover and cook on High for 20 minutes.
4. Release the pressure, uncover, add tomatoes, plus more salt and pepper if needed and set the pot on Simmer mode.
5. Stir and simmer for 20 minutes more, add cilantro and serve in brightly colored bowls to compliment your Indian style feast!

(**C**alories 210|**F**at 4.3 g| **P**rotein 13 g| **F**iber 8.7 g| **C**arbohydrates 33 g)

Navy Beans with Bacon and Cabbage

(**Prep Time:** 10 MIN| **Cook Time:** 40 MIN| **Serve:** 8)

Ingredients:

6 bacon slices, chopped
1 yellow onion, chopped
1 ½ cups navy beans, soaked for 8 hours and drained
¼ tsp cloves
3 cups chicken stock
1 bay leaf
1 cabbage head, chopped
3 tbsp honey
3 tbsp white wine vinegar
Salt and black pepper to taste

Directions:

1. Set your instant pot on Sauté mode, add bacon, stir and brown it for 4 minutes before adding onions, then cook for 4 more minutes.
2. Add stock, beans, clove and bay leaf, stir, cover and cook on High for 35 minutes.
3. Release the pressure fast, uncover, add vinegar, honey and cabbage, cover and cook on High for 12 minutes more.
4. Release pressure again, uncover and add salt and pepper to taste, before dividing into bowls.

(Calories 150|Fat 1 g| Protein 7 g| Fiber9.5 g| Carbohydrates 27 g)

Full Mudammas

(**Prep** Time: 10 MIN| **C**ook Time: 25 MIN| **S**erve: 2)

Ingredients:

2 cups cooked fava beans
4 roasted garlic cloves, chopped
1 small red onion, chopped
1 tbsp olive oil
1 tsp cumin
½ cup water
Salt and black pepper to taste
Juice from 2 lemons
1 egg, hard boiled, peeled and sliced
1 tomato, finely chopped
1 yellow onion, cut into thin rigs
A pinch of red chili flakes
A pinch of paprika

Directions:

1. Set your instant pot on Sauté mode, add oil and fry red onion for 3 minutes.
2. Add cumin and garlic, stir and cook for a minute, before adding beans, salt, pepper and water, then covering and cooking on High for 15 minutes.
3. Release the pressure, uncover and set pot on Simmer mode and cook for 10 more minutes.
4. Transfer to a bowl, add more salt, pepper and lemon juice and mash using a potato masher.
5. Garnish with egg slices, tomato pieces, yellow onion rings, red chili flakes and paprika sprinkled on top. Serve this pretty color-fest hot!

(**C**alories 154|**F**at 1.4 g| **P**rotein 8.6 g| Fiber 3 g| Carbohydrates 30 g)

Butter Beans and Bacon

(**Prep Time:** 10 MIN| **Cook Time:** 1 HOUR| **Serve:** 8)

Ingredients:

1 pound butter beans, soaked for 8 hours and drained
1 pound bacon, chopped
4 cups water
1 garlic clove, minced
1 jalapeno pepper, chopped
½ tsp cumin, ground
12 ounces beer
Salt and black pepper to taste

Directions:

1. Set your instant pot on Sauté mode, add bacon and brown it for 10 minutes.
2. Transfer bacon to paper towels, drain grease, put in a bowls and leave aside.
3. Add the water, cumin and beer to your pot and stir, before adding beans and cooking with lid on High for 30 minutes.
4. Release the pressure, uncover pot and add garlic, bacon, jalapeno, salt and pepper, cover again and cook on High for 3 minutes more.
5. Release pressure and transfer to bowls and serve.

(**Calories** 156|**Fat** 4 g| **Protein** 1 g| **Fiber** 3 g| **Carbohydrates** 6 g)

Split Pea and Squash Curry

(**P**rep Time: 10 MIN| **C**ook Time: 25 MIN| **S**erve: 4)

Ingredients:

1 cup split peas, soaked in water for a few hours and drained
¼ tsp fenugreek seeds
¼ tsp udad dhal
1 tbsp peanut oil
½ tsp mustard seeds
A pinch of hing (asafetida)
1 tbsp ginger, minced
1 garlic clove, minced
½ cup onion, chopped
2 cups squash, peeled and chopped
1/3 cup tomato, cut into chunks
2 cups water
Salt and pepper to taste
½ tsp turmeric
1 tsp cumin, ground
1 tsp coriander, ground
2 tsp garam masala
½ cup cilantro, chopped

Directions:

1. Set your instant pot on Sauté mode, add oil and stir-fry udad dhal, mustard seeds and fenugreek for 1 minute.
2. Add hing, onions, ginger, garlic, stir and cook for 3 minutes more.
3. Add split peas, water, tomato, turmeric, salt, pepper, coriander, cumin, squash and half of the cilantro, stir, cover and cook on High for 10 minutes.
4. Release the pressure naturally and uncover pot. Then add the rest of the cilantro and garam masala and mix well, divide into bowls and enjoy!

(**C**alories 275|**F**at 2.7 g| **P**rotein 12 g| **F**iber 12.5 g| **C**arbohydrates 53 g)

Pea and Pineapple Curry

(**Prep Time:** 10 MIN| **Cook Time:** 35 MIN| **Serve:** 4)

Ingredients:

1 cup peas, soaked in water for a few hours and drained
4 cups water
3 tbsp extra virgin olive oil
1 yellow onion, chopped
1 cup brown lentils
1 tsp curry powder
½ tsp turmeric
¼ tsp cinnamon
½ tsp cumin
2/3 cup canned pineapple, cut into chunks
¼ cup cashew butter

Directions:

1. In a bowl, mix cashew butter with some water, stir very well and set aside.
2. Put lentils and beans in your instant pot, add 3 ½ cups water, stir, cover and cook on High for 25 minutes.
3. Release the pressure, drain peas and lentils and put them in a bowl.
4. Set your instant pot on Sauté mode, add oil and fry turmeric, cumin, curry powder and cinnamon for 3 minutes, stirring all the time.
5. Add onions and cook for 4 minutes.
6. Then set the pot on Simmer mode, add peas and lentils, cashew butter, pineapple and the remaining ½ cup water, stir and simmer for 5 minutes, then divide into bowls and enjoy this creamy curry.

(**C**alories 333|**F**at 11 g| **P**rotein 16 g| Fiber 17 g| Carbohydrates 43 g)

Vegetables & Sides

Artichoke Hearts with Garlic

(**Prep Time:** 10 MIN| **Cook Time:** 40 MIN| **Serve:** 4)

Ingredients:

4 big artichokes, washed, stems and petal tips cut off
Salt and black pepper to taste
2 tbsp lemon juice
¼ cup extra virgin olive oil
2 tsp balsamic vinegar
1 tsp oregano
2 cups water
2 garlic cloves, minced

Directions:

1. Put artichokes in the steamer basket of your instant pot and add 2 cups water to the pot, cover and steam them for 8 minutes.
2. Meanwhile, in a bowl, mix lemon juice with vinegar, oil, salt, pepper, garlic and oregano and stir very well.
3. Release the pressure from the pot, transfer artichokes to a plate, cut them in halves, take out the hearts and arrange them on a platter.
4. Drizzle the vinaigrette over artichokes and leave them on one side for 30 minutes.
5. Heat up your kitchen grill over medium heat, add artichokes and cook for 3 minutes on each side. Serve them warm.

(**Calories** 120|**Fat** 2 g| **Protein** 4 g| **Fiber** 1 g| **Carbohydrates**1 g)

Blue Cheese Beet Crumble

(**P**rep Time: 10 MIN| **C**ook Time: 20 MIN| **S**erve: 6)

Ingredients:

6 beets
Salt and black pepper to taste
¼ cup blue cheese, crumbled
1 cup water

Directions:

1. Put the beets in the steamer basket of your instant pot, add 1 cup water into the pot, cover and cook on High for 20 minutes.
2. Release the pressure naturally, uncover and transfer beets to a cutting board to cool. Peel and cut them into quarters.
3. Put beet pieces in a bowl, add crumbled blue cheese, salt and pepper to taste, and enjoy!

(**C**alories 160|**F**at 1 g| **P**rotein 7 g| Fiber 5 g| **C**arbohydrates 10 g)

Mexican Stuffed Bell Peppers

(**Prep Time:** 15 MIN| **Cook Time:** 15 MIN| **Serve:** 4)

Ingredients:

1 pound turkey meat, ground
1 cup water
2 green onions, chopped
5 ounces canned green chilies, chopped
1 jalapeno pepper, chopped
2 tsp chili powder
½ cup whole wheat Panko crumbs
1 tsp garlic powder
1 tsp cumin, ground
Salt to taste
4 bell peppers, tops and seeds discarded
4 pepper jack cheese slices
1 avocado, chopped
Crushed tortilla chips
Pico de gallo

For the chipotle sauce:
Zest from 1 lime
Juice from 1 lime
½ cup sour cream
2 tbsp chipotle in adobo sauce
1/8 tsp garlic powder

Directions:

1. In a bowl, mix sour cream with chipotle in adobo sauce, lime zest and lime juice and garlic powder, stir well and keep in the fridge until you serve it.
2. In a bowl, mix turkey with green onions, green chilies, bread crumbs, jalapeno, cumin, salt, chili powder and garlic powder, stir very well and stuff your peppers with this mix.
3. Add 1 cup water in your instant pot, add peppers in the steamer basket, cover and cook on High for 15 minutes.
4. Release the pressure naturally for 10 minutes and transfer bell peppers to a pan, add cheese on top, place in your preheated broiler and broil until cheese is browned.

5. Divide bell peppers on plates, top with chipotle sauce you've made earlier and serve.

(Calories 177|Fat 5 g| **Protein** 13 g| Fiber 3.3 g| **Carbohydrates** 22 g)

Stuffed Bell Peppers with Beef

(**Prep Time:** 10 MIN| **Cook Time:** 15 MIN| **Serve:** 4)

Ingredients:

4 bell peppers, tops and seeds removed
Salt and black pepper to taste
16 ounces beef meat, ground
1 cup white rice, already cooked
1 egg
½ cup milk
2 onions, chopped
8 ounces water
10 ounces canned tomato soup

Directions:

1. Put some water in a pot, bring to a boil over medium heat and add the bell peppers. Blanch them for 3 minutes, drain and transfer them to a working surface.
2. In a bowl, mix beef with rice, salt, pepper, egg, milk and onions and stir very well.
3. Stuff bell peppers with this mince mixture and place them in your instant pot.
4. Add tomato soup mixed with water, cover pot and cook on High for 12 minutes.
5. Release the pressure fast and divide the stuffed bell peppers onto individual serving plates, drizzle tomato sauce over them and serve.

(Calories 200|Fat 12 g| **Protein** 12 g| Fiber 1.5 g| **Carbohydrates** 13 g)

Brussels Sprouts with Bacon

(**Prep Time:** 4 MIN| **Cook Time:** 6 MIN| **Serve:** 4)

Ingredients:

1 pound Brussels sprouts, trimmed and cut into halves
Salt and black pepper to taste
½ cup bacon, chopped
1 tbsp mustard
1 cup chicken stock
1 tbsp butter
2 tbsp dill, finely chopped

Directions:

1. Set your instant pot on Sauté mode, add bacon and fry until it's crispy.
2. Add sprouts and cook for 2 minutes.
3. Add stock, mustard, salt and pepper, stir, cover and cook on High for 4 minutes.
4. Release pressure, uncover and add butter and dill, set the pot on Sauté mode again while you stir the vegetables to coat before spooning onto serving plates.

(**Calories** 175|**Fat** 11 g| **Protein** 6.6 g| **Fiber** 5.6 g| **Carbohydrates** 14 g)

Brussels Sprouts with Parmesan

(**P**rep Time: 10 MIN| **C**ook Time: 6 MIN| **S**erve: 4)

Ingredients:

1 pound Brussels sprouts, washed
Juice of 1 lemon
Salt and black pepper to taste
2 tbsp butter
1 cup water
3 tbsp parmesan, grated

Directions:

1. Put sprouts in your instant pot, add salt, pepper and water before covering and cooking on High for 3 minutes.
2. Release the pressure and transfer sprouts to a bowl, discard water and clean your pot.
3. Set your pot on Sauté mode, add butter and melt it.
4. Add lemon juice to the melted butter and stir well.
5. Add sprouts, stir to coat with butter and transfer to plates.
6. Add more salt and pepper if needed and sprinkle parmesan cheese on top.

(**C**alories 160|**F**at 2 g| **P**rotein 12 g| **F**iber 1 g| **C**arbohydrates 7 g)

Turmeric Cabbage and Sausages

(**Prep Time:** 10 MIN| **Cook Time:** 5 MIN| **Serve:** 4)

Ingredients:

3 tbsp butter
1 green cabbage head, chopped
Salt and black pepper to taste
1 pound sausage links, sliced
15 ounces canned tomatoes, chopped
½ cup yellow onion, chopped
2 tsp turmeric

Directions:

1. Set your instant pot on Sauté mode, add sausage slices and cook until they brown.
2. Drain excess grease, add butter, cabbage, tomatoes salt, pepper, onion and turmeric, stir, cover and cook on High for 2 minutes.
3. Release the pressure fast and uncover, spoon cabbage and sausages onto plates and enjoy.

(**C**alories 140|**F**at 6 g| **P**rotein 10 g| **F**iber 4 g| **C**arbohydrates 11 g)

Sweet and Spicy Cabbage

(**Prep Time:** 10 MIN| **Cook Time:** 8 MIN| **Serve:** 4)

Ingredients:

1 cabbage, cut into 8 wedges
1 tbsp sesame seed oil
1 carrots, grated
¼ cup apple cider vinegar
1 ¼ cups apple+2 tbsp water
1 tsp raw sugar
½ tsp cayenne pepper
½ tsp red pepper flakes
2 tsp cornstarch

Directions:

1. Set your instant pot on Sauté mode, add oil and heat before adding cabbage, cook for 3 minutes.
2. Add carrots, 1 ¼ cups water, sugar, vinegar, cayenne and pepper flakes, cover and cook on High for 5 minutes.
3. Release the pressure and uncover pot, divide cabbage and carrots mixture onto plates.
4. Add cornstarch mixed with 2 tbsp water to the pot, set the pot on Simmer mode, stir very well as it thickens and bring to a boil.
5. Drizzle over cabbage and serve.

(**C**alories 90|**F**at 4.5 g| **P**rotein 1 g| Fiber 2.1 g| Carbohydrates 11 g)

Cauliflower and Spinach Pasta

(Prep Time: 10 MIN| Cook Time: 10 MIN| Serve: 4)

Ingredients:

2 tbsp butter
8 cups cauliflower florets
2 garlic cloves, minced
1 cup chicken stock
Salt to taste
2 cups spinach, chopped
1 pound fettuccine paste
2 green onions, chopped
1 tbsp gorgonzola cheese, grated
3 sun dried tomatoes, chopped
A splash of balsamic vinegar

Directions:

1. Set your instant pot on Sauté mode, add butter and melt before adding garlic, cook for 2 minutes.
2. Add stock, salt and cauliflower, stir, cover and cook on High for 6 minutes.
3. Release the pressure for 10 minutes and transfer cauliflower to your blender and pulse well.
4. Add spinach and green onions and stir gently.
5. Heat up a pot with some water and a pinch of salt over medium high heat, bring to a boil, add pasta and cook according to instructions, drain and dish into bowls.
6. Add cauliflower sauce, gorgonzola, sun dried tomatoes and a splash of vinegar on top, toss to coat and serve.

(Calories 160|Fat 5 g| Protein 13 g| Fiber 3 g| Carbohydrates 23 g)

Endives with Ham

(**Prep Time:** 10 MIN| **Cook Time:** 20 MIN| **S**erve:4)

Ingredients:

4 endives, trimmed
Salt and black pepper to taste
1 tbsp white flour
4 slices ham
2 tbsp butter
½ tsp nutmeg
14 ounces milk

Directions:

1. Put the endives in the steamer basket of your instant pot, add some water in the pot, cover and cook on High for 10 minutes.
2. Meanwhile, heat up a pan and melt butter over medium heat before adding flour, stirring well and cooking for 3 minutes.
3. Add milk, salt, pepper and nutmeg, reduce heat to low and cook for 10 minutes.
4. Release the pressure from the pot and uncover it, transfer endives to a cutting board and roll each in a slice of ham.
5. Arrange endives in a pan, pour milk mixture over them and place in preheated broiler for 10 minutes.
6. Slice, arrange on plates and serve.

(**Calories** 120|**Fat** 1 g| **Protein** 23 g| **Fiber** 2 g| **Carbohydrates** 6 g)

Eggplant Ratatouille

(**Prep Time:** 15 MIN| **Cook Time:** 8 MIN| **Serve:** 6)

Ingredients:

1 big eggplant, peeled and thinly sliced
2 garlic cloves, minced
3 tbsp extra virgin olive oil
Salt and black pepper to taste
1 cup onion, chopped
1 green bell pepper, chopped
1 red bell pepper, chopped
½ cup water
1 tsp thyme
14 ounces canned tomatoes, chopped
A pinch of sugar
1 cup basil, chopped

Directions:

1. Set your instant pot on Sauté mode, add oil and fry green and red bell pepper, onion and garlic for 3 minutes.
2. Add eggplant, water, salt, pepper, thyme, sugar and tomatoes, cover and cook on High for 4 minutes.
3. Release the pressure fast and uncover, add basil, stir gently and dish up onto plates!

(**Calories** 109|**Fat** 5 g| **Protein** 2 g| **Fiber** 3 g| **Carbohydrates** 4 g)

Eggplant Supreme

(**Prep Time:** 10 MIN| **Cook Time:** 8 MIN| **Serve:** 2)

Ingredients:

4 cups eggplant, cubed
1 tbsp extra virgin olive oil
3 garlic cloves, minced
1 tbsp garlic powder
Salt and black pepper to taste
1 cup marinara sauce
½ cup water

Directions:

1. Set your instant pot on Sauté mode, add the oil and fry garlic for 2 minutes.
2. Add eggplant, salt, pepper, garlic powder, marinara sauce and water, stir gently, cover and cook on High for 8 minutes.
3. Release the pressure fast and uncover, serve your eggplant supreme right away with your favorite spaghetti.

(**C**alories 130|**F**at 3 g| **P**rotein 3 g| **F**iber 2 g| **C**arbohydrates 3 g)

Babaganoush

(**Prep Time:** 10 MIN| **Cook Time:** 4 MIN| **Serve:** 6)

Ingredients:

2 pounds eggplant, peeled and cut into medium chunks
Salt and black pepper to taste
¼ cup extra virgin olive oil
½ cup water
4 garlic cloves
¼ cup lemon juice
1 bunch thyme, chopped
1 tbsp tahini
A drizzle of olive oil
3 olives, pitted and sliced

Directions:

1. Put the eggplant pieces in your instant pot, add ¼ cup oil, set the pot on Sauté mode and heat before adding garlic, water and salt and pepper, cover and cook on High for 3 minutes.
2. Release the pressure and uncover pot, transfer eggplant pieces and garlic to your blender, add lemon juice and tahini and pulse well.
3. Add thyme and blend again.
4. Transfer eggplant spread to a bowl, top with olive slices and a drizzle of oil and serve.

(**Calories** 70|**Fat** 2 g| **Protein** 1 g| **Fiber** 2 g| **Carbohydrates** 7 g)

Fennel Risotto

(**P**rep Time: 10 MIN| **C**ook Time: 10 MIN| **S**erve: 2)

Ingredients:

1 ½ cups Arborio rice
1 yellow onion, chopped
3 cups chicken stock
1 fennel bulb, trimmed and chopped
2 tbsp butter
1 tbsp extra virgin olive oil
¼ cup white wine
Salt and black pepper to taste
½ tsp thyme, dried
3 tbsp tomato paste
1/3 cup parmesan cheese, grated

Directions:

1. Set your instant pot on Sauté mode, add butter and sauté fennel and onion for 4 minutes and transfer to a bowl.
2. Add oil to your pot and heat before adding rice and cooking for 3 minutes.
3. Add tomato paste, stock, fennel, onions, wine, salt, pepper and thyme, cover and cook on High for 8 minutes.
4. Release the pressure and uncover, add cheese, stir to melt and spoon onto plates.

(**C**alories 200|**F**at 10 g| **P**rotein 12 g| Fiber 2 g| **C**arbohydrates 20 g)

Smoked Kale and Bacon

(**Prep Time:** 10 MIN| **Cook Time:** 10 MIN| **Serve:** 4)

Ingredients:

6 bacon slices, chopped
1 tbsp vegetable oil
1 onion, thinly sliced
6 garlic cloves, chopped
1 ½ cups chicken stock
1 tbsp brown sugar
2 tbsp apple cider vinegar
10 ounces kale leaves, chopped
1 tsp red chili, crushed
1 tsp liquid smoke
Salt and black pepper to taste

Directions:

1. Set your instant pot on Sauté mode, add oil and fry bacon for 1-2 minutes.
2. Add onion and cook for 3 minutes before adding garlic and cooking for 1 minute.
3. Add vinegar, stock, sugar, liquid smoke, red chilies, salt, pepper, kale, stir, cover and cook on High for 5 minutes.
4. Release the pressure fast and uncover, spoon onto plates and enjoy!

(**Calories** 140|**Fat** 7 g| **Protein** 2 g| **Fiber** 1 g| **Carbohydrates** 7 g)

Crispy Potatoes

(**Prep Time:** 10 MIN| **Cook Time:** 7 MIN| **Serve:** 4)

Ingredients:

½ cup water
1 pound gold potatoes, cubed
Salt and black pepper to taste
2 tbsp ghee
Juice from ½ lemon
¼ cup parsley leaves, chopped

Directions:

1. Put the water in your instant pot, add potatoes in the steamer basket, cover and cook on High for 5 minutes.
2. Release the pressure naturally and uncover pot, set it on Sauté mode.
3. Add ghee, lemon juice, parsley, salt and pepper, stir and cook for 2 minutes.
4. Transfer to plates and serve.

(Calories 132|Fat 1 g| Protein 3 g| Fiber 0 g| Carbohydrates 23 g)

Zucchinis and Cherry Tomatoes

(Prep Time: 10 MIN| Cook Time: 12 MIN| Serve: 4)

Ingredients:

6 zucchinis, roughly chopped
2 yellow onions, chopped
1 tbsp vegetable oil
1 cup tomato puree
1 pound cherry tomatoes, cut into halves
A drizzle of olive oil
Salt and black pepper to taste
2 garlic cloves, minced
1 bunch basil, chopped

Directions:

1. Set your instant pot on Sauté mode, add vegetable oil and fry onion, stirring for 5 minutes.
2. Add tomatoes, tomato puree, zucchinis, salt and pepper, stir, cover and cook on High for 5 minutes.
3. Release the pressure, uncover pot and add garlic and basil before dishing onto plates.
4. Drizzle some olive oil over plate and serve.

(Calories 155|Fat 2 g| Protein 22 g| Fiber 4 g| Carbohydrates 12 g)

Spicy Turnips

(**Prep** Time: 10 MIN| **Cook** Time: 22 MIN| **Serve**: 4)

Ingredients:

20 ounces turnips, peeled and chopped
1 tsp garlic, minced
1 tsp ginger, grated
2 yellow onions, chopped
2 tomatoes, chopped
1 tsp sugar
1 tsp cumin powder
1 tsp coriander powder
2 green chilies, chopped
½ tsp turmeric powder
1 cup water
2 tbsp butter
Salt to taste
A handful coriander leaves, chopped

Directions:

1. Set your instant pot on Sauté mode, add butter and melt before adding green chilies, garlic and ginger and cooking for 1 minute.
2. Add onions, stir and cook for a further 3 minutes.
3. Add salt, tomatoes, turmeric, cumin and coriander powder and cook for 3 more minutes.
4. Add turnips and water, stir, cover and cook on Low for 15 minutes.
5. Release the pressure and uncover pot, add sugar and coriander, stir well and dish onto plates and serve.

(Calories 80|Fat 2.4 g| Protein 3 g| Fiber 4 g| Carbohydrates 12 g)

Stuffed Tomatoes

(**Prep Time:** 10 MIN| **Cook Time:** 10 MIN| **Serve:** 4)

Ingredients:

4 tomatoes, tops cut off and pulp scooped
Salt and black pepper to taste
1 yellow onion, chopped
1 tbsp butter
2 tbsp celery, chopped
½ cup mushrooms, chopped
1 slice of bread, crumbled
1 cup cottage cheese
¼ tsp caraway seeds
1 tbsp parsley, chopped
½ cup water

Directions:

1. Chop tomato pulp and put it in a bowl.
2. Heat up a pan with the butter over medium high heat, add onion and celery, stir and cook for 3 minutes.
3. Add tomato pulp and mushrooms and cook for 1 minute more.
4. Add salt, pepper, crumbled bread, cheese, caraway seeds and parsley, stir and cook for a further 4 minutes.
5. Fill each tomato with this mixture and arrange them in the steamer basket of your instant pot.
6. Add the water to the pot, cover and cook on High for 2 minutes.
7. Release the pressure fast, uncover the pot and transfer the stuffed potatoes onto plates and serve.

(Calories 140|Fat 3 g| Protein 4 g| Fiber 1.4 g| Carbohydrates 10 g)

Rosemary Baby Potatoes

(**P**rep Time: 10 MIN| **C**ook Time: 10 MIN| **S**erve: 4)

Ingredients:
3 lbs baby potatoes, rinsed and dry
1 tbsp rosemary
½ tsp oregano
1 tsp dried thyme
¼ tsp garlic powder
1 tsp salt
½ tsp freshly ground black pepper
2 tbsp extra-virgin olive oil
¾ cup vegetable stock

Directions:
1. Place the Instant Pot over medium heat and set on "Sauté".
2. In a bowl, toss the potatoes with the herbs and spices.
3. Add the olive oil into the pot. Drop in the potatoes into the pot and stir for 5 minutes until golden brown.
4. Pour in the vegetable stock and cover the pot. Set the timer to 8 minutes.
5. Once the time is finished, carefully release the pressure and uncover the pot.
6. Transfer the potatoes to a bowl and serve warm.

(Calories 270|Fat 7.8g| Protein 9.8 g| Carbohydrates 43.6 g)

Indian-style Potato Cubes

(Prep Time: 10 MIN| Cook Time: 10 MIN| Serve: 4)

Ingredients:
2 tbsp unsalted butter
1 large onion, diced
2 jalapeno peppers, pitted and diced
½ tsp cumin seeds
2 tsp ground ginger
½ tsp Indian Chili
½ tsp ground turmeric
¼ tbsp Garam Masala
1 tsp salt
¾ cup water, for cooking
2 lbs potatoes, peeled and cubed
3 cups cauliflower florets, chopped
Fresh cilantro, to garnish

Directions:
1. Melt the butter in the Instant Pot over medium heat. Stir in the onion and sauté for 4 minutes.
2. Add the jalapeno and cumin seeds.
3. Season with ground ginger, chili, turmeric, garam masala and the salt. Keep stirring for 1 minutes.
4. Pour in the water and stir, make sure nothing is sticking to the pot.
5. Drop in the potato cubes and stir until evenly coated.
6. Cover the pot and set the timer for 5 minutes.
7. Once the time is finished, carefully released the pressure.
8. Uncover the pot and add the cauliflower florets and cook, uncovered, for 5 minutes.
9. Transfer the mixture to serving bowl and top with fresh cilantro

(Calories 250|Fat 6.4g| Protein 6.1 g| Carbohydrates 44.8 g)

Wild Rice, Faro and Cherry Pilaf

(**Prep Time:** 10 MIN| **Cook Time:** 35 MIN| **Serve:** 12)

Ingredients:

1 shallot, finely chopped
1 tsp garlic, minced
A drizzle of extra virgin olive oil
1 and ½ cups whole grain faro
¾ cup wild rice
6 cups chicken stock
Salt and black pepper to taste
1 tbsp parsley and sage, finely chopped
½ cup hazelnuts, toasted and chopped
¾ cup cherries, dried
Some chopped chives for serving

Directions:

1. Set your instant pot on Sauté mode, add a drizzle of oil and fry onion and garlic for 2-3 minutes.
2. Add farro, rice, salt, pepper, stock and 1 tbsp mixed sage and parsley, stir, cover and cook on High for 25 minutes.
3. Meanwhile, put cherries in a pot, add hot water to cover, set aside for 10 minutes and drain them.
4. Release the pressure from the pot for 5 minutes, drain excess liquid, add hazelnuts and cherries, stir gently and spoon onto plates, before garnishing with chopped chives.

(Calories 120|Fat 1 g| Protein 4.5 g| Fiber 1.5 g| Carbohydrates 21 g)

Quinoa Pilaf

(**Prep Time:** 10 MIN| **Cook Time:** 2 MIN| **Serve:** 4)

Ingredients:

2 cups quinoa
2 garlic cloves, minced
2 tbsp extra virgin olive oil
Salt to taste
2 tsp turmeric
3 cups water
1 handful parsley, chopped
2 tsp cumin, ground

Directions:

1. Set your instant pot on Sauté mode, add oil and fry garlic for 30 seconds.
2. Add water, quinoa, cumin, turmeric and salt, stir, cover and cook on High for 1 minute.
3. Release the pressure naturally for 10 minutes and fluff quinoa with a fork, transfer to plates, season with more salt if needed, sprinkle parsley on top and serve as a side dish.

(Calories 130|Fat 0.9 g| Protein 6.9 g| Fiber 3.2 g| Carbohydrates 12 g)

Quinoa with Almonds

(**Prep Time:** 10 MIN| **Cook Time:** 11 MIN| **Serve:** 4)

Ingredients:

½ cup yellow onion, finely chopped
1 tbsp butter
1 celery stalk, chopped
1 ½ cups quinoa, rinsed
14 ounces chicken stock
Salt and black pepper to taste
¼ cup water
½ cup almonds, toasted and sliced
2 tbsp parsley, chopped

Directions:

1. Set your instant pot on Sauté mode, add butter and melt before add onion and celery and cooking for 5 minutes.
2. Add quinoa, water, stock, salt and pepper, stir, cover and cook on High for 3 minutes.
3. Release the pressure for 5 minutes and uncover, fluff quinoa with a fork, add almonds and parsley before spooning onto plates and serving as a side dish.

(Calories 140|Fat 3 g| Protein 12.4 g| Fiber 2 g| Carbohydrates 12 g)

Mushroom Risotto

(**Prep Time:** 10 MIN| **Cook Time:** 15 MIN| **Serve:** 4)

Ingredients:

2 cups risotto rice
4 cups chicken stock
2 garlic cloves, crushed
2 ounces extra virgin olive oil
1 yellow onion, chopped
8 ounces mushrooms, sliced
4 ounces heavy cream
4 ounces sherry vinegar
2 tbsp parmesan cheese, grated
1 ounce basil, finely chopped

Directions:

1. Set your instant pot on Sauté mode, add the oil and heat before adding onions, garlic and mushrooms and cook for 3 minutes.
2. Add rice, stock and vinegar, stir, cover and cook on High for 10 minutes.
3. Release the pressure, uncover and add cream and parmesan and stir until well combined.
4. Divide among plates, sprinkle basil over risotto and serve.

(Calories 340|Fat 1 g| Protein 4 g| Fiber 1 g| Carbohydrates 15 g)

Simple Pumpkin Risotto

(**Prep Time:** 5 MIN| **Cook Time:** 10 MIN| **Serve:** 4)

Ingredients:

2 ounces extra virgin olive oil
1 small yellow onion, chopped
2 garlic cloves, minced
12 ounces risotto rice
4 cups chicken stock
6 ounces pumpkin puree
½ tsp nutmeg
1 tsp thyme, chopped
½ tsp ginger, grated
½ tsp cinnamon
½ tsp allspice
4 ounces heavy cream

Directions:

1. Set your instant pot on Sauté mode, add oil and fry onion and garlic for 1-2 minutes.
2. Also add risotto rice, chicken stock, pumpkin puree, thyme, nutmeg, cinnamon, ginger and allspice and stir well in figure of eight.
3. Cover and cook on High for 10 minutes
4. Release the pressure and add cream, stir very well before serving as a side dish.

(Calories 263|Fat 5 g| Protein 6 g| Fiber 2 g| Carbohydrates 37 g)

Spicy Veggie Rice

(Prep Time: 6 MIN| Cook Time: 15 MIN| Serve: 4)

Ingredients:

2 cups basmati rice
1 cup mixed frozen carrots, peas, corn, green beans
2 cups water
½ tsp green chili, minced
½ tsp ginger, grated
3 garlic cloves, minced
2 tbsp butter
1 cinnamon stick
1 tbsp cumin seeds
2 bay leaves
3 whole cloves
5 black peppercorns
2 whole cardamoms
1 tbsp sugar
Salt to taste

Directions:

1. Put the water in your instant pot and add rice, mixed frozen veggies, green chili, grated ginger, garlic cloves, cinnamon stick, whole cloves and butter.
2. Also add cumin seeds, bay leaves, cardamoms, black peppercorns, salt and sugar.
3. Stir, cover and cook on High for 15 minutes
4. Release the pressure and divide among plates and serve with your favorite steaks.

(Calories 340|Fat 6 g| Protein 14.2 g| Fiber 5.5 g| Carbohydrates 40 g)

Herby Mashed Potatoes

(**Prep Time:** 10 MIN| **Cook Time:** 9 MIN| **Serve:** 8)

Ingredients:

2 garlic cloves
3 pounds sweet potatoes, peeled and chopped
Salt and black pepper to taste
½ tsp parsley, dried
¼ tsp sage, dried
½ tsp rosemary, dried
½ tsp thyme dried
1 ½ cups water
¼ cup milk
½ cup parmesan, grated
2 tbsp butter

Directions:

1. Put potatoes and garlic in the steamer basket of your instant pot and add 1 ½ cups of water to the pot, cook on High for 10 minutes.
2. Release the pressure quickly and drain water, transfer the potatoes and garlic to a bowl and mash them using your kitchen mixer.
3. Add butter, parmesan, milk, salt, pepper, parsley, sage, rosemary and thyme and blend everything well.
4. Spoon mashed potato onto plates and serve.

(Calories 240|Fat 1 g| Protein 4.5 g| Fiber 8.2 g| Carbohydrates 34 g)

Saffron Risotto

(**Prep Time:** 10 MIN| **Cook Time:** 10 MIN| **Serve:** 10)

Ingredients:

2 tbsp extra virgin olive oil
½ tsp saffron threads, crushed
½ cup onion, chopped
2 tbsp hot milk
1 ½ cups Arborio rice
3 ½ cups veggie stock
A pinch of salt
1 tbsp honey
1 cinnamon stick
1/3 cup almonds, chopped
1/3 cup currants, dried

Directions:

1. In a bowl, mix hot milk with saffron, stir and set aside to infuse.
2. Set your instant pot on Sauté mode, add oil and fry onions for 5 minutes.
3. Add rice, veggie stock, saffron and milk, honey, salt, almonds, cinnamon stick and currants.
4. Stir, cover and cook on High for 5 minutes.
5. Release the pressure quickly and fluff the rice a bit, discard cinnamon and spoon the risotto onto plates and serve.

(Calories 260|Fat 7 g| Protein 3.9 g| Fiber 2 g| Carbohydrates 41 g)

Farro with Cherries

(**P**rep Time: 10 MIN| **C**ook Time: 40 MIN| **S**erve: 6)

Ingredients:

1 tbsp apple cider vinegar
1 cup whole grain farro
1 tsp lemon juice
Salt to taste
3 cups water
1 tbsp extra virgin olive oil
½ cup cherries, dried and chopped
¼ cup green onions, chopped
10 mint leaves, chopped
2 cups cherries, pitted and cut into halves

Directions:

1. Put the water in your instant pot, add rinsed farro, stir, cover and cook on High for 40 minutes.
2. Release the pressure quickly and drain farro, transfer to a bowl and mix with salt, oil, lemon juice, vinegar, dried cherries, fresh cherries, green onions and mint.
3. Fold everything together well and serve.

(Calories 160|Fat 1 g| Protein 4 g| Fiber 2 g| Carbohydrates 12 g)

Herbed Polenta

(**Prep Time:** 15 MIN| **Cook Time:** 6 MIN| **Serve:** 6)

Ingredients:

4 cups veggie stock
2 tbsp extra virgin olive oil
2 tsp garlic, minced
½ cup yellow onion, chopped
1/3 cup sun dried tomatoes, chopped
Salt to taste
1 cup polenta
1 bay leaf
2 tsp oregano, finely chopped
3 tbsp basil, finely chopped
1 tsp rosemary, finely chopped
2 tbsp parsley, finely chopped

Directions:

1. Set your instant pot on Sauté mode, add the oil and heat before adding onion, cook for 1 minute.
2. Add garlic, stir again and cook for a further minute.
3. Add stock, salt, tomatoes, bay leaf, rosemary, oregano, half of the basil, half of the parsley and polenta.
4. Do not stir, cover and cook on High for 5 minutes and release pressure naturally for 10 minutes.
5. Uncover, discard bay leaf, stir polenta gently, add the rest of the parsley, basil and more salt, stir and serve.

(Calories 150|Fat 1.6 g| Protein 3.7 g| Fiber 3.6 g| Carbohydrates 35 g)

Mexican Rice

(**Prep Time:** 10 MIN| **Cook Time:** 4 MIN| **Serve:** 8)

Ingredients:

1 cup long grain rice
1 and ¼ cups veggie stock
½ cup cilantro, chopped
½ avocado, pitted, peeled and chopped
Salt and black pepper to taste
¼ cup green hot sauce

Directions:

1. Put the rice in your instant pot, add stock, stir, cover and cook on High for 4 minutes.
2. Release the pressure naturally for 10 minutes, uncover and fluff rice with a fork and transfer to a bowl.
3. Meanwhile, in your food processor, mix avocado with hot sauce and cilantro and blend well.
4. Pour this over the rice, stir well, add salt and pepper to taste, stir again and serve.

(Calories 100|Fat 2 g| Protein 2 g| Fiber 1 g| Carbohydrates 18 g)

Cauliflower and Barley Risotto

(**Prep Time:** 10 MIN| **Cook Time:** 1 HOUR| **Serve:** 4)

Ingredients:

4 tbsp extra virgin olive oil
Salt and black pepper to taste
1 cauliflower head, florets separated
½ cup parmesan, grated
2 garlic cloves, minced
1 cup pearl barley
1 yellow onion, chopped
3 cups chicken stock
2 thyme springs
2 tbsp parsley, chopped
1 tbsp butter

Directions:

1. Spread cauliflower florets on a lined baking dish, add 3 tbsp oil, salt and pepper, toss to coat and place in the oven at 425 degrees F and bake for 20 minutes, turning them every 10 minutes.
2. Take cauliflower out of the oven, sprinkle ¼ cup parmesan and bake for 5 minutes more.
3. Meanwhile, set your instant pot on Sauté mode, add 1 tbsp oil and heat
4. Add onion, stir and cook for 5 minutes before adding garlic and cooking for a further minute.
5. Add stock, thyme and barley and cover before cooking on High for 25 minutes.
6. Release the pressure quickly and uncover the pot, stir the barley, discard thyme and add butter, the rest of the parmesan, roasted cauliflower, salt, pepper to taste and parsley.
7. Stir the risotto well before serving.

(Calories 350|Fat 16 g| Protein 14.6 g| Fiber 10 g| Carbohydrates 25 g)

Lemon, Parmesan and Pea Risotto

(Prep Time: 10 MIN| Cook Time: 17 MIN| Serve: 6)

Ingredients:

1 ½ cups rice
2 tbsp butter
1 yellow onion, chopped
1 tbsp extra virgin olive oil
2 tbsp lemon juice
1 tsp lemon zest, grated
3 and ½ cups chicken stock
2 tbsp parsley, finely chopped
Salt and black pepper to taste
1 ½ cups peas
2 tbsp parmesan, finely grated

Directions:

1. Set your instant pot on Sauté mode, add 1 tbsp butter and the oil and heat before adding onions, stir and cook for 5 minutes.
2. Add rice and cook for 3 more minutes, stirring constantly.
3. Add 3 cups stock and the lemon juice, stir, cover and cook on High for 5 minutes.
4. Release the pressure quickly and set the pot on Simmer, add peas and the rest of the stock and cook for 2 minutes.
5. Add parmesan, parsley, the rest of the butter, lemon zest, salt and pepper to taste and serve.

(Calories 140|Fat 1.5 g| Protein 5 g| Fiber 1 g| Carbohydrates 27 g)

Spinach and Goat Cheese Risotto

(Prep Time: 10 MIN| Cook Time: 10 MIN| Serve: 6)

Ingredients:

2 garlic cloves, minced
2 tbsp extra virgin olive oil
¾ cup yellow onion, chopped
1 ½ cups Arborio rice
½ cup white wine
12 ounces spinach, chopped
3 ½ cups hot veggie stock
Salt and black pepper to taste
4 ounces goat cheese, soft and crumbled
2 tbsp lemon juice
1/3 cup pecans, toasted and chopped

Directions:

1. Set your instant pot on Sauté mode, add the oil and fry garlic and onions for 5 minutes.
2. Add rice and cook for 1 minute more.
3. Add wine and cook until it's absorbed, stirring constantly.
4. Add 3 cups stock, cover and cook on High for 4 minutes.
5. Release the pressure quickly and uncover, add spinach and cook on Simmer mode for 3 minutes.
6. Add salt, pepper, the rest of the stock, lemon juice and goat cheese and stir before dishing onto plates and garnishing with pecans.

(Calories 340|Fat 23 g| Protein 18.9 g| Fiber 4.5 g| Carbohydrates 24 g)

Creamy Rice and Artichoke Pilaf

(Prep Time: 10 MIN| Cook Time: 20 MIN| Serve:4)

Ingredients:

1 tbsp extra virgin olive oil
5 ounces Arborio rice
2 garlic cloves crushed
1 ¼ cups chicken broth
1 tbsp white wine
6 ounces graham cracker crumbs
1 ¼ cups water
15 ounces canned artichoke hearts chopped
16 ounces cream cheese
1 tbsp grated parmesan cheese
1 ½ tbsp thyme, chopped
Salt and black pepper to taste

Directions:

1. Set your instant pot on Sauté mode, add the oil, heat up, add rice and cook for 2 minutes.
2. Add garlic, stir and cook for a further minute before transferring to a heat proof dish.
3. Add stock, crumbs, salt, pepper and wine, stir and cover with tin foil.
4. Place the dish in the steamer basket of the pot, add water, cover and cook on High for 8 minutes
5. Release the pressure, take the dish out, uncover and add cream cheese, parmesan, artichoke hearts and thyme.
6. Mix well and serve while it's hot!

(Calories 240|Fat 7.2 g| Protein 6 g| Fiber 5.1 g| Carbohydrates 34 g)

Potatoes Au Gratin

(Prep Time: 10 MIN| Cook Time: 17 MIN| Serve: 6)

Ingredients:

1 cup chicken stock
½ cup yellow onion, chopped
2 tbsp butter
6 potatoes, peeled and sliced
Salt and black pepper to taste
½ cup sour cream
1 cup Monterey jack cheese, shredded

For the topping:
3 tbsp melted butter
1 cup bread crumbs

Directions:

1. Set your instant pot on Sauté mode, add butter and melt before adding onion, cook for 5 minutes.
2. Add stock, salt, pepper and put the steamer basket in the pot as well.
3. Add potatoes, cover and cook on High for 5 minutes.
4. In a bowl, mix 3 tbsp butter with bread crumbs and stir well.
5. Release pressure from the pot fast, take the steamer basket out and transfer potatoes to a baking dish.
6. Pour cream and cheese into instant pot and stir.
7. Pour over potatoes and stir gently.
8. Spread bread crumbs mixture all over potatoes, place in preheated broiler and broil for 7 minutes.
9. Serve right away!

(Calories 340|Fat 22 g| Protein 11 g| Fiber2 g| Carbohydrates 32 g)

Crunchy Sweet Potato Casserole

(**Prep Time:** 15 MIN| **Cook Time:** 10 MIN| **Serve:** 4)

Ingredients:

3 pounds sweet potatoes, scrubbed
1 cup water
¼ cup coconut milk
1/3 cup palm sugar
½ tsp nutmeg, ground
2 tbsp coconut flour
1 tsp cinnamon
¼ tsp allspice
Salt to taste

For the topping:
½ cup almond flour
½ cup walnuts, soaked, drained and ground
¼ cup pecans, soaked, drained and ground
¼ cup shredded coconut
1 tbsp chia seeds
¼ cup palm sugar
A pinch of salt
1 tsp cinnamon, ground
5 tbsp salted butter

Directions:

1. Prick potatoes with a fork and place them in the steamer basket of your instant pot, add 1 cup water to the pot, cover and cook on High for 20 minutes.
2. Meanwhile, in a bowl, mix almond flour with pecans, walnuts, ¼ cup coconut, ¼ cup palm sugar, chia seeds, 1 tsp cinnamon, a pinch of salt and the butter and stir all ingredients well.
3. Release the pressure naturally from the pot and remove potatoes, peel them and add ½ cup water to the pot.

4. Chop potatoes and place them in a baking dish.
5. Add the crumble mixture you've made, stir everything, spread evenly in the dish, cover, place in the steamer basket, cover again and cook on High for 10 minutes.
6. Release the pressure quickly, take the dish out of the pot, uncover and leave to cool down before cutting and serving as a side dish.

(Calories 150|Fat 9 g| Protein 4 g| Fiber 3 g| Carbohydrates 25 g)

Classic French Fries

(Prep Time: 10 MIN| Cook Time: 10 MIN| Serve: 4)

Ingredients:

8 medium potatoes, peeled, cut into medium matchsticks and pat dried
1 cup water
Salt to taste
¼ tsp baking soda
Oil for frying

Directions:

1. Put the water in your instant pot, add salt and the baking soda and stir.
2. Put potatoes in the steamer basket and place it in the pot.
3. Cover and cook on High for 3 minutes.
4. Release the pressure naturally and take fries out of the pot to put them in a bowl.
5. Heat up a pan with enough oil over medium high heat and add fries, spread them and cook until they become golden.
6. Transfer fries to paper towels in order to drain excess grease and then put them in a bowl.
7. Add salt, toss to coat and serve.

(Calories 300|Fat 10 g| Protein 3.4 g| Fiber 3.7 g| Carbohydrates 41 g)

Pineapple and Cauliflower Rice

(**P**rep Time: 10 MIN| **C**ook Time: 20 MIN| **S**erve: 6)

Ingredients:

2 cups rice
4 cups water
1 cauliflower, florets separated and chopped
½ pineapple, peeled and chopped
Salt and black pepper to taste
2 tsp extra virgin olive oil

Directions:

1. In your instant pot, mix rice with pineapple, cauliflower, water, oil, salt and pepper, cover and cook for 20 minutes on Low.
2. Release the pressure naturally for 10 minutes, uncover and fluff with a fork, add more salt and pepper to taste and serve.

(Calories 100|Fat 2.7 g| Protein 4.9 g| Fiber 2.9 g| Carbohydrates 12 g)

Red Beans and Herb Rice

(**Prep Time:** 10 MIN| **Cook Time:** 25 MIN| **Serve:** 6)

Ingredients:

1 pound red kidney beans, soaked overnight and drained
Salt to taste
1 tsp vegetable oil
1 pound smoked sausage, cut into wedges
1 yellow onion, chopped
1 celery stalk, chopped
4 garlic cloves, chopped
1 green bell pepper, chopped
1 tsp thyme, dried
2 bay leaves
5 cups water
Long grain rice already cooked
2 green onions, minced for serving
2 tbsp parsley, minced for serving
Hot sauce for serving

Directions:

1. Set your instant pot on Sauté mode, add the oil and heat.
2. Add sausage, onion, bell pepper, celery, garlic, thyme and salt to taste, stir and cook for 8 minutes.
3. Add beans, bay leaves and the water, stir, cover and cook on High for 15 minutes.
4. Release the pressure naturally for 20 minutes before discarding bay leaves and put 2 cups of beans and some liquid in your blender.
5. Pulse them well and return to your pot.
6. Spoon the rice onto plates, add beans, sausage and veggies on top, sprinkle green onions and parsley and serve with hot sauce on top.

(Calories 160|Fat 3.8 g| Protein 4.6 g| Fiber 3.4 g| Carbohydrates 24 g)

Golden Cauliflower Mash

(**Prep Time:** 10 MIN| **Cook Time:** 6 MIN| **Serve:** 4)

Ingredients:

1 cauliflower, florets separated
Salt and black pepper to taste
1 ½ cups water
½ tsp turmeric
1 tbsp butter
3 chives, finely chopped

Directions:

1. Put the water in your instant pot, place cauliflower in the steamer basket, cover and cook on High for 6 minutes.
2. Release the pressure naturally for 2 minutes and then release the rest quickly.
3. Transfer cauliflower to a bowl and mash it with a potato masher.
4. Add salt, pepper, butter and turmeric, transfer to a blender and pulse well.
5. Serve with chives sprinkled on top.

(Calories 70|Fat 5 g| Protein 2 g| Fiber 2 g| Carbohydrates 5 g)

Garlic and Parmesan Asparagus

(Prep Time: 5 MIN| Cook Time: 8 MIN| Serve: 4)

Ingredients:

3 garlic cloves, minced
1 bunch asparagus, trimmed
1 cup water
3 tbsp butter
3 tbsp parmesan cheese, grated

Directions:

1. Put the water in your instant pot.
2. Place asparagus on a tin foil, add garlic and butter and curve the edges of the foil to prevent butter running off.
3. Place this in your pot, cover it and cook on High for 8 minutes.
4. Release the pressure quickly and arrange asparagus on plates, sprinkle parmesan and serve.

(Calories 70|Fat 5.2 g| Protein 4 g| Fiber 1.8 g| Carbohydrates 3.8 g)

"Drunken" Peas with Pancetta

(**Prep Time:** 10 MIN| **Cook Time:** 7 MIN| **Serve:** 4)

Ingredients:

4 ounces smoked pancetta, chopped
1 pound fresh peas
1 green onion, sliced
1 tbsp mint, chopped
¼ cup beer
1 tbsp butter
Salt and black pepper to taste
2 cups water

Directions:

1. Put the water in your instant pot, place the steamer basket inside as well and set aside.
2. In a heat proof pan, mix pancetta with half of the onion and heat this up on the stove over medium high heat for 3 minutes, add beer, peas and salt, stir and take off heat.
3. Cover this pan with some tin foil, place in the steamer basket, cover and cook on High for 1 minute.
4. Release the pressure quickly and uncover the pan, add more salt, pepper, mint and butter, stir and spoon onto plates and serve with the rest of the onions sprinkled on top.

(Calories 134|Fat 2 g| Protein 4.3 g| Fiber 2.5 g| Carbohydrates 10 g)

Eggplant and Anchovies

(**Prep Time:** 10 MIN| **Cook Time:** 13 MIN| **Serve:** 4)

Ingredients:

2 eggplants, cubed
Salt and black pepper to taste
2 tbsp extra virgin olive oil
1 garlic clove, crushed
A pinch of hot pepper flakes
1 bunch oregano, chopped
½ cup water
2 anchovies, chopped

Directions:

1. Sprinkle eggplant pieces with salt and place them in a strainer, press them with a plate and then drain them.
2. Set your instant pot on Sauté mode, add the oil and the garlic and fry anchovies, oregano and pepper flakes for 5 minutes.
3. Discard the garlic, add eggplants, salt and pepper, toss to coat and cook for 5 minutes.
4. Add the water, cover and cook on High for 3 minutes.
5. Release the pressure quickly and transfer eggplant mixture to plates. Enjoy!

(Calories 130|Fat 5 g| Protein 15 g| Fiber 10 g| Carbohydrates 12 g)

Ginger Bok Choy

(**Prep Time:** 10 MIN| **Cook Time:** 10 MIN| **Serve:** 4)

Ingredients:

5 bok choy bunches, end cut off
5 cups water
2 garlic cloves, minced
1 tsp ginger, grated
1 tbsp coconut oil
Salt to taste

Directions:

1. Put bok choy in your instant pot, add the water, cover and cook on High for 7 minutes.
2. Release the pressure and drain bok choy, chop and put them in a bowl.
3. Heat up a pan with the oil over medium heat, add bok choy and cook for 3 minutes.
4. Add more salt to taste, garlic and ginger and cook for 2 more minutes.
5. Serve with your favorite meat.

(Calories 60|Fat 0.4 g| Protein 2.4 g| Fiber 1.3 g| Carbohydrates 6.5 g)

Sauce Recipes

Eggplant Oregano Dip

(**P**rep **T**ime: 10 MIN| **C**ook **T**ime: 9 MIN| **S**erve: 4)

Ingredients:

1 tsp Italian Seasoning
2 cups water
4 medium eggplants, sliced
3 tbsp extra-virgin olive oil
2 cloves garlic, minced
1 tsp salt
½ tsp freshly ground black pepper
Juice of ½ organic lemon
½ tbsp dried oregano

Directions:

1. Place the Instant Pot over medium heat and add the water and Italian Seasoning.
2. Place the trivet into the pot.
3. Slice the eggplants and arrange in the trivet, with the skin side down. Cover the pot and set the timer for 9 minutes. When the time is finished, carefully release the pressure.
4. Uncover the pot and transfer the eggplant slices to a plate.
5. Remove the trivet and discard the water.
6. In a food processor, blend the eggplant slices with the olive oil and rest of the ingredients.
7. Transfer the puree into a bowl and serve with tortilla chips.

(Calories 235|Fat 11.9g| Protein 5.6 g| Carbohydrates 33.4 g)

Hot Double Cheese Corn Dip

(**Prep Time:** 10 MIN| **Cook Time:** 15 MIN| **Serve:** 4)

Ingredients:

2 tbsp extra-virgin olive oil
5 bacon strips, slices
1 small onion, diced
2 cups corn kernels (frozen is fine)
2 jalapeno pepper, seeds removed and diced (optional)
2 garlic cloves, crushed
1 can tomatoes, diced
1 tsp salt
1 tsp chili powder
½ tsp paprika
¼ tsp red pepper flakes
½ tsp ground cumin
1 package 8 ounce full fat cream cheese
1 ½ cups Cheddar cheese, grated
Fresh cilantro, to garnish

Directions:

1. Heat the olive oil in the Instant Pot over medium heat. Stir in the bacon and sauté until crispy. Transfer the bacon to a bowl and add the onions in the pot.
2. Stir the onions for 4 minutes until translucent. Add in the corn, jalapeno, garlic and tomatoes.
3. Season with salt, chili, paprika, red pepper flakes and cumin.
4. Stir in the cream cheese and cover the pot.
5. Set the time for 6 minutes. Once the time is finished, carefully release the pressure.
6. Uncover the pot and return the bacon and stir in the Cheddar.
7. Transfer to serving bowl and top with fresh cilantro.

(Calories 539|Fat 40.8| Protein 22.5 g| Carbohydrates 25.2 g)

Something Meaty Sauce

(**Prep Time:** 10 MIN| **Cook Time:** 30 MIN| **Serve:** 8)

Ingredients:

½ tsp salt
¼ tsp black pepper
1 Tbsp olive oil
1 pound ground beef
½ pound Italian sausage
28 ounces diced tomatoes, undrained
½ cup dry red wine
½ tsp chili powder
½ tsp minced garlic
2 bay leaves
6 ounces tomato paste
8 ounces mushrooms, sliced
1 cup chopped onion
¾ cup chopped green bell pepper
1/3 cup water
2.25 ounces ripe olives, drained and sliced
2 tsp sugar
½ tsp Worcestershire sauce

Directions:

1. Turn Instant Pot on to sauté mode.
2. Season the ground beef with salt and freshly ground black pepper.
3. Add 1 Tbsp of olive oil into the IP. Ensure the oil has coated the bottom of the insert entirely.
4. Then, add the ground beef and Italian sausage into the IP.
5. After 5 minutes drain sauce from the pot into a separate bowl and set aside. Sauté meat for another 3 – 4 minutes until brown. Stirring occasionally for browning on all sides.
6. Add all the remaining ingredients except diced tomatoes
7. Sauté for another 5 minutes to develop flavor and add in another pinch of salt
8. Then add diced tomatoes but do not mix them in.
9. Lock lid and cook on High Pressure for 10 minutes.
10. Then, 5 minutes Quick Release.

11. Stir and change the setting back to sauté. Let the sauce simmer on low for a few minutes to reduce to the desired thickness
12. Serve your Something Meaty Sauce over cooked spaghetti and sprinkle with Parmesan cheese.

(Calories 309|Fat 20 g| Protein 18 g| Fiber 3 g| Carbohydrates 14 g)

Infused Mushroom Sauce

(Prep Time: 10 MIN| Cook Time: 20 MIN| Serve: 8)

Ingredients:

1 Tbsp olive oil
8 ounces mushrooms, sliced
1 cup chopped onion
1 tsp minced garlic
½ tsp oregano
¼ cup grated Parmesan cheese
1 can tomato paste
24 ounces tomato sauce
½ tsp salt
½ tsp pepper

Directions:

1. Turn Instant Pot on to sauté.
2. Heat oil and add onions, mushrooms and garlic until onions are transparent, about 5 mins.
3. Add remaining ingredients.
4. Close the lid and set the IP to High Pressure for 10 minutes. Quick release the pressure.
5. Change the setting back to sauté, and let the sauce simmer on low for a few minutes to reduce to the desired thickness.
6. Divide into two parts and puree one half in a blender.
7. Combine and serve warm over pasta.

(Calories 92|Fat 3 g| Protein 4 g| Fiber 3 g| Carbohydrates 13 g)

Overnight Marinara Sauce

(**Prep Time:** 15 MIN| **Cook Time:** 8:30 HRS| **Serve:** 12)

Ingredients:

2 Tbsp olive oil
1 cup finely chopped onion
½ cup finely chopped carrots
½ tsp chopped garlic
2 cans crushed tomatoes
½ tsp dried oregano
½ tsp dried marjoram
1 Tbsp brown sugar
Pinch of salt

Directions:

1. In a skillet, sauté onion, carrots, and garlic in oil until tender. Do not brown.
2. Combine onion mixture, tomatoes, and brown sugar in instant pot. Stir well.
3. Cover and turn the steam release handle to venting position.
4. Select the slow cooker setting and cook on low for 8 hours.
5. Stir well. Cook on high uncovered for 30 minutes for a thicker marinara sauce.

(Calories 54|Fat 2 g| Protein 1 g| Fiber 2 g| Carbohydrates 8 g)

Cream Cheese Corn Dip with Cotija

(**Prep Time:** 10 MIN| **Cook Time:** 5 MIN| **Serve:** 4)

Ingredients:

2 cups sweetened corn kernels
package 4 ounces full fat cream cheese
½ cup mayonnaise
1 tsp salt
½ tsp ground black pepper
2 tsp ground chili
1 tsp red pepper flakes
½ tsp paprika
½ tsp ground cumin
½ tsp garlic powder
Juice of ½ lemon
½ cup Cotija cheese, crumbled
Fresh cilantro, to garnish

Directions:

1. Place the Instant Pot over medium heat and add the corn, cheese and mayonnaise.
2. Season with salt, black pepper, chili, red pepper, paprika, cumin and garlic powder.
3. Cover the pot and set the time on for 4 minutes.
4. Once the time is finished, carefully release the pressure. Uncover the pit and ass the lemon juice.
5. Transfer the corn mix to your serving bowl and top with Cotija crumbles and fresh cilantro.

(Calories 464|Fat 34.2g| Protein 18.1 g| Carbohydrates 27.4 g)

Classic Salsa Recipe

(**Prep Time:** 10 MIN| **Cook Time:** 20 MIN| **Serve:** 4)

Ingredients:

4 cans diced tomatoes
1 bell pepper , diced
2 onions, diced
3 jalapeno peppers, pitted and diced
2 cans tomato paste
1/3 cup white vinegar
¼ cup sugar
2 tsp salt
2 tsp garlic powder
2 tsp paprika
Fresh cilantro, finely chopped

Directions:

1. Place the Instant Pot over medium heat and add in all the ingredients and stir to combine.
2. Cover the pot and set the timer for 20 minutes.
3. Once the time is finished, allow the pressure to be release naturally.
4. Uncover the pot and transfer to a bowl and top with fresh cilantro.

(Calories 171|Fat 0.9g| Protein 5.4 g| Carbohydrates 40 g)

Ancho Chili Sauce

(**Prep Time:** 10 MIN| **Cook Time:** 10 MIN| **Serve:** 8)

Ingredients:

5 ancho chilies, dried, seedless and chopped
2 garlic cloves, crushed
Salt and black pepper to taste
1 ½ cups water
1 ½ tbsp sugar
½ tsp oregano, dried
½ tsp cumin, ground
2 tbsp apple cider vinegar

Directions:

1. In your instant pot mix water chilies, garlic, salt, pepper, sugar, cumin and oregano, stir, cover and cook on High for 8 minutes.
2. Release the pressure for 5 minutes, uncover pot and pour sauce into a blender.
3. Add vinegar, blend well and transfer sauce to a bowl.

(Calories 50|Fat 2 g| Protein 0 g| Fiber 0 g| Carbohydrates 2 g)

BBQ Sauce

(**P**rep Time: 10 MIN| **C**ook Time: 10 MIN| **S**erve: 8)

Ingredients:

1 tbsp sesame seed oil
½ cup tomato puree
1 yellow onion, chopped
½ cup water
4 tbsp white wine vinegar
4 tbsp honey
1 tsp salt
½ tsp granulated garlic
1 tsp liquid smoke
1 tsp Tabasco sauce
1/8 tsp cumin powder
1/8 tsp clove powder
5 ounces plumps, dried and deedless

Directions:

1. Set your instant pot on Sauté mode, add oil and fry onion for 5 minutes.
2. Add tomato puree, honey, water, vinegar, salt, garlic, Tabasco sauce, liquid smoke, cumin and clove powder and stir everything very well.
3. Add plumps and stir again well before covering pot and cooking on High for 10 minutes.
4. Release the pressure, uncover and blend sauce with an immersion blender, transfer to a bowl and serve.

(Calories 20|Fat 0.4 g| Protein 0.1 g| Fiber 0.4 g| Carbohydrates 3.5 g)

Giblet Gravy

(**Prep Time:** 10 MIN| **Cook Time:** 1 HOUR 30 MIN| **Serve:** 2)

Ingredients:

Turkey neck, gizzard, but and heart
1 tbsp vegetable oil
½ cup dry vermouth
1 yellow onion, chopped
1 quart turkey stock
1 bay leaf
4 tbsp butter
2 thyme springs
4 tbsp white flour
Salt and black pepper to taste

Directions:

1. Set your instant pot on Sauté mode, add oil and brown turkey pieces and onion for 6 minutes.
2. Add vermouth, stock, bay leaf and thyme and stir.
3. Cover pot and cook on High for 36 minutes.
4. Release the pressure for 20 minutes, then strain stock (reserving turkey gizzard and heart), leave them to cool down, remove gristle and chop it along with the heart.
5. Heat up a pan with the butter over medium heat and add flour, stir and cook flour for 3 minutes.
6. Add strained stock, stir well as it begins to thicken, increase heat to medium high and simmer for 20 minutes.
7. Add salt and pepper, heart and gizzard, stir well and serve with rice.

(Calories 181|Fat 10 g| Protein 10.5 g| Fiber 1 g| Carbohydrates 11.4 g)

Zucchini Pesto

(**P**rep **T**ime: 10 MIN| **C**ook **T**ime: 10 MIN| **S**erve: 4)

Ingredients:
1 yellow onion, chopped
1 tbsp extra virgin olive oil
1 and ½ pounds zucchini, chopped
Salt to taste
½ cup water
1 bunch basil, chopped
2 garlic cloves, minced

Directions:
1. Set your instant pot on Sauté mode, add oil and fry onion for 4 minutes.
2. Add zucchini, salt and water, stir, cover and cook on High for 3 minutes.
3. Release the pressure, uncover pot, add garlic and basil and blend contents using an immersion blender.
4. Transfer to a bowl and serve.

(Calories 71|Fat 5 g| Protein 1.2 g| Fiber2.3 g| Carbohydrates 2 g)

Cheese and Tomato Sauce

(**P**rep **T**ime: 10 MIN| **C**ook **T**ime: 5 MIN| **S**erve: 4)

Ingredients:
2 cups processed cheese, cut into chunks
1 cup Italian sausage, cooked and chopped
5 ounces canned tomatoes and green chilies, finely chopped
4 tbsp water

Directions:
1. In your instant pot, mix sausage with cheese, tomatoes and chilies and water.
2. Stir, cover and cook on High for 5 minutes.
3. Release pressure, uncover pot, transfer sauce to a bowl and serve with your favorite macaroni.

(Calories 110|Fat 8.5 g| Protein 4.3 g| Fiber 0.4 g| Carbohydrates4.3 g)

Mushroom Sauce

(**Prep Time:** 10 MIN| **Cook Time:** 35 MIN| **Serve:** 6)

Ingredients:

1 yellow onion, chopped
¼ cup olive oil
1 tbsp flour
Salt and black pepper to taste
1 tbsp thyme, chopped
3 garlic cloves, minced
1 and ¼ cup chicken stock
¼ cup dry sherry
10 ounces shiitake mushrooms, chopped
10 ounces cremini mushrooms, chopped
10 ounces Portobello mushrooms, chopped
1 ounce parmesan cheese, grated
½ cup heavy cream
1 tbsp parsley, finely chopped

Directions:

1. Set your instant pot on Sauté mode, add oil and fry onion, salt and pepper for 5 minutes.
2. Add garlic, flour and thyme and cook for a further minute.
3. Add sherry, stock and all mushrooms, stir, cover and cook on High for 25 minutes.
4. Release pressure quickly and add cream, cheese and parsley, stir and set the pot on Simmer mode.
5. Cook for 5 minutes before transferring to a bowl and serving.

(Calories 140|Fat 5.7 g| Protein 7.4 g| Fiber 3.1 g| Carbohydrates 13 g)

Spicy Mango Chutney

(**Prep Time:** 10 MIN| **Cook Time:** 30 MIN| **Serve:** 4)

Ingredients:

1 shallot, chopped
1 tbsp vegetable oil
¼ tsp cardamom powder
2 tbsp ginger, minced
½ tsp cinnamon
2 mangos, chopped
2 red hot chilies, chopped
1 apple, cored and chopped
2 tsp salt
¼ cup raisins
1 ¼ cup raw sugar
1 ¼ apple cider vinegar

Directions:

1. Set your instant pot on Sauté mode, add oil and fry ginger and shallots for 5 minutes.
2. Add cinnamon, hot peppers and cardamom and cook for 2 more minutes.
3. Add mangos, apple, raisins, sugar and cider, stir and cook until sugar melts.
4. Cover and cook on High for 7 minutes.
5. Release the pressure, uncover and transfer to a pan and simmer on medium heat for 15 minutes more, stirring from time to time.
6. Transfer to jars and serve when needed.

(Calories 80|Fat 0.3 g| Protein 0.9 g| Fiber 1 g| Carbohydrates 9 g)

Tomato Chutney

(Prep Time: 10 MIN| Cook Time: 10 MIN| Serve: 6)

Ingredients:

3 pounds tomatoes, peeled and chopped
1 cup red wine vinegar
1 ¾ cups sugar
1 inch ginger piece, grated
3 garlic cloves, minced
2 onions, chopped
¼ cup raisins
¾ tsp cinnamon, ground
¼ tsp cloves
½ tsp coriander, ground
¼ tsp nutmeg
¼ tsp ginger, ground
1 pinch paprika
1 tsp chili powder

Directions:

1. Mix tomatoes and grated ginger in your blender, pulse well and transfer to your instant pot.
2. Add vinegar, sugar, garlic, onions, raisins, cinnamon, cloves, coriander, nutmeg, ground ginger, paprika and chili powder, stir, cover and cook on High for 10 minutes.
3. Release the pressure and transfer to clean sterilized jars and serve when needed.

(Calories 140|Fat 10 g| Protein 4 g| Fiber 0 g| Carbohydrates 10 g)

Date and Tomato Sauce

(**Prep Time:** 10 MIN| **Cook Time:** 15 MIN| **Serve:** 20)

Ingredients:

2 pounds tomatoes, peeled and chopped
1 apple, cored and chopped
1 yellow onion, chopped
6 ounces sultanas, chopped
3 ounces dates chopped
Salt to taste
3 tsp allspice
½ pint vinegar
½ pound brown sugar

Directions:

1. Put tomatoes in your instant pot and add apple, onion, sultanas, dates, salt, whole spice and half of the vinegar, stir, cover and cook on High for 10 minutes.
2. Release the pressure, uncover and set it on Simmer mode, add the rest of the vinegar and sugar, stir and simmer until sugar dissolves.
3. Transfer to sterilized jars and serve when needed.

(Calories 70|Fat 4 g| Protein 1.7 g| Fiber 1 g| Carbohydrates 8 g)

Green Tomato Sauce

(**Prep Time:** 5 MIN| **Cook Time:** 10 MIN| **Serve:** 12)

Ingredients:

2 pounds green tomatoes, chopped
1 white onion, chopped
¼ cup currants
1 Anaheim chili pepper, chopped
4 red chili peppers, chopped
2 tbsp ginger, grated
¾ cup brown sugar
¾ cup white vinegar

Directions:
1. In your instant pot, mix green tomatoes with onion, currants, Anaheim pepper, chili pepper, ginger, sugar and vinegar, stir, cover and cook on High for 10 minutes.
2. Release the pressure for 5 minutes and transfer sauce to sterilized jars and serve as needed.

(Calories 50|Fat 2 g| Protein1.5 g| Fiber 2.4 g| Carbohydrates 10 g)

Orange and Ginger Sauce

(**Prep Time:** 5 MIN| **Cook Time:** 7 MIN| **Serve:** 4)

Ingredients:

1 cup fish stock
Salt and black pepper to taste
1 tbsp olive oil
4 spring onions, chopped
1 inch ginger piece, chopped
Zest and juice from 1 orange

Directions:
1. In your instant pot, mix fish stock with salt, pepper, olive oil, spring onions, ginger, orange juice and zest and stir well.
2. Cover pot and cook on High for 7 minutes.
3. Release pressure, uncover pot and serve your sauce.

(Calories 100|Fat 1 g| Protein 4 g| Fiber 1 g| Carbohydrates 2 g)

Plum Sauce

(**P**rep Time: 10 MIN| **C**ook Time: 15 MIN| **S**erve: 20)

Ingredients:
3 pounds plums, pitted and chopped
2 onions, chopped
2 apples, cored and chopped
4 tbsp ginger, ground
4 tbsp cinnamon
4 tbsp allspice
1 ½ tbsp salt
1 pint vinegar
¾ pound sugar

Directions:
1. Put plums, apples and onions in your instant pot and add ginger, cinnamon, allspice, salt and almost all the vinegar, stir, cover and cook on High for 10 minutes.
2. Release the pressure, uncover and set it on Simmer mode, add the rest of the vinegar and the sugar, stir and cook until sugar dissolves.

(Calories 100|Fat 10 g| Protein 26 g| Fiber 3 g| Carbohydrates 23 g)

Simple Onion Sauce

(**P**rep Time: 10 MIN| **C**ook Time: 30 MIN| **S**erve: 8)

Ingredients:
6 tbsp butter
3 pounds yellow onion, thinly chopped
Salt and black pepper to taste
½ tsp baking soda

Directions:
1. Set your instant pot on Sauté mode, add butter and heat before adding onions and soda and cooking for 3 minutes.
2. Cover your pot and cook on High for 20 minutes.
3. Release the pressure, uncover and set it on Sauté mode again and cook for 5 minutes more, stirring often. Serve when needed.

(Calories 100|Fat0.4 g| Protein 0 g| Fiber 0 g| Carbohydrates 9 g)

Spiced Pineapple Sauce

(Prep Time: 10 MIN| Cook Time: 3 MIN| Serve: 4)

Ingredients:

3 cups pineapple tidbits

3 tbsp rum

3 tbsp butter

4 tbsp brown sugar

1 tsp cinnamon

1 tsp allspice

1 tsp nutmeg

1 tsp ginger

Directions:
1. Set your instant pot on Sauté mode, add butter and melt before adding sugar, pineapple tidbits, rum, allspice, nutmeg, cinnamon and ginger, stir, cover and cook on High for 3 minutes.
2. Release pressure, uncover and stir sauce one more time and serve.

(Calories 160|Fat 0 g| Protein 0 g| Fiber 0 g| Carbohydrates 23 g)

Clementine and Cranberry Sauce

(Prep Time: 10 MIN| Cook Time: 6 MIN| Serve: 4)

Ingredients:

12 ounces cranberries

1 cup water

Juice and peel from 1 clementine

1 cup sugar

Directions:
1. In your instant pot, mix cranberries with clementine juice and peel, water and sugar, stir, cover and cook on High for 6 minutes.
2. Release pressure, uncover and serve your sauce.

(Calories 50|Fat 0 g| Protein 0 g| Fiber 0 g| Carbohydrates 0.3 g)

Chili Orange Sauce

(Prep Time: 10 MIN| Cook Time: 7 MIN| Serve: 6)

Ingredients:

¼ cup white wine vinegar
1 tsp ginger paste
2 tbsp tomato paste
3 tbsp sugar
1 cup orange juice
1 tsp garlic, finely chopped
2 tbsp agave nectar
1 tsp sesame oil
1 tsp chili sauce
2 tbsp soy sauce
¼ cup veggie stock
2 tbsp cornstarch

Directions:

1. Set your instant pot on Sauté mode, add oil and heat before frying garlic and ginger paste for 2 minutes.
2. Add tomato paste, sugar, orange juice, vinegar, agave nectar, soy and chili sauce, stir, cover and cook on High for 3 minutes more.
3. Release pressure, uncover and add stock and cornstarch, stir, cover again and cook on High for 4 minutes.
4. Release pressure again and serve your sauce.

(Calories 80|Fat 7 g| Protein 13 g| Fiber 1.4 g| Carbohydrates 5 g)

Sriracha Hot Sauce

(Prep Time: 10 MIN| Cook Time: 17 MIN| Serve: 6)

Ingredients:

4 ounces red chilies, seeded and chopped
3 tbsp palm sugar
3 ounces bird's eye chilies
12 garlic cloves, minced
5 ounces distilled vinegar
5 ounces water

Directions:

1. In your instant pot, mix water with palm sugar and stir.
2. Add all chilies and garlic, stir, cover and cook on High for 7 minutes.
3. Release pressure, uncover and blend sauce using an immersion blender.
4. Add vinegar, stir and set pot on Simmer mode and cook sauce for 10 minutes.
5. Serve when needed.

(Calories 90|Fat 0.4 g| Protein 2.4 g| Fiber 0.3 g| Carbohydrates 19 g)

Pomegranate Sauce

(Prep Time: 10 MIN| Cook Time: 25 MIN| Serve: 4)

Ingredients:

5 cups pomegranate juice
½ cup lemon juice
1 cup white sugar

Directions:

1. In your instant pot, mix pomegranate juice with sugar and lemon juice, stir, cover and cook on High for 25 minutes.
2. Release pressure, uncover and ladle sauce into sterilized jars and serve when needed.

(Calories 136|Fat 0.4 g| Protein 1.2 g| Fiber0.8 g| Carbohydrates 35 g)

Mustard Sauce

(**P**rep Time: 10 MIN| **C**ook Time: 7 MIN| **S**erve: 4)

Ingredients:

6 ounces mushrooms, chopped
3 tbsp olive oil
3.5 ounces dry sherry
1 thyme spring
1 garlic clove, minced
3.5 ounces beef stock
1 tbsp balsamic vinegar
1 tbsp mustard
2 tbsp crème fraiche
2 tbsp parsley, finely chopped

Directions:

1. Set your instant pot on Sauté mode, add oil and heat before frying garlic, thyme and mushrooms for 5 minutes.
2. Add sherry, vinegar and stock, cover and cook on High for 3 minutes.
3. Release pressure and discard thyme before adding crème fraiche, mustard, and parsley, stir well and set pot on Simmer mode and cook sauce for 3 minutes.
4. Serve right away.

(Calories 67|Fat 0.4 g| Protein 1 g| Fiber 0.2 g| Carbohydrates 4 g)

Apricot Sauce

(**Prep Time:** 10 MIN| **Cook Time:** 32 MIN| **Serve:** 6)

Ingredients:

3 ounces apricots, dried and cut into halves
2 cups water
2/3 cup sugar
1 tsp vanilla extract

Directions:
1. In your instant pot mix apricots with water, sugar and vanilla, stir, cover and cook on Medium for 20 minutes.
2. Release pressure and transfer sauce to your blender and pulse well.
3. Divide into jars and serve with a poultry dish.

(Calories 100|Fat 0.6 g| Protein 1 g| Fiber 0 g| Carbohydrates 10 g)

Creamy Broccoli Sauce

(**Prep Time:** 10 MIN| **Cook Time:** 6 MIN| **Serve:** 4)

Ingredients:

6 cups water
3 cups broccoli florets
2 garlic cloves, minced
Salt and black pepper to taste
1/3 cup coconut milk
1 tbsp white wine vinegar
1 tbsp nutritional yeast
1 tbsp olive oil

Directions:
1. Put the water in your instant pot and add broccoli, salt, pepper and garlic, cover and cook on High for 6 minutes.
2. Release pressure, uncover and strain broccoli and garlic and transfer to a food processor.
3. Add coconut milk, vinegar, yeast, olive oil, salt and pepper and blend very well.
4. Serve over pasta.

(Calories 128|Fat 10 g| Protein 5.4 g| Fiber 1.4 g| Carbohydrates 6 g)

Eggplant Sauce

(**Prep Time:** 10 MIN| **Cook Time:** 20 MIN| **Serve:** 6)

Ingredients:

1 pound ground meat
28 ounces canned tomatoes, chopped
5 garlic cloves, minced
5 ounces canned tomato paste
1 sweet onion, chopped
1 eggplant, chopped
½ cup olive oil
½ tsp turmeric
1 cup bone stock
1 tbsp apple cider vinegar
½ tsp dill, dried
Salt and black pepper to taste
¼ cup parsley, chopped

Directions:

1. Set your instant pot on Sauté mode, add meat, brown for a few minutes and transfer to a bowl.
2. Heat up the oil in your instant pot, add onion and some salt and fry for 2 minutes before adding eggplant and garlic and cooking for 1 more minute.
3. Add vinegar and cook for a further 2 minutes.
4. Add tomato paste, tomatoes, meat, salt, pepper, parsley, dill, turmeric and stock, stir, cover and cook on High for 15 minutes.
5. Release pressure, uncover and add more salt and pepper and a splash of lemon juice, stir well and serve.

(Calories 142|Fat 11 g| Protein 2.1 g| Fiber 4.4 g| Carbohydrates 10 g)

Cherry Sauce

(**Prep Time:** 10 MIN| **Cook Time:** 5 MIN| **Serve:** 4)

Ingredients:
1 tbsp lemon juice
¼ cup water
1 tsp kirsch
A pinch of salt
1 tbsp sugar
2 tbsp cornstarch
2 cups cherries

Directions:
1. In your instant pot, mix water with lemon juice, salt, sugar, kirsch and cornstarch.
2. Add cherries, stir, cover and cook on High for 5 minutes.
3. Release pressure, uncover and transfer sauce to a bowl and serve once it cools down.

(Calories 60|Fat 0 g| Protein 0 g| Fiber 0 g| Carbohydrates 13 g)

Elderberry Honey Sauce

(**Prep Time:** 10 MIN| **Cook Time:** 10 MIN| **Serve:** 20)

Ingredients:
4 cups water
1 cup elderberries
1 inch ginger piece, grated
1 cinnamon stick
1 vanilla bean, split
5 cloves
1 cup honey

Directions:
1. In your instant pot, mix elderberries with water, ginger, cinnamon, vanilla and cloves, stir, cover and cook on High for 10 minutes.
2. Release pressure, strain sauce and keep in sterilized jars.

(Calories 55|Fat 0 g| Protein 0 g| Fiber 0 g| Carbohydrates 13 g)

Pear and Cinnamon Sauce

(**P**rep Time: 10 MIN| **C**ook Time: 15 MIN| **S**erve: 20)

Ingredients:

10 cups pears, sliced
2 tsp cinnamon
1 cup pear juice
½ tsp nutmeg

Directions:
1. Put pear pieces in your instant pot and add cinnamon, nutmeg and pear juice.
2. Stir, cover pot and cook on High for 10 minutes.
3. Release pressure, uncover and blend using an immersion blender. Serve when needed. Delicious over ice-cream!

(Calories 80|Fat 0.1 g| Protein 0.1 g| Fiber 0 g| Carbohydrates 20 g)

Melon and Wine Sauce

(**P**rep Time: 5 MIN| **C**ook Time: 10 MIN| **S**erve: 6)

Ingredients:

Flesh from 1 small melon
1 ounce sugar
1 cup sweet wine
1 tbsp butter
1 tsp starch
Juice of 1 lemon

Directions:
1. Put melon and sweet wine in your instant pot, cover and cook on High for 7 minutes.
2. Release pressure, transfer sauce to a blender and add lemon juice, sugar, butter and starch and blend very well.
3. Return this sauce to your instant pot, set it on Simmer mode and cook sauce for 3 minutes until it thickens. Serve right away.

(Calories 68|Fat 0.3 g| Protein 1 g| Fiber 0.1 g| Carbohydrates 1 g)

Gingered Guava Sauce

(**Prep Time:** 10 MIN| **Cook Time:** 20 MIN| **Serve:** 6)

Ingredients:

1 can guava shells and syrup
2 onions, chopped
¼ cup vegetable oil
Juice from 2 lemons
2 garlic cloves, chopped
1 inch ginger piece, minced
½ tsp nutmeg
2 bird chilies, chopped

Directions:

1. Put guava shells and syrup in your blender, pulse well and set aside.
2. Set your instant pot on Sauté mode, add oil and fry onion and garlic for 4 minutes.
3. Add guava mixture, ginger, lemon juice, chilies and nutmeg, stir, cover and cook on High for 15 minutes.
4. Release pressure, uncover and serve sauce with fish.

(Calories 85|Fat 2.3 g| Protein 3 g| Fiber 8 g| Carbohydrates 22 g)

Peaches & Whiskey Sauce

(**Prep Time:** 10 MIN| **Cook Time:** 10 MIN| **Serve:** 6)

Ingredients:

1 cup brown sugar
3 cups peaches, pureed
6 tbsp whiskey
1 cup white sugar
2 tsp lemon zest, grated

Directions:

1. In your instant pot mix peaches with brown and white sugar, whiskey and lemon zest, stir, cover and cook on High for 10 minutes.
2. Release pressure, uncover and stir sauce and transfer it to sterilized jars.

(Calories 100|Fat 0.7 g| Protein 7 g| Fiber 0.6 g| Carbohydrates 7 g)

Peach Sauce

(**Prep Time:** 5 MIN| **Cook Time:** 3 MIN| **Serve:** 6)

Ingredients:

10 ounces peaches, stoned and chopped

1/8 tsp nutmeg, ground

2 tbsp cornstarch

3 tbsp sugar

½ cup water

A pinch of salt

1/8 tsp cinnamon

1/8 tsp almond extract

Directions:
1. In your instant pot, mix peaches with nutmeg, cornstarch, sugar, cinnamon and salt, stir, cover and cook on High for 3 minutes.
2. Release pressure, uncover and add almond extract, stir and serve sauce.

(Calories 100|Fat 1 g| Protein 6 g| Fiber 0.6 g| Carbohydrates 4 g)

Quince Sauce

(**Prep Time:** 10 MIN| **Cook Time:** 15 MIN| **Serve:** 6)

Ingredients:

2 pounds grated quince

Juice of 1 lemon

10 cloves

2 pounds sugar

¼ cup water

Directions:
1. In your instant pot, mix quince with sugar and stir well before adding water and stir again.
2. Tie cloves in a cheesecloth and add to the pot as well.
3. Cover and cook on High for 10 minutes.
4. Release pressure for 10 minutes, uncover and stir sauce again and transfer to clean sterilized storage jars. Serve on top of cakes.

(Calories 60|Fat 0 g| Protein 1 g| Fiber 1 g| Carbohydrates 16 g)

Creamy Parsley Sauce

(Prep Time: 10 MIN| Cook Time: 7 MIN| Serve: 6)

Ingredients:

2 cups chicken stock
1 yellow onion, finely chopped
2 tbsp butter
2 tbsp flour
¾ cup whole milk
4 tbsp parsley, chopped
1 egg yolk
¼ cup heavy cream
Salt and white pepper to taste

Directions:

1. Put stock and onion in your instant pot, set the pot on Simmer mode and bring to the boil.
2. Heat up a pan with the butter over medium heat, add flour and stir well to combine.
3. Pour this mixture and whole milk over stock and stir very well to prevent lumps forming.
4. Bring to a boil, add parsley, stir, cover and cook on High for 2 minutes.
5. Release pressure, uncover and set it back on Simmer mode.
6. In a bowl, mix cream with egg yolk and some of the sauce from the pot.
7. Stir this well, pour over sauce and whisk vigorously.
8. Add salt and pepper to taste, stir again and cook for a couple of minutes until it thickens and serve with chicken and rice.

(Calories 70|Fat 2.5 g| Protein 2.5 g| Fiber 0.5 g| Carbohydrates 7.3 g)

Cilantro Sauce

(**P**rep Time: 5 MIN| **C**ook Time: 6 MIN| **S**erve: 6)

Ingredients:

3 garlic cloves, minced
1 tbsp olive oil
2 red chilies, minced
3 shallots, minced
3 scallions, chopped
3 tomatoes, chopped
Salt and black pepper to taste
2 tbsp cilantro, chopped
¼ cup water

Directions:

1. Set your instant pot on Sauté mode, add oil and fry garlic, shallots and chilies for 3 minutes.
2. Add scallions, tomatoes, water, salt, pepper and cilantro, stir, cover and cook on High for 3 minutes.
3. Release the pressure, uncover and blend using an immersion blender and serve.

(Calories 67|Fat 1 g| Protein 0.5 g| Fiber 0.4 g| Carbohydrates 1 g)

Chestnut Sauce

(**Prep Time:** 10 MIN| **Cook Time:** 20 MIN| **Serve:** 6)

Ingredients:
11 ounces sugar
11 ounces water
1 ½ pounds chestnuts, cut into halves and peeled
1/8 cup rum liquor

Directions:
1. In your instant pot, mix sugar with water, rum and chestnuts.
2. Stir well, cover and cook on High for 20 minutes.
3. Release pressure for 10 minutes, uncover and blend contents with an immersion blender.
4. Serve when needed.

(Calories 50|Fat 0 g| Protein 0 g| Fiber 0 g| Carbohydrates 10 g)

Spiced Rhubarb Sauce

(**Prep Time:** 10 MIN| **Cook Time:** 13 MIN| **Serve:** 6)

Ingredients:
8 ounces rhubarb, trimmed and chopped
1 tbsp cider vinegar
1 small onion, chopped
A pinch of cardamom, ground
1 garlic clove, minced
2 jalapeno peppers, chopped
1/3 cup honey
¼ cup raisins
¼ cup water

Directions:
1. In your instant pot, mix rhubarb with vinegar, onion, cardamom, garlic, jalapenos, honey, water and raisins, stir, cover and cook on High for 7 minutes.
2. Release the pressure, uncover and set it on Simmer mode and cook for 3 more minutes.

(Calories 90|Fat 0 g| Protein 1 g| Fiber 1 g| Carbohydrates 23 g)

Jams & Spreads

Mixed Berry Breakfast Jam

Serve (**Prep Time:** 20 MIN| **Cook Time:** 1 HOUR 15 MIN| **Serve:** 12)

Ingredients:
16 ounces cranberries
16 ounces strawberries, chopped
Zest from 1 lemon
4 ounces raisins
Pinch of salt
3 ounces water
2 ½ pounds sugar

Directions:
1. In your instant pot, mix strawberries with cranberries, lemon zest and raisins.
2. Add sugar, stir and set pot aside for 1 hour.
3. Add water and a pinch of salt, cover and cook on High for 15 minutes.
4. Release the pressure and set jam aside for 5 minutes, stir and pour into small sterilized jars and enjoy on toasted bread slices!

(Calories 60|Fat 0 g| Protein 1 g| Fiber 0 g| Carbohydrates 12 g)

Instant Lemon Marmalade

(**Prep Time:** 10 MIN| **Cook Time:** 15 MIN| **Serve:** 8)

Ingredients:
2 pounds lemons, washed and sliced with a mandolin
4 pounds sugar
1 tbsp vinegar

Directions:
1. Put lemon slices in your instant pot.
2. Cover and cook the marmalade on High for 10 minutes.
3. Release the pressure, add the sugar, cover again and cook on High for 4 more minutes.
4. Release the pressure again and stir your marmalade, pour it into sterilized jars .

(Calories 60|Fat 1 g| Protein g| Fiber 0 g| Carbohydrates 12 g)

Orange Marmalade

(**P**rep Time: 10 MIN| **C**ook Time: 25 MIN| **S**erve: 8)

Ingredients:
Juice from 2 lemons
3 pounds sugar
1 pound oranges, cut into halves
1 pint water

Directions:
1. Squeeze juice from the oranges and cut the peel into small pieces.
2. Put peel in a bowl, cover with water and set aside overnight.
3. In your instant pot, mix lemon juice with orange juice, water and peel.
4. Cover pot, cook on High for 15 minutes, release pressure and, add sugar and stir before setting the pot on Simmer mode.
5. Cook until sugar dissolves, spoon into jars and serve when needed.

(Calories 50|Fat 0 g| Protein 0.1 g| Fiber 0.1 g| Carbohydrates 12 g)

Pear and Apple Jam

(**P**rep Time: 10 MIN| **C**ook Time: 4 MIN| **S**erve: 12)

Ingredients:
8 pears, cored and cut into quarters
2 apples, peeled, cored and cut into quarters
¼ cup apple juice
1 tsp cinnamon, ground

Directions:
1. In your instant pot, mix pears with apples, cinnamon and apple juice, stir, cover and cook on High for 4 minutes.
2. Release the pressure naturally and blend using an immersion blender.
3. Spoon hot jam into jars and keep in refrigerator until you eat it.

(Calories 90|Fat 0 g| Protein 0 g| Fiber 1 g| Carbohydrates 20 g)

Mixed Berry Jam

(**Prep Time:** 1 HOUR| **Cook Time:** 20 MIN| **Serve:** 12)

Ingredients:

1 pound cranberries
1 pound strawberries
½ pound blueberries
3.5 ounces black currant
2 pounds sugar
Zest from 1 lemon
A pinch of salt
2 tbsp water

Directions:

1. In your instant pot, mix strawberries with cranberries, blueberries, currants, lemon zest and sugar.
2. Stir to distribute sugar evenly and set aside for 1 hour.
3. Add salt and water, set the pot on Simmer mode and bring to the boil.
4. Cover pot, cook on Low for 10 minutes and release pressure for 10 minutes.
5. Uncover pot and set it on Simmer mode again, bring to the boil and simmer for 4 minutes.
6. Spoon into sterilized jars and keep in the fridge until you need it.

(Calories 60|Fat 0 g| Protein 0 g| Fiber 0 g| Carbohydrates 12 g)

Peach and Ginger Jam

(**Prep Time:** 10 MIN| **Cook Time:** 5 MIN| **Serve:** 6)

Ingredients:

4 ½ cups peaches, peeled and cubed
6 cups sugar
¼ cup crystallized ginger, chopped
1 box fruit pectin

Directions:

1. Set your instant pot on Simmer mode, add peaches, ginger and pectin, stir and bring to the boil.
2. Add sugar, stir, cover and cook on High for 5 minutes.
3. Release pressure and pour hot jam into sterilized jars and seal. Serve as needed.

(Calories 50|Fat 0 g| Protein 0 g| Fiber 1 g| Carbohydrates 3 g)

Raspberry Curd

(**Prep Time:** 10 MIN| **Cook Time:** 5 MIN| **Serve:** 4)

Ingredients:

1 cup sugar
12 ounces raspberries
2 egg yolks
2 tbsp lemon juice
2 tbsp butter

Directions:

1. Put raspberries in your instant pot and add sugar and lemon juice, stir well before covering and cook on High for 2 minutes.
2. Release pressure for 5 minutes, uncover and strain raspberries, discarding seeds.
3. In a bowl, mix egg yolks with hot raspberries and stir well to avoid lumps of cooked egg yolk forming.
4. Return this to your instant pot, set it on Sauté mode and simmer for 2 minutes before stirring in butter. Transfer to a container and serve cold with waffles or toast.

(Calories 110|Fat 4 g| Protein 1 g| Fiber 0 g| Carbohydrates 16 g)

Blackberry Jam

(**Prep Time:** 10 MIN| **Cook Time:** 20 MIN| **Serve:** 4)

Ingredients:
4 pints blackberries
Juice from 1 small lemon
5 cups sugar
3 tbsp pectin powder

Directions:
1. Put the blackberries in your instant pot and add the sugar, stir, select Sauté mode and cook for 3 minutes.
2. Transfer the jam to clean jars, close them and place them in the steamer basket of your instant pot.
3. Add water to cover the jars halfway, select Canning mode on your pot, cover and leave them for 20 minutes.
4. Remove jars after 20 minutes and leave them to cool down.
5. Keep your jam in the fridge until you serve it in the morning with some toast and butter.

(Calories 63|Fat 6 g| Protein 2 g| Fiber 7.6 g| Carbohydrates 12 g)

Berry Compote

(**Prep Time:** 10 MIN| **Cook Time:** 5 MIN| **Serve:** 8)

Ingredients:
1 cup blueberries
2 cups strawberries, sliced
2 tbsp lemon juice
¾ cup sugar
1 tbsp cornstarch
1 tbsp water

Directions:
1. In your instant pot, mix blueberries with lemon juice and sugar, stir, cover and cook on High for 3 minutes.
2. Release pressure naturally for 10 minutes and uncover pot.

3. In a bowl, mix cornstarch with water, stir well and add to the pot, stirring continuously to avoid lumps.
4. Set pot on Sauté mode and cook compote for a further 2 minutes before spooning hot compote into jars and keeping in the fridge until you serve it.

(Calories 260|Fat 0 g| Protein 3 g| Fiber 3 g| Carbohydrates 23 g)

Cinnamon Apple Butter

(**Prep Time:** 10 MIN| **Cook Time:** 1:15 HRS| **Serve:** 48)

Ingredients:
12 tart apples
1 cup apple cider
1 cup honey
1 tsp cinnamon
¼ tsp cloves

Directions:
1. Core and chop apples into squares but do not peel.
2. Combine with cider, honey and spices in your Instant Pot.
3. Cover and cook for 15 minutes at high pressure. Naturally release pressure.
4. Puree the contents of the pot.
5. Return the contents to your IP and sauté on low for 30 minutes.
6. Stir after the first 30 minutes and if it has not reached the desired consistency, repeat and sauté on low for another 30 minutes.
7. This recipe makes quite a lot of apple butter, but it freezes well and you can keep it frozen for up to a month.

(Calories 39|Fat 0 g| Protein 0 g| Fiber 0 g| Carbohydrates 11 g)

Candied Lemon Peel

(**Prep Time:** 20 MIN| **Cook Time:** 20 MIN| **Serve:** 80 pieces)

Ingredients:

5 big lemons
2 ¼ cups white sugar
5 cups water

Directions:

1. Wash lemons, slice them in half, reserve juice for another use, slice each half in quarters, take out the pulp and cut peel in thin strips.
2. Put strips in your instant pot, add 4 cups water, cover and cook on High for 3 minutes.
3. Release pressure fast and uncover, strain peel and rinse and put in a bowl.
4. Clean your instant pot and add 2 cups sugar and 1 cup water into it.
5. Add lemon strips and set pot on Simmer mode before cooking for 5 minutes.
6. Cover pot, cook on High for 10 more minutes and release pressure naturally for 20 minutes
7. Strain candied peel again and spread them on a cutting board to cool down for 10 minutes.
8. Keep them in sterilized jars until you serve them as an accompaniment to cakes or desserts.

(Calories 7|Fat 0 g| Protein 0 g| Fiber 0.2 g| Carbohydrates 2 g)

Chickpea Spread

(**Prep Time:** 5 MIN| **Cook Time:** 20 MIN| **Serve:** 8)

Ingredients:

1 cup chickpeas soaked and drained
6 cups water
1 bay leaf
4 garlic cloves crushed
2 tbsp tahini paste
Juice of 1 lemon
¼ tsp cumin
Salt to taste
¼ cup chopped parsley
A pinch of paprika
Extra virgin olive oil

Directions:

1. Put chickpeas and water in your instant pot and add bay leaf, 2 garlic cloves, cover and cook on High for 18 minutes
2. Release the pressure, discard excess liquid and bay leaf and reserve some of the cooking liquid.
3. Add tahini paste, the cooking liquid you've reserved, lemon juice, cumin, the rest of the garlic and salt to taste.
4. Transfer all ingredients to your food processor and pulse well.
5. Transfer your chickpea spread into a serving bowl, sprinkle olive oil and paprika on top and enjoy!

(Calories 270|Fat 19 g| Protein 6.8 g| Fiber 5.1 g| Carbohydrates 21.5 g)

Mushroom Pate

(**Prep Time: 6 MIN| Cook Time: 18 MIN| Serve: 6**)

Ingredients:

1 ounce dry porcini mushrooms
1 pound button mushrooms sliced
1 cup boiled water
1 tbsp butter
1 tbsp extra virgin olive oil
1 shallot finely chopped
¼ cup white wine
Salt and pepper to taste
1 bay leaf
1 tbsp truffle oil
3 tbsp grated parmesan cheese

Directions:

1. Put dry mushrooms in a bowl, add 1 cup boiling water over them and set them aside to absorb the water.
2. Set your instant pot on Sauté mode, add butter and the olive oil and heat before frying shallots for 2 minutes
3. Add reconstituted mushrooms and their liquid, fresh mushrooms, wine, salt, pepper and bay leaf.
4. Stir, cover and cook on High for 16 minutes.
5. Release the pressure, discard bay leaf and some of the liquid, transfer mixture to your blender and pulse until you obtain a creamy spread.
6. Add truffle oil and grated parmesan cheese, blend again and transfer to a bowl and serve.

(Calories 220|Fat 15 g| Protein 5 g| Fiber 0 g| Carbohydrates 15 g)

Ricotta Cheese Spread

(**Prep Time:** 10 MIN| **Cook Time:** 5 MIN| **Serve:** 4)

Ingredients:

10 ounces canned tomatoes and green chilies, chopped

1 ¾ cups Italian sausage, ground

4 cups processed cheese, cut into chunks

4 tbsp water

Directions:

1. In your instant pot, mix tomatoes and chilies with water, ground sausage and cheese.
2. Stir, cover and cook on High for 5 minutes.
3. Release the pressure naturally for 5 minutes, uncover and transfer to a bowl and serve.

(Calories 294|Fat 18 g| Protein 7 g| Fiber 1 g| Carbohydrates 4 g)

Pumpkin Butter

(**Prep Time:** 15 MIN| **Cook Time:** 10 MIN| **Serve:** 18)

Ingredients:

30 ounces pumpkin puree

3 apples, peeled, cored and chopped

1 tbsp pumpkin spice

1 cup sugar

A pinch of salt

12 ounces apple cider

½ cup honey

Directions:

1. In your instant pot, mix pumpkin puree with pumpkin spice, apple pieces, sugar, honey, cider and a pinch of salt,
2. Stir well, cover and cook on High for 10 minutes.
3. Release the pressure naturally for 15 minutes and transfer the butter to small jars and keep it in the fridge until you serve it.

(Calories 50|Fat 1 g| Protein 1 g| Fiber 0 g| Carbohydrates 10 g)

Chili Jam

(**Prep Time:** 10 MIN| **Cook Time:** 40 MIN| **Serve:** 12)

Ingredients:

4 garlic cloves, minced
2 red onions, finely chopped
4 red chili peppers, seeded and chopped
17 ounces cranberries
4 ounces sugar
A drizzle of olive oil
Salt and black pepper to taste
2 tbsp red wine vinegar
3 tbsp water

Directions:

1. Set your instant pot on Sauté mode, add oil and heat before frying onions, garlic and chilies for 8 minutes.
2. Add cranberries, vinegar, water and sugar, stir, cover pot and cook on High for 14 minutes.
3. Release the pressure, uncover and mash sauce using an immersion blender, set the pot on Simmer mode and cook sauce for 15 minutes.
4. Add salt and pepper to taste and transfer to jars and serve when needed.

(Calories 20|Fat 0.2 g| Protein 0.2 g| Fiber 0.4 g| Carbohydrates 4 g)

Dessert Recipes

Chocolate Cheesecake

(**Prep Time:** 60 MIN| **Cook Time:** 50 MIN| **Serve:** 12)

Ingredients:

For the crust:
4 tbsp melted butter
1 and ½ cups chocolate cookie crumbs

For the filling:
24 ounces cream cheese, soft
2 tbsp cornstarch
1 cup sugar
3 eggs
1 tbsp vanilla extract
Cooking spray
1 cup water
½ cup Greek yogurt
4 ounces white chocolate
4 ounces milk chocolate
4 ounces bittersweet chocolate

Directions:

1. In a bowl mix cookie crumbs with butter and stir well.
2. Spray a spring form pan with some cooking oil, line with parchment paper, press crumbs and butter mixture on the bottom and keep in the freezer for now.
3. In a bowl, mix cream cheese with cornstarch and sugar and stir using your mixer.
4. Add eggs, yogurt and vanilla and stir again to combine everything and divide into 3 bowls.
5. Put milk chocolate in a heat proof bowl and heat up in the microwave for 30 seconds before adding this into one of the bowls with the batter you've made earlier and stir well.
6. Put dark and white chocolate in 2 heat proof bowls and heat them up in the microwave for 30 seconds.
7. Add these to the other 2 bowls with cheesecake batter, stir and introduce them all in the fridge for 30 minutes.

8. Take bowls out of the fridge and layer your cheesecake.
9. Pour the dark chocolate batter in the center of the crust.
10. Add white chocolate batter on top and spread evenly and end with milk chocolate batter.
11. Put pan in the steamer basket of your pot, add 1 cup water into the pot, cover and cook on High for 45 minutes.
12. Release pressure for 10 minutes and take cake out of the pot, set aside to cool down and serve.

(Calories 470|Fat 31 g| Protein 8 g| Fiber 2 g| Carbohydrates 45 g)

Apple Bread

(**P**rep Time: 10 MIN| **C**ook Time: 1 HOUR 10 MIN| **S**erve: 6)

Ingredients:

3 cups apples, cored and cubed
1 cup sugar
1 tbsp vanilla
2 eggs
1 tbsp apple pie spice
2 cups white flour
1 tbsp baking powder
4 ounces butter
1 cup water

Directions:

1. In a bowl mix egg with butter, apple pie spice and sugar and stir using your mixer.
2. Add apples and stir again well.
3. In another bowl, mix baking powder with flour and stir.
4. Combine the 2 mixtures, stir and pour into a spring form pan.
5. Place in the steamer basket of your instant pot, add 1 cup water to the pot, cover and cook on High for 1 hour and 10 minutes.
6. Release pressure fast, leave bread to cool down before cutting and serving.

(Calories 89|Fat 3 g| Protein 0 g| Fiber 1 g| Carbohydrates 17 g)

Pumpkin Chocolate Cake

(**Prep Time:** 10 MIN| **Cook Time:** 45 MIN| **Serve:** 12)

Ingredients:

¾ cup white flour
¾ cup whole wheat flour
A pinch of salt
1 tsp baking soda
¾ tsp pumpkin pie spice
¾ cup sugar
1 banana, mashed
½ tsp baking powder
2 tbsp canola oil
½ cup Greek yogurt
8 ounces canned pumpkin puree
Cooking spray
1 quart water
1 egg
½ tsp vanilla extract
2/3 cup chocolate chips

Directions:

1. In a bowl, mix white flour with whole wheat flour, salt, baking soda and powder and pumpkin spice and stir.
2. In another bowl, mix sugar with oil, banana, yogurt, pumpkin puree, vanilla and egg and stir using a mixer.
3. Combine the 2 mixtures, add chocolate chips and mix together well.
4. Pour this into a greased Bundt pan, cover pan with paper towels and foil and place in the steamer basket of your instant pot.
5. Add 1 quart water to the pot, cover and cook on High for 35 minutes.
6. Release the pressure for 10 minutes, uncover pot and leave the cake to cool down, before cutting and serving.

(Calories 270|Fat 9 g| Protein 3 g| Fiber 1 g| Carbohydrates 45 g)

Banana Bread

(**P**rep Time: 10 MIN| **C**ook Time: 30 MIN| **S**erve: 6)

Ingredients:

¾ cup coconut sugar
1/3 cup ghee, soft
1 tsp vanilla
1 egg
2 bananas, mashed
1 tsp baking powder
1 ½ cups flour
A pinch of salt
½ tsp baking soda
1/3 cup cashew milk
1 ½ tsp cream of tartar
2 cups water
Cooking spray

Directions:

1. In a bowl, mix milk with cream of tartar and stir well before adding sugar, ghee, egg, vanilla and bananas and stir again.
2. In another bowl, mix flour with salt, baking powder and soda.
3. Combine the 2 mixtures, stir well and pour batter into a cake pan which you've greased with some cooking spray. Place pan in the steamer basket of your instant pot.
4. Add the water to your pot, cover and cook on High for 30 minutes.
5. Release the pressure, uncover and take bread out, leave aside to cool down before removing from the pan, slice and serve.

(Calories 325|Fat 2 g| Protein 4.5 g| Fiber 1.1 g| Carbohydrates 44 g)

Chocolate Lava Cake

(Prep Time: 10 MIN| Cook Time: 6 MIN| Serve: 3

Ingredients:

1 egg
4 tbsp sugar
2 tbsp olive oil
4 tbsp milk
4 tbsp flour
A pinch of salt
1 tbsp cocoa powder
½ tsp baking powder
½ tsp orange zest
1 cup water

Directions:

1. In a bowl, mix egg with sugar, oil, milk, flour, salt, cocoa powder, baking powder and orange zest and stir very well.
2. Pour this into greased ramekins and place them in the steamer basket of your instant pot.
3. Add 1 cup water to the pot, cover and cook on High for 6 minutes.
4. Release pressure, uncover and take lava cakes out and serve them after they cool down a little. The centers should be liquid and yummy!

(Calories 200|Fat 5 g| Protein 2 g| Fiber 1 g| Carbohydrates 24 g)

Tasty Apple Crisp

(**P**rep Time: 10 MIN| **C**ook Time: 8 MIN| **S**erve: 4)

Ingredients:

2 tsp cinnamon

5 apples, cored and cut into chunks

½ tsp nutmeg

1 tbsp maple syrup

½ cup water

4 tbsp butter

¼ cup flour

¾ cup old fashioned rolled oats

¼ cup brown sugar

A pinch of salt

Directions:

1. Put the apples in your instant pot and add cinnamon, nutmeg, maple syrup and water.
2. In a bowl, mix butter with oats, sugar, salt and flour and stir well.
3. Drop spoonfuls of oats mixture on top of the apples, cover pot and cook on High for 8 min.
4. Release the pressure and serve warm.

(Calories 180|Fat 7 g| Protein 1.4 g| Fiber 2.5 g| Carbohydrates 30 g)

Grandma's Baked Apples

(**P**rep Time: 10 MIN| **C**ook Time: 10 MIN| **S**erve: 6)

Ingredients:

6 apples, cored

1 cup red wine

¼ cup raisins

1 tsp cinnamon powder

½ cup raw sugar

Readymade vanilla custard for serving

Directions:

1. Put the apples in your instant pot and add wine, raisins, sugar and cinnamon, cover pot and cook on High for 10 minutes.
2. Release pressure naturally, uncover and transfer apples and their cooking juice to plates and serve with vanilla custard.

(Calories 188|Fat 0.4 g| Protein 0.5 g| Fiber 3.5 g| Carbohydrates 34 g)

Decadent Chocolate Fondue

(**Prep Time:** 10 MIN| **Cook Time:** 2 MIN| **Serve:** 4)

Ingredients:

3.5 ounces crème fraiche

3.5 ounces dark chocolate, cut into chunks

1 tsp liquor

1 tsp sugar

2 cups water

Fresh fruit, marshmallows and cookies for serving

Directions:

1. In a heat proof container, mix chocolate chunks with sugar, crème fraiche and liquor.
2. Put the water in your instant pot, place container in the steamer basket, cover pot and cook on High for 2 minutes.
3. Release the pressure naturally, uncover and take container out, stir your fondue well and serve it right away with some fresh fruit pieces, marshmallows and cookies.

(Calories 210|Fat 20 g| Protein 2 g| Fiber 3 g| Carbohydrates 6.5 g)

Classic Tapioca Pudding

(**Prep Time:** 10 MIN| **Cook Time:** 8 MIN| **Serve:** 6)

Ingredients:

1 ¼ cups milk

1/3 cup tapioca pearls, rinsed

½ cup water

½ cup sugar

Zest from ½ lemon

1 cup water

Directions:

1. In a heat-proof bowl, mix tapioca with milk, sugar, ½ cup water and lemon zest, stir well.
2. Put this bowl into the steamer basket of your instant pot, add 1 cup water to the pot, cover and cook on High for 8 minutes.
3. Release the pressure and set it aside for 5 more minutes before uncovering and taking your pudding out. Serve it warm.

(Calories 180|Fat 2.5 g| Protein 2.5 g| Fiber 0.1 g| Carbohydrates 90 g)

Steamed Cranberry and Apricot Pudding

(**Prep Time:** 10 MIN| **Cook Time:** 40 MIN| **Serve:** 4)

Ingredients:

4 ounces dried cranberries, soaked in hot water for 30 minutes, drained and chopped
A drizzle of olive oil
2 cups water
4 ounces dried apricots, chopped
1 cup white flour
3 tsp baking powder
1 cup raw sugar
1 tsp ginger powder
A pinch of cinnamon powder
A pinch of salt
5 tbsp butter
3 tbsp maple syrup
4 eggs
1 carrot, grated
Pouring cream for serving

Directions:

1. Grease a heat proof pudding mould with a drizzle of oil and set aside.
2. In a blender, mix flour with baking powder, sugar, cinnamon, salt and ginger and pulse a few times before adding butter and pulsing again.
3. Add maple syrup and eggs and pulse again.
4. Add dried fruits and carrot and fold them into the batter with a spatula.
5. Spoon this mixture into the pudding mold, place into the steamer basket of your instant pot and add 2 cups water in the pot.
6. Set the pot on Sauté mode and steam your pudding for 10 minutes without a lid.
7. Cover your pot and cook pudding on High for 30 minutes.
8. Release the pressure naturally for 10 minutes, set the pot aside for another 10 minutes before uncovering, take your delicious pudding out and leave to cool before serving with cream.

(Calories 310|Fat 15 g| Protein3.6 g| Fiber 2 g| Carbohydrates 27.9 g)

Mini Pumpkin Pies

(**Prep Time:** 10 MIN| **Cook Time:** 20 MIN| **Serve:** 8)

Ingredients:

2 pounds butternut squash, peeled and chopped
2 eggs
2 cups water
1 cup whole milk
¾ cup maple syrup
1 tsp cinnamon powder
½ tsp powdered ginger
¼ tsp powdered cloves
A pinch of salt
1 tbsp cornstarch
Whipped cream for serving
Chopped pecans

Directions:

1. Put squash cubes in the steamer basket of your instant pot, add 1 cup water, cover pot and cook on High for 4 minutes, release pressure and transfer squash to a strainer, cool it down and mash it a bit in a bowl with a fork.
2. Add maple syrup, milk, eggs, cinnamon, ginger, cloves, salt and cloves and stir very well.
3. Pour this mixture into ramekins, place them in the steamer basket of your pot, add 1 cup water to the pot before covering and cook on High for 10 minutes.
4. Release the pressure and take ramekins out, garnish your individual pumpkin pies with whipped cream and chopped pecans and serve.

(Calories 143|Fat 3 g| Protein 3.3 g| Fiber 2.1 g| Carbohydrates 19 g)

Upside-Down Apple Cake

(**Prep Time:** 10 MIN| **Cook Time:** 20 MIN| **Serve:** 8)

Ingredients:

1 apple, sliced
1 apple, chopped
2 cup water
1 cup ricotta cheese
¼ cup raw sugar
1 tbsp lemon juice
1 egg
1 tsp vanilla extract
3 tbsp olive oil
1 cup white flour
2 tsp baking powder
1/8 tsp cinnamon powder
1 tsp baking soda

Directions:

1. Put chopped and sliced apple in a bowl, add lemon juice, toss to coat and set aside.
2. Line a heat proof dish with some parchment paper, grease with some oil and dust with some flour before sprinkling some sugar on the bottom and arranging sliced apple on top.
3. In a bowl, mix egg with cheese, sugar, vanilla extract and oil and stir well.
4. Add flour, baking powder and soda and cinnamon and stir again.
5. Add chopped apple, toss to coat and pour mixture into the pan.
6. Place the pan in the steamer basket of your instant pot, add the water to the pot before covering and cooking on High for 20 minutes.
7. Release the pressure and turn cake onto a plate and serve warm.

(Calories 241|Fat 10 g| Protein 5.8 g| Fiber 2 g| Carbohydrates 20 g)

Brownie Cake with Almonds

(Prep Time: 10 MIN| Cook Time: 50 MIN| Serve: 6)

Ingredients:

1 cup borlotti beans, soaked for 8 hours and drained
4 cups water

For the cake:
1/8 tsp almond extract
½ cup cocoa powder
½ cup raw sugar
3 tbsp extra virgin olive oil
A pinch of salt
2 eggs
2 tsp baking powder
¼ cup almonds, sliced

Directions:

1. Put beans and water in your instant pot, cover, cook on High for 12 minutes, release pressure and strain beans before transferring them to a blender and pureeing them.
2. Discard water from the pot but keep 1 cup aside.
3. Grease a heat proof bowl with some olive oil and set aside.
4. Add cocoa powder, almond extract, honey, salt, eggs and oil to your blender with the beans and puree for 1 minute.
5. Transfer mixture to greased bowl, spread evenly and place bowl in the steamer basket of your pot, add reserved water from cooking the beans, cover and cook on High for 20 minutes.
6. Release the pressure and take cake out of the pot, set aside for 15 minutes to cool before transferring to a plate and garnishing with almonds. Slice and serve.

(Calories 164|Fat 7.8 g| Protein 4.4 g| Fiber 4 g| Carbohydrates 24 g)

Crème Brûlée

(**Prep Time:** 1 HOUR| **Cook Time:** 15 MIN| **Serve:** 6)

Ingredients:

2 cups fresh cream
1 tsp cinnamon powder
6 egg yolks
5 tbsp white sugar
Zest from 1 orange
A pinch of nutmeg for serving
4 tbsp raw sugar
2 cups water

Directions:

1. In a pan, mix cream with cinnamon and orange zest, stir and bring to a boil over medium high heat.
2. Take pan off heat and set aside for 30 minutes to infuse flavors.
3. In a bowl, mix egg yolks with white sugar and whisk well.
4. Add this to cooled cream and whisk well again.
5. Strain this mixture and then pour into ramekins.
6. Cover each one with foil and place them in the steamer basket of your instant pot, add 2 cups water to the pot, cover and cook on Low for 10 minutes.
7. Release the pressure naturally and take ramekins out and leave them to continue setting and cool for 30 minutes.
8. Sprinkle nutmeg and raw sugar on top of each ramekin and melt this with a culinary torch. Serve right away for a classy desert that is sure to impress!

(Calories 210|Fat 10 g| Protein 13 g| Fiber 3 g| Carbohydrates 18 g)

Old-Fashioned Bread Pudding

(**Prep Time:** 5 MIN| **Cook Time:** 25 MIN| **Serve:** 4)

Ingredients:

4 egg yolks
3 cups brioche, cubed
2 cups half and half
½ tsp vanilla extract
1 cup sugar
2 tbsp butter, soft
1 cup cranberries
2 cups warm water
½ cup raisins
Zest from 1 lime

Directions:

1. Grease a baking dish with some butter and set aside.
2. In a bowl mix, egg yolks with half and half, cubed brioche, vanilla extract, sugar, cranberries, raisins and lime zest and stir well
3. Pour this mixture into your greased dish, cover with some tin foil and set aside for 10 minutes for flavors to infuse.
4. Put dish in the steamer basket of your instant pot, add warm water to the pot before covering and cooking on High for 20 minutes.
5. Release the pressure naturally and leave your bread pudding to cool on the kitchen counter before slicing and serving.

(Calories 300|Fat 7 g| Protein 11 g| Fiber 2 g| Carbohydrates 46 g)

Poached Pears with Wine Sauce

(**Prep Time:** 10 MIN| **Cook Time:** 10 MIN| **Serve:** 6)

Ingredients:
6 green pears
1 vanilla pod
1 clove
A pinch of cinnamon
7 oz sugar
1 glass red wine

Directions:
1. In your instant pot, mix wine with sugar, vanilla and cinnamon.
2. Add pears and clove, cover and cook on High for 10 minutes.
3. Release pressure, uncover and leave pears to cool down for 10 minutes.
4. Transfer them to serving bowls with a generous amount of wine sauce and enjoy!

(Calories 151|Fat 7.7 g| Protein 1.1 g| Fiber 3 g| Carbohydrates 14 g)

Rich Ruby Pears

(**Prep Time:** 10 MIN| **Cook Time:** 10 MIN| **Serve:** 4)

Ingredients:
4 pears
Juice and zest from 1 lemon
26 ounces grape juice
11 ounces currant jelly
4 garlic cloves
½ vanilla bean
4 peppercorns
2 rosemary springs

Directions:
1. Pour the jelly and grape juice in your instant pot and mix with lemon zest and juice.
2. Dip each pear in this mixture to soak up flavor, wrap them in tin foil and arrange them in the steamer basket of your pot.

3. Add garlic cloves, peppercorns, rosemary and vanilla bean to the juice mixture, cover pot and cook on High for 10 minutes.
4. Release pressure and take the pears out, unwrap them carefully and arrange them in pudding bowls with a little lake of spicy cooking liquid surrounding them. Serve cold.

(Calories 145|Fat 5.6 g| Protein 12 g| Fiber 6 g| Carbohydrates 12g)

Citrus Ricotta Cake

(**Prep Time:** 30 MIN| **Cook Time:** 30 MIN| **Serve:** 6)

Ingredients:
1 pound ricotta
6 oz dates, soaked for 15 minutes and drained
2 ounces honey softened
4 eggs
2 ounces sugar
Some vanilla extract
17 ounces water
Orange juice and zest from ½ orange

Directions:
1. In a bowl, whisk ricotta until it softens.
2. In another bowl, whisk eggs well.
3. Combine the 2 mixtures, stirring very well.
4. Add honey, vanilla, dates, orange zest and juice to the ricotta mixture and stir again
5. Pour the batter in a heatproof dish and cover with tin foil.
6. Place dish in the steamer basket of your instant pot, add water to the pot, cover and cook on High for 20 minutes.
7. Release pressure, uncover and allow cake to cool down before transferring to a platter. Slice and serve.

(Calories 211|Fat 8.6 g| Protein 12 g| Fiber 0.5 g| Carbohydrates 21 g)

Pumpkin Rice Pudding

(**Prep Time:** 30 MIN| **Cook Time:** 35 MIN| **Serve:** 6)

Ingredients:

1 cup brown rice
½ cup water
3 cups cashew milk
½ cup dates, chopped
A pinch of salt
1 cinnamon stick
1 cup pumpkin puree
½ cup maple syrup
1 tsp pumpkin spice mix
1 tsp vanilla extract

Directions:

1. Put the rice in your instant pot, add boiling water to cover and set aside for 10 minutes before draining.
2. Put the water in milk in your instant pot, add rice, cinnamon stick, dates and salt, stir, cover and cook on High for 20 minutes.
3. Release pressure, uncover and add maple syrup, pumpkin pie spice and pumpkin puree, stir, set the pot on Simmer mode and cook for 5 minutes.
4. Discard cinnamon stick, add vanilla, stir, spoon pudding into bowls and leave for 30 minutes to cool before serving.

(Calories 100|Fat 1 g| Protein 4.1 g| Fiber 4 g| Carbohydrates 21g)

Key Lime Pie

(**Prep Time:** 10 MIN| **Cook Time:** 15 MIN| **Serve:** 6)

Ingredients:

For the crust:
1 tbsp sugar
3 tbsp butter, melted
5 graham crackers, crumbled

For the filling:
4 egg yolks
14 ounces canned condensed milk
½ cup key lime juice
1/3 cup sour cream
Cooking spray
1 cup water
2 tbsp key lime zest, grated

Directions:

1. In a bowl, whisk egg yolks very well and add milk gradually, stirring continuously.
2. Add lime juice, sour cream and lime zest and stir again.
3. In a bowl, whisk butter with crackers and sugar, stir well and spread evenly on the bottom of a spring form pan (greased with some cooking spray).
4. Cover pan with some tin foil and place it in the steamer basket of your instant pot.
5. Add 1 cup water to the pot, cover and cook on High for 15 minutes.
6. Release the pressure for 10 minutes and take pie out, leave to cool before placing in the fridge for 4 hours.
7. Slice and enjoy!

(Calories 400|Fat 21 g| Protein 7 g| Fiber 0.5 g| Carbohydrates 34 g)

Spiced Carrot Cake

(**Prep Time:** 10 MIN| **Cook Time:** 30 MIN| **Serve:** 6)

Ingredients:

5 ounces flour
A pinch of salt
¾ tsp baking powder
½ tsp baking soda
½ tsp cinnamon powder
¼ tsp nutmeg, ground
½ tsp allspice
1 egg
3 tbsp yogurt
½ cup sugar
¼ cup pineapple juice
4 tbsp coconut oil, melted
1/3 cup carrots, grated
1/3 cup pecans, toasted and chopped
1/3 cup coconut flakes
Cooking spray
2 cups water

Directions:

1. In a bowl, mix flour with baking soda and powder, salt, allspice, cinnamon and nutmeg and combine well.
2. In another bowl, mix egg with yogurt, sugar, pineapple juice, oil, carrots, pecans and coconut flakes and stir.
3. Combine the two mixtures, stirring very well.
4. Pour this into a spring form pan greased with some cooking spray, add 2 cups water in your instant pot and place the pan into the steamer basket.
5. Cover the instant pot and cook on High for 32 minutes.
6. Release pressure for 10 minutes before removing cake from the pot and cooling. Cut and serve your delicious, healthy cake.

(Calories 140|Fat 3.5 g| Protein 4.3 g| Fiber 4.1 g| Carbohydrates 23.4 g)

Zucchini Nut Bread

(**Prep Time:** 10 MIN| **Cook Time:** 25 MIN| **Serve:** 6)

Ingredients:

1 cup applesauce
3 eggs, whisked
1 tbsp vanilla extract
2 cups sugar
2 cups zucchini, grated
1 tsp salt
2 ½ cups white flour
½ cup baking cocoa
1 tsp baking soda
¼ tsp baking powder
1 tsp cinnamon
½ cup walnuts, chopped
½ cup chocolate chips
1 ½ cups water

Directions:

1. In a bowl, mix zucchini with sugar, vanilla, eggs and applesauce and stir well.
2. In another bowl, combine flour with salt, cocoa, baking soda, baking powder, cinnamon, chocolate chips and walnuts.
3. Combine the 2 mixtures, stir and pour into a Bundt pan, place pan in the steamer basket of your instant pot, add the water to the pot, cover and cook on High for 25 minutes.
4. Release the pressure naturally and transfer bread to a plate to cool before cutting and serving.

(Calories 217|Fat 8 g| Protein 3 g| Fiber 2 g| Carbohydrates 35 g)

Samoa Cheesecake

(**Prep** Time: 15 MIN| **Cook Time:** 1 HOUR| **S**erve: 6)

Ingredients:

For the crust:
2 tbsp butter, melted
½ cup chocolate graham crackers, crumbled

For the filling:
¼ cup heavy cream
½ cup sugar
12 ounces cream cheese, soft
1 ½ tsp vanilla extract
¼ cup sour cream
1 tbsp flour
1 egg yolk
2 eggs
Cooking spray
1 cup water

For the topping:
3 tbsp heavy cream
12 caramels
1 ½ cups coconut, shredded
¼ cup chocolate, chopped

Directions:

1. Grease a spring form pan with some cooking spray and set aside.
2. In a bowl, mix crackers with butter and spread in the bottom of the pan, pressing down well with the back of a spoon. Keep in the freezer for 10 minutes.
3. Meanwhile, in another bowl, mix cheese with sugar, heavy cream, vanilla, flour, sour cream and eggs and beat very well using a mixer.
4. Pour this mixture into the pan on top of the cold crust, cover with tin foil and place in the steamer basket of your instant pot.

5. Add 1 cup water to the pot, cover and cook on High for 35 minutes.
6. Release the pressure for 10 minutes, uncover and remove tin foil and leave cake to cool down in the fridge for 4 hours.
7. Spread coconut onto a lined baking sheet, place in the oven at 300 degrees F and toast for 20 minutes, stirring often.
8. Put caramels in a heat proof bowl, place in the microwave for 2 minutes to melt, stir every 20 seconds and then fold into the toasted coconut.
9. Spread this evenly on top of your cheesecake and set aside.
10. Put chocolate in another heat proof bowl, place in your microwave for a few seconds until it melts and drizzle over your cake in any pattern you choose.
11. Serve this delicious dessert right away and watch it disappear!

(Calories 310|Fat 8 g| Protein 10 g| Fiber 2 g| Carbohydrates 20 g)

Autumn Cobbler

(Prep Time: 10 MIN| Cook Time: 12 MIN| Serve: 4)

Ingredients:

3 apples, cored and cut into chunks
2 pears, cored and cut into chunks
1 ½ cups hot water
¼ cup date syrup
1 cup steel-cut oats
1 tsp cinnamon
Ice cream for serving

Directions:

1. Put apples and pears in your instant pot and mix with hot water, date syrup, oats and cinnamon.
2. Stir, cover and cook on High for 12 minutes.
3. Release pressure naturally and spoon cobbler to bowls, serving with a scoop of ice cream

(Calories 170|Fat 4 g| Protein 3 g| Fiber 2.4 g| Carbohydrates 10 g)

Pina Colada Rice Pudding

(Prep Time: 10 MIN| Cook Time: 5 MIN| Serve: 8)

Ingredients:

1 tbsp coconut oil
A pinch of salt
1 ½ cups water
1 cup Arborio rice
14 ounces canned coconut milk
2 eggs
½ cup milk
½ cup sugar
½ tsp vanilla extract
8 ounces canned pineapple tidbits, drained and halved

Directions:

1. In your instant pot, mix oil, water, rice and salt, stir, cover and cook on High for 3 minutes.
2. Release the pressure for 10 minutes, uncover pot, add sugar and coconut milk and stir well.
3. In a bowl, mix eggs with milk and vanilla, stir and pour over rice.
4. Stir to combine well and set the pot on Sauté mode to bring to the boil.
5. Add pineapple tidbits and spoon into dessert bowls and serve.

(Calories 113|Fat 3.2 g| Protein 4.2 g| Fiber 0.2 g| Carbohydrates 15 g)

Caramel Custard Flan

(**Prep Time:** 10 MIN| **Cook Time:** 15 MIN| **Serve:** 6)

Ingredients:

For the caramel:
¼ cup water
¾ cup sugar

For the custard:
2 egg yolks
3 eggs
1 ½ cups water
A pinch of salt
2 cups milk
1/3 cup sugar
½ cup whipping cream
2 tbsp hazelnut syrup
1 tsp vanilla extract

Directions:

1. Heat up a pot over medium heat, add ¼ cup water and ¾ cup sugar, stir, cover, bring to a boil, boil for 2 minutes, uncover and boil for a few more minutes.
2. Pour this into custard cups and coat bottoms evenly.
3. In a bowl, mix eggs with yolks, a pinch of salt and 1/3 cup sugar and beat using your mixer.
4. Put the milk in a pan and heat up over medium heat.
5. Add warm milk to eggs mix and stir well to avoid lumps.
6. Add hazelnut syrup, vanilla and cream, stir and strain this mixture.
7. Pour into custard cups, place them in the steamer basket of your instant pot, add 1 ½ cups water to the pot, cover and cook on High for 6 minutes.
8. Release pressure and place custard cups on a cooling rack before putting the cool puddings in the fridge for 4 hours. Serve and enjoy!

(Calories 145|Fat 4 g| Protein 4.5 g| Fiber 0 g| Carbohydrates 23 g)

Decadent Chocolate Pudding

(**Prep Time:** 10 MIN| **Cook Time:** 20 MIN| **Serve:** 4)

Ingredients:

6 ounces bittersweet chocolate, chopped
½ cup milk
1 ½ cups heavy cream
5 egg yolks
1/3 cup brown sugar
2 tsp vanilla extract
1 ½ cups water
¼ tsp cardamom, ground
A pinch of salt
Crème fraiche for serving
Chocolate shavings for serving

Directions:

1. Put cream and milk in a pot, bring to a simmer over medium heat, remove from heat before adding chocolate and whisking well.
2. In a bowl, mix egg yolks with vanilla, sugar, cardamom and a pinch of salt, strain and combine with chocolate mixture.
3. Pour this into a soufflé dish, cover with tin foil, place in the steamer basket of your instant pot, add water to the pot and cover, cook on Low for 18 minutes before releasing pressure naturally.
4. Take pudding out to cool down and keep in the fridge for 3 hours before you serve it with crème fraiche and chocolate shavings on top.

(Calories 200|Fat 3 g| Protein 14 g| Fiber 1 g| Carbohydrates 20 g)

Sticky Date Pudding

(**Prep Time:** 15 MIN| **Cook Time:** 20 MIN| **Serve:** 8)

Ingredients:

2 cups water
1 ¼ cups dates, chopped
¼ cup blackstrap molasses
¾ cup hot water
1 tsp baking powder
1 ¼ cups white flour
A pinch of salt
¾ cup brown sugar
1/3 cup butter, soft
1 tsp vanilla extract
1 egg

For the caramel sauce:
1/3 cup whipping cream
2/3 cup brown sugar
¼ cup butter
1 tsp vanilla extract

Directions:

1. In a bowl, mix dates with hot water and molasses, stir and set aside.
2. In another bowl, mix baking powder with flour and salt.
3. In a third bowl, mix sugar, butter, egg and 1 tsp vanilla extract and beat, using a mixer.
4. Add flour and date mixtures to third bowl and stir very well.
5. Spoon this mixture into 8 ramekins which you've greased with some butter, cover with tin foil, place them in the steamer basket of your instant pot, add 2 cups water to the pot before covering and cooking on Low for 20 minutes.
6. Meanwhile, heat up a pan with the butter for the caramel sauce over medium high heat.
7. Add cream, vanilla extract and brown sugar, stir and bring to a boil.
8. Reduce temperature to medium low and simmer for 5 minutes stirring often.

9. Release pressure from the pot and take ramekins out, remove foil and drizzle sauce over puddings, before serving immediately.

(Calories 260|Fat 14 g| Protein 2 g| Fiber 1 g| Carbohydrates 33 g)

Simple Chocolate Cake

(**Prep Time:** 10 MIN| **Cook Time:** 40 MIN| **Serve:** 6)

Ingredients:

¾ cup cocoa powder
¾ cup white flour
½ cup butter
1 cup water
1 ½ cups white sugar
½ tsp baking powder
3 eggs, whites and yolks separated
1 tsp vanilla extract

Directions:

1. In a bowl, beat egg whites with your mixer until they form soft peaks.
2. In another bowl, beat egg yolks with your mixer.
3. In a third bowl, mix flour with baking powder, sugar and cocoa powder.
4. Add egg white, egg yolks and vanilla extract and fold in very well with a metal spoon.
5. Grease a spring form pan with butter, line with parchment paper, pour cake batter into it and place in the steamer basket of your pot, add 1 cup water to the pot, cover and cook on Low for 40 minutes.
6. Release the pressure and remove cake, leave to cool before transferring to a platter and serving.

(Calories 379|Fat 5 g| Protein 5 g| Fiber 2 g| Carbohydrates 53 g)

Carrot and Pecan Pudding

(**Prep Time:** 10 MIN| **Cook Time:** 1 HOUR| **Serve:** 8)

Ingredients:

1 ½ cups water
Cooking spray
½ cup brown sugar
2 eggs
¼ cup molasses
½ cup flour
½ tsp allspice
½ tsp cinnamon
A pinch of salt
A pinch of nutmeg
½ tsp baking soda
2/3 cup shortening, frozen, grated
½ cup pecans, chopped
½ cup carrots, grated
½ cup raisins
1 cup bread crumbs

For the sauce:
4 tbsp butter
½ cup brown sugar
¼ cup heavy cream
2 tbsp rum
¼ tsp cinnamon

Directions:

1. In a bowl, mix molasses with eggs and ½ cup sugar.
2. Add flour, shortening, carrots, nuts, raisins, bread crumbs, salt, ½ tsp cinnamon, allspice, nutmeg and baking soda and combine well.

3. Pour this mixture into a Bundt pan which you've greased with some cooking spray, cover with foil, place in the steamer basket of your instant pot, add the water to the pot, cover and cook on High for 1 hour.
4. Release the pressure, uncover and take pudding out. Leave to cool down.
5. Meanwhile, heat up a pan for the sauce over medium heat and melt butter.
6. Add ½ cup brown sugar and cook for 2 minutes, stirring continuously.
7. Add cream, rum, ½ tsp cinnamon and simmer for 2 more minutes.
8. Serve your pudding with rum sauce drizzled on top.

(Calories 316|Fat 16 g| Protein 7 g| Fiber 5 g| Carbohydrates 44 g)

Eggnog Cheesecake

(Prep Time: 15 MIN| Cook Time: 20 MIN| Serve: 6)

Ingredients:

2 cups water
2 tsp butter, melted
½ cup ginger cookies, crumbled
16 ounces cream cheese, soft
2 eggs
½ cup sugar
1 tsp rum
½ tsp vanilla
½ tsp nutmeg, ground

Directions:

1. Grease a pan with the butter, add cookie crumbs and spread them evenly.
2. In a bowl, beat cream cheese with a mixer and add nutmeg, vanilla, rum and eggs and mix very well.
3. Pour this into the pan on top of the crumbs and place in the steamer basket of your instant pot, add the water to your pot, cover and cook on High for 15 minutes.
4. Release pressure and take cheesecake out, leave to cool before placing in the fridge for 4 hours. Slice and enjoy!

(Calories 400|Fat 25 g| Protein 6 g| Fiber 0 g| Carbohydrates 30 g)

Lemon Crème Pots

(**Prep Time:** 30 MIN| **Cook Time:** 5 MIN| **Serve:** 4)

Ingredients:

1 cup whole milk
Zest from 1 lemon
6 egg yolks
1 cup fresh cream
1 cup water
2/3 cup sugar
Blackberry syrup for serving
½ cup fresh blackberries

Directions:

1. Heat up a pan over medium heat, add milk, lemon zest and cream, stir and bring to a boil, take off heat and set aside to infuse for 30 minutes.
2. In a bowl, mix egg yolks with sugar and the cold cream mixture and stir well.
3. Pour this into ramekins, cover them with tin foil and place in the steamer basket of your instant pot, add 1 cup water to the pot, cover and cook on High for 5 minutes.
4. Release the pressure for 10 minutes and remove ramekins, leave them to cool and serve with blackberries and blackberry syrup drizzled on top.

(Calories 145|Fat 4 g| Protein 1 g| Fiber 3 g| Carbohydrates 10 g)

Conclusion

Thank you again for purchasing this book!

I hope this Instant Pot Cookbook helps you understand the dynamics and principles of this revolutionary kitchen appliance, why you should use it and how it's going to change your outlook on food preparation and healthy living.

The next step is to get into the right frame of mind and decide that it's time to take charge of your eating habits by only putting the best organic and free range ingredients in your Instant Pot

Even if you have never tried the Instant Pot before, I can promise you one thing, after the 30 days, you will be kicking yourself for having not discovered this sooner.

I hope it was able to inspire you to clean up your kitchen from all the useless appliances that clutter your countertop and start putting the Instant Pot to good use.

The Instant Pot is definitely a change in lifestyle that will make things much easier for you and your family. You'll discover increased energy, decreased hunger, a boosted metabolism and of course a LOT more free time!

I encourage you to share these recipes with family and friends, tell them about this book, and let them know that the Instant Pot can be the best investment that one can make.

Finally, if you feel that you have received any value from this book, then I'd like to ask if you would be kind enough to click on the link below and leave a review on Amazon to share your positive experience with other readers.

It'd be greatly appreciated!